INTERCULTURAL LIVING
Explorations in Missiology

Edited by
Lazar T. Stanislaus, SVD
Martin Ueffing, SVD

ORBIS BOOKS
Maryknoll, New York

ORBIS BOOKS
Maryknoll, New York 10545

Fathers and Brothers
MARYKNOLL™

Founded in 1970, Orbis Books endeavors to publish works that enlighten the mind, nourish the spirit, and challenge the conscience. The publishing arm of the Maryknoll Fathers and Brothers, Orbis seeks to explore the global dimensions of the Christian faith and mission, to invite dialogue with diverse cultures and religious traditions, and to serve the cause of reconciliation and peace. The books published reflect the views of their authors and do not represent the official position of the Maryknoll Society. To learn more about Maryknoll and Orbis Books, please visit our website at www.maryknollsociety.org.

Library of Congress Cataloging-in-Publication Data

Names: Stanislaus, L., editor. | Ueffing, Martin, editor.
Title: Intercultural living : explorations in missiology / Lazar T.
    Stanislaus, SVD, Martin Ueffing, SVD, editors.
Description: Maryknoll : Orbis Books, 2018. | Originally published as 2
    volumes; this volume selected articles. Delhi : Steyler
    Missionswissenschaftliches Institut : ISPCK, 2015. | Includes
    bibliographical references and index.
Identifiers: LCCN 2018005223 (print) | LCCN 2018022444 (ebook) | ISBN
    9781608337446 (e-book) | ISBN 9781626982789 (pbk.)
Subjects: LCSH: Christianity and culture. | Christianity and other religions.
    | Missions—Theory. | Intercultural communication—Religious
    aspects—Christianity.
Classification: LCC BR115.C8 (ebook) | LCC BR115.C8 I49225 2018 (print) | DDC
    266—dc23
LC record available at https://lccn.loc.gov/2018005223

INTERCULTURAL LIVING

*Dedicated to
Divine Word Missionaries (SVD),
Sisters Servants of the Holy Spirit (SSpS)
and Sisters Servants of the Holy Spirit
of Perpetual Adoration (SSpSAP)—
men and women of the "Anthropos Tradition,"
committed to intercultural living and intercultural mission.*

Contents

Preface

As the meaning and value in cultures, religions, and national pride cannot be denied to any human being, living in a society with respect and concern for other human beings should lead us to recognize the others' cultures, religions, and nationalities. This can happen not just by tolerating and understanding other human beings' cultures and religions but by interacting with them to mold a more humane society. This interaction, interchange, sharing, and living together like a family lead to the concept of interculturality.

This concept gains more significance as part of the church's engagement in fulfilling the will of God to realize the reign of God here and now. Thus, interculturality has to be studied more deeply by the church and religious congregations so that we can commit ourselves more fruitfully in our missionary endeavors. All Christian communities—church hierarchies, priests, sisters, lay people, and religious communities of males and females—need to live and work interculturally among peoples. Many churches and congregations have begun to study this subject, and the Society of the Divine Word has done much in discussing and promoting this vital concept.

We would like to thank Fr. Heinz Kulüke, SVD, superior general of the Society of the Divine Word, and his council for encouraging us to undertake this project and for supporting us in the publishing of this volume. All the authors who have contributed articles have shown immense interest, done valuable research, and worked hard, and we are very grateful to all of them.

The editing work was greatly assisted by Christian Tauchner, SVD, and we acknowledge his skill, depth of knowledge, and patient work. We appreciate his commitment and valuable suggestions. Dr. Eric Barnsley has also acted as a lector, and we highly value his dedicated service. We thank Brian O'Reilly, SVD, for translating an article. We are indebted to Orbis Books for their professional work.

We hope that this volume will be helpful for the whole church and beyond. The value of this volume will depend on how these writings serve to enrich meaningful living and effective mission in today's world.

Abbreviations

AG	*Ad Gentes*
CST	Catholic Social Teaching
CTU	Catholic Theological Union
DH	*Dignitatis Humanae* (Declaration on Religious Liberty)
DMIS	Developmental Model of Intercultural Sensitivity
DV	*Dei Verbum* (Dogmatic Constitution on Divine Revelation)
EA	Pope John Paul II, *Ecclesia in Asia* (The Church in Asia, apostolic exhortation)
EG	Pope Francis, *Evangelii Gaudium* (The Joy of the Gospel, apostolic exhortation)
EN	Pope Paul VI, *Evangelii Nuntiandi* (Evangelization in the Modern World, apostolic exhortation)
FABC	Federation of Asian Bishops' Conference
FAPA	*For All the Peoples of Asia*
FMM	Franciscan Missionaries of Mary
GS	*Gaudium et Spes* (Pastoral Constitution on the Church in the Modern World)
ICS	Intercultural Competence Scale
IDI	Intercultural Development Inventory
IDW	*In Dialogue with the Word*
IM	*Inter Mirifica* (Decree on the Means of Social Communication)
IMF	International Monetary Fund
ISPCK	Indian Society for Promoting Christian Knowledge
JW	*Justice in the World*
LAC	Linguistic Awareness of Culture
LF	Pope Francis, *Lumen Fidei* (The Light of Faith, encyclical letter)
LGBT	Lesbian, Gay, Bisexual, Transgender persons
LGBTQIA	Lesbian, Gay, Bisexual, Transgender, Queer/Questioning, Intersexual, and Asexual/Ally persons
ML	Martial Law
NA	*Nostra Aetate* (Declaration on the Relationship of the Church to Non-Christian Religions)
NGO	Non-Governmental Organization
NVC	Non-Violent Communication
OTP	Overseas Training Program

PIH	Partners In Health
PNG	Papua New Guinea
PT	Pope John XXIII, *Pacem in Terris* (Peace on Earth, encyclical letter)
RM	Pope John Paul II, *Redemptoris Missio* (Mission of the Redeemer, encyclical letter)
RSVB	Revised Standard Version Bible
SEDOS	Service of Documentation and Study on Global Mission
SS	Pope Benedict XVI, *Spe Salvi* (Christian Hope, encyclical letter)
SVD	Society of the Divine Word
UISG	International Union of Superiors General
UNCSW	United Nations Commission on the Status of Women
USAID	United States Agency for International Development
USG	Union of Superiors General
WCC	World Council of Churches

Introduction

More so now than at any other time in world history people are on the move. This movement is a global phenomenon—people move inside their own country, from one country to another, and from continent to continent. The reasons as well as the consequences are manifold. Due to globalization, economic reasons, or poverty, and increasingly because of wars, violent conflicts, and persecution, people are leaving their homes. Many do not know what the future has in store for them, and with much insecurity they enter the often-unknown world of another culture, nation, and people. Others are on the move for reasons of tourism and because they can afford short visits in "exotic" places and are curious to explore new cultures and to encounter local people.

As they move they leave their own traces behind them. Their own lives are strongly affected, but also the lives and cultures of the local people among whom they settle. Formerly homogenous cultures become increasingly heterogeneous, and intercultural living brings about its own challenges. How do local people welcome people of other cultures? How do both—local people and their new neighbors—deal with cultural diversity, change, pluralism, and so forth? Interaction with other cultures has become a norm of this century. In this context, many people are searching for appropriate interactions that will give meaning to one's life in a heterogeneous culture.

Scholars in various fields would name this mixing or interaction of cultures in their own normative way; some may call it multicultural, others cross-cultural or intercultural life. We observe that there is hardly a society left in the world with a monocultural life. Even if there are groups that are not mixing with other cultures in their territorial life, due to the influence of media and cyberspace every cultural group is affected or influenced by another culture. Therefore, there is a greater need to understand this interaction between cultures and peoples.

The church exists for the purpose of its mission—a mission related to the Divine, Christ, the Good News, people, cultures, religions, creatures, and the cosmos. In this context, the need to understand the cultures of different peoples and the changes that happen in the interaction of cultures in the contemporary world is profoundly significant. For this reason, the study of cultures and the matrix of cultural exchanges, as well as the emergence of interculturality, become prominent aspects of the church's mission.

More than ever, missionaries around the globe go from south to north and from east to west, and the earlier paradigm and pattern of missionaries coming from west and north have changed. Due to this emerging phenomenon, the missionary life in a congregation or diocese has changed too. There are many multicultural groups, and church communities themselves have become increasingly heterogeneous communities.

To have a deeper understanding of interculturality, we, the editors, have previously published two volumes on *Intercultural Living* and *Intercultural Mission*, studying various aspects of missionaries' lives and endeavors. This volume, *Intercultural Living: Explorations in Missiology*, contains some of the key articles from those earlier volumes. In this volume, the richness of living together and the enrichment of intercultural life are explained. The challenges of living in such a community are articulated, and the prospective ways to face these challenges are explored. The ever-changing scenario of the world calls for new approaches and new methods to do mission. Deeper analyses on intercultural mission, and new ideas or proposals to work effectively in mission, challenge missionaries to explore various possibilities of doing mission today. Some pathways of intercultural mission are explored in this volume.

Understanding Culture

Culture is one of the central topics of multidisciplinary discussions. Every group tries to evolve definitions and descriptions according to its contextual setting and need. The social sciences have developed the meaning of culture in various ways. Culture is a complex concept, and no single definition of it has achieved consensus in the literature, but it affects everything people do in their society because of their ideas, values, attitudes, and normative or expected patterns of behavior. Culture is not genetically inherited, and cannot exist on its own but is always shared by members of a society.

Edward Tyler's definition of culture lasted a long time in the academic arena: "Culture . . . is that complex whole which includes knowledge, belief, art, morals, law, custom, and any other capabilities and habits acquired by man as a member of society."[1] Many scholars have started from this definition and his understanding and have evolved theories to understand various behavioral patterns of human beings. Today, one goes beyond these acquired capabilities and mere habits and tries to go in depth into the communications and interactions among groups and cultures.

The classical definitions are being contested today. In the present context of rapidly globalizing societies, "cultures" no longer tend to be coherent and permanent "wholes" that guide their adherents' ways of thinking and liv-

---

1. Edward Tyler, *Primitive Culture* (London: John Murray, 1871), 1.

ing. Culture is now preferably understood as a dynamic and changing set of beliefs and values that inform common ways of interpreting reality and interacting with one another.

Culture is often manifested in two distinct ways. The first is as values, beliefs, schemas, and implicit theories commonly held among members of a collectivity (society or organization); these are variously called the *attributes* or *content* of culture. The second is as commonly observed and reported practices of entities such as families, schools, work organizations, economic and legal systems, political institutions, and the like, which are often referred to as the *process* of culture. When we consider a community, we take into account the content of its culture and also how the process of culture is practiced in the respective community.

Clearly, the field of whatever goes under the concept of "culture" is extremely wide and complex. Different perspectives of social sciences take their own definitions and approaches, which are often mutually exclusive.

The Divine Word Missionaries have become ever more conscious of the importance of culture and the need to take it seriously—the founding of Anthropos more than one hundred years ago is one indication of their recognition of this need. Recently, this congregation has set up a program to promote intercultural competence in the fields of cultural anthropology and spirituality. Likewise many congregations, dioceses, and organizations give importance to culture in their approach to mission and formation. Since Vatican II, the church has given more prominence to the importance of culture.

Interculturality

Interculturality refers to the sustained interaction of people raised in different cultural backgrounds. In contrast to multicultural or cross-cultural settings, it denotes mutual exchange between cultures that can lead to transformation and enrichment of all involved.

It also means that there are mutually reciprocal relationships among and between cultures; people from different cultural groups interact with one another, learn and grow together; build relationships and become transformed, shaped, and molded from one another's experiences. The focus is on relationship building (not survival), deep connections, interactions, mutual gifting, respect, and learning from one another. Here, the racial and cultural power imbalances are addressed, the commonness is more highlighted than the differences, people are enabled to learn from each other, people appreciate and work together for a common cause, and this leads toward the transformation of all peoples.[1]

---

1. See www.united-church.ca/files/intercultural/multicultural-crosscultural-intercultural. pdf.

Interculturality stands for movement from toleration of differences to appreciation and celebration of differences in cultures. Therefore, acceptance and joining with the other cultures in celebration are some signs of integration. Imbibing the values of other cultures and living joyfully become a sign of growth. Interculturality can be nurtured when one enters the sphere of spirituality with the concept that everyone is created in the image of God and that cultural diversity is part of God's plan. Therefore, living and interaction with other cultures are participation in God's plan, and transforming cultures takes a person to another level.

After a basic understanding of culture, we are aware that in today's context the significance of interculturality has to go deeper. Here, we go beyond mere diversity of cultures in a society, where people consider others just as guests or workers. Multiculturalism seems to emphasize the value of each culture in a society, but this seems to overemphasize ethnicity and distinctiveness and thus promotes tolerance but not real unity. Often the cultures of migrants and minority communities are respected but not integrated; they are valued but are not assumed important for growth of the majority.

Interculturality recognizes strongly the need to enable each culture to survive and flourish but underlines also the right of all cultures to contribute to the growth of the society in which they live. In a society where people of various religions, peoples, and cultures live, the interaction of cultural values, customs, and other religious values may lead to the easing of cultural conflict and tensions. Interculturality seeks to reinforce intercultural interaction as a means of building trust, openness and confidence as necessary parts of the fabric of a community.

Today's church has to become intercultural in its living and approach to mission. This is the reality that the church faces today—some local churches have recognized this trend and moved ahead; others are still figuring out how to cope with the situation. Every local church or religious congregation must embrace this intercultural aspect in its life and mission. The present and the future of the church are intercultural living and mission. The more one is prepared for this approach and task, the better will be one's life and mission.

This volume consists of various chapters that are written by experienced authors, innovative thinkers, path finders, academicians, and activists. They explore the problems, difficulties, and complexities of interculturality, as well as the significance, new orientations, innovative actions, and future visions of intercultural living and intercultural mission.

Lazar T. Stanislaus, SVD
Martin Ueffing, SVD

1

The Challenge of Intercultural Living
Anthropological and Theological Implications

Anthony J. Gittins, CSSp

Overview

Community and identity today are very different from what they were a century ago, in membership, missiology, focus, and works. The impact of geographical and social mobility has reshaped the contours of international religious institutions. *Assimilation* was *the* recruitment model: culturally or linguistically different aspirants were expected to "fit in," while the broader community continued, with minimum disturbance.

My thesis is this: given the global changes occurring in the lifetime of today's senior members, the future of international religious communities must increasingly and intentionally become intercultural. Without the tectonic shift from "international" to "intercultural" there will simply be no viable future for international religious orders.

The challenge facing *everyone* now, old and new alike, is to identify and respond to the demands of intercultural living. The broader community must engage with the cultural identity of newer members and abandon the assimilation model as "unfit for purpose," and individual members must respond to the challenge of intercultural living by embracing it wholeheartedly or halfheartedly, or by resisting it and waiting for death. Everyone must stand and be counted: the future, viable or not, depends on it.

Anthony J. Gittins, CSSp, is emeritus professor of theology and culture at Catholic Theological Union, Chicago, USA. A missionary anthropologist, he spent a decade in Sierra Leone, West Africa, and three decades teaching graduate theology in London and Chicago.

Clearing the Field

For more than half a century, the need for cross-cultural communication and cooperation has been identified by multinational companies and addressed by the social sciences. The term *multicultural* has been largely replaced by *intercultural* in order to focus not simply on the social fact that people of diverse cultures live in close proximity but on the specific challenges facing multinational corporations attempting to create a concerted workforce of culturally diverse personnel. For us, *intercultural* (as used by international religious communities) carries a further significance. As with *inculturation,* it has a deeply theological connotation; and as the theological component of *inculturation* is unknown or insignificant to social scientists, so the theological connotations of *intercultural* would not interest them. So it is important for us to identify some of the specific features of intercultural living. Here are ten.

- It is an intentional, faith-based undertaking, not just an international workforce.
- Faith can only be lived *culturally*; it is expressed in the (cultural) practice of daily life.
- It is a *challenge* (not a "problem"), not just for some but for all. A polarized group will never achieve intercultural living; only a true community can succeed.
- It does not come naturally, yet it is possible from a *supernatural* perspective. As a form of faith-based living, it is not achieved by mastery of new techniques alone.
- It is far from easy but is highly desirable and seems to be desired by God, lest one culture dominate, causing individuals to be seriously distressed and distraught.
- Good intentions and good will are necessary but quite insufficient; they have perpetrated many human tragedies. Also required are commitment and sustained work, necessary for the acquisition of skills (expertise) and virtue (conversion).
- Diplomacy, compromise, dialogue, and a common vision must inspire a common effort and provide appropriate means to sustain it.
- For people in established international religious communities, it is something new. Most of us are monocultural, even in multicultural or international environments.
- It is necessary, but costly for viable international religious life. If successful, it will revolutionize religious life; but it is obligatory if dry bones are to live.
- In some form, it is not only for religious communities; it challenges everyone in ministry in relation to any other person whether by gender, age, ethnicity, religion, culture, or any other criterion.

Guiding Principles

The following might provide a framework for intercultural living. Based on certain principles a community is built, its operational methodologies are worked out, and the community members interact with one another.

We Must Build a Home for All

Theoretically, a religious community is the primary group to which we belong by profession; in practice, it can be far from that. We are called to build something in which all can live harmoniously, to which each can lay equal claim, and for which everyone assumes responsibility. Jonathan Sacks contrasts various places of residence, from family home to hotel, nursing home or prison, distinguished according to rights and responsibilities, degrees of freedom or ownership, and comfort level. Reflection on the sense of belonging that each one evokes, and on their advantages and disadvantages, might help us visualize whether a particular community is suited to its various purposes.[1]

"A house is not a home"; and a religious community is not a retirement home. A family home is more than a group of relatives living under one roof; it is an *evolving, organic entity*. Its shape constantly changes as spouses become parents, as a child gains a sibling, and as siblings mature. Each person has needs, rights, and has different temperaments. Family survival depends on the quality of interaction between each member and requires compromise and adaptability to unforeseen circumstances. As the children begin to leave home, everyone is affected. A family exhibits elements of stability and change and cannot survive without drama, trauma, fusion, and fission.

Intercultural communities can be compared to a family home. They bear a great responsibility for becoming "fit for purpose" as nurturers of faith and places of mutual support and challenge. They are public witnesses to the possibility that people of different cultures and languages, but a common faith and vision, can thrive for a purpose beyond individual whim or comfort, and as a sign of the kingdom or realm of God. But "if identity resembles a hotel, identity will be, not in integration, but separation."[2]

We Must Learn to Appreciate Our Differences

An enduring human challenge is to value difference positively and constructively. The "cultural flaw" is the human propensity to define by differentiation, and to use the differences to justify discrimination. "To define" is

---

1. Jonathan Sacks, *The Home We Build Together: Recreating Society* (New York: Continuum Books, 2007).

2. Ibid., 82.

to set boundaries, mark off, delimit, or distinguish. While it is quite true that I am *not* Chinese, young, female, a physiotherapist, artist or activist, defining myself in this negative fashion discloses very little about my actual identity. The great human paradox is that we are all the same and all different, simultaneously; the great folly is for humanity to be alienated itself by using differences to disagree, dissent and discriminate, and with appalling consequences.

Genesis tells of a community: individuals in unity. Man, woman, and creator are a community-of-difference. The Fall drove a wedge between the humans and God, and between the man and the woman, fracturing the community now marked by enmity and opposition: an original "we" becomes polarized and opposed, as "us" and "them."

In an old rabbinic story,[3] the teacher asks the disciples: "When do you know it is dawn?" One says, "when you can distinguish a white thread from a black one." "No," says the teacher. "When you can see the outline of a tree against the horizon," ventures another. "No," says the teacher, to this and to all other efforts to answer the question. Finally he says, "when you can look into the eyes of a stranger and see a sister or a brother, then it is dawn; until then, it is still night." This summarizes the process and challenge of becoming intercultural communities. We certainly have to identify and learn the skills to engage with our own cultural conditioning, during which, and subtly, the cataracts of ethnocentrism and other biases and prejudices cloud our vision. Such skills are not easily attained, especially during mid- and later life. But we have a model to help us negotiate our prejudices and can take comfort from the fact that it is not through deliberate fault that we create misunderstanding and frustration; they are from our cultural conditioning. The lesson is to learn to overcome our prejudices.

The Letter to the Ephesians identifies the "cultural flaw" that opposed and alienated Jew and Greek (Gentile) until Jesus himself came to remove the barrier between "us" (Jews) and "them" (Greeks) by bridging that barrier with his own body and thus drawing each side to a new relationship with himself as mediator or link. Ephesians 2:1–2 and 11–16 bear serious reflection and discussion. The passages dramatically describe an "us/them" world becoming a world of "we." It required cultural imperatives to yield to grace. What God created was good, declared seven times in the first creation story, culminating with God's verdict that "indeed it was very good" (Gen 1:31). We must urgently rediscover the dignity of difference and celebrate it in our intercultural communities.

---

3. This story, officially cited as "source unknown," abounds in various forms. Mine is a paraphrase—as indeed are they all. Versions can be found at https://tinw.org (search The Face of Our Brother), or philipchircop.wordpress.com.

The "cultural flaw" is a residual sign of the sin marking every culture and person; but we are also touched by grace. We must identify both sin and grace in self and others, not comparing the grace in our lives and cultures with the sin we find in others. The agenda of those striving for intercultural community is taxing and not accomplished painlessly. But by God's grace and our commitment, we can put our hands to the plow and not look back. "Peace involves a profound crisis of identity. The boundaries of self and other, friend and foe, must be re-drawn."[4]

We Need to Rethink the Way We Think

People influenced by Western cultures operate out of a largely *dialectical* (oppositional or exclusive) mode of thought; either/or thinking pursues an argument until it concludes that one person or thesis is right and another is wrong. By contrast, *analogical* (complementary or inclusive) thinking looks for compromise between two extremes, finding truth or validity in each: this is both/and thinking. As we develop principles and practices of intercultural living, we need to shift from dialectical to analogical thinking. Each side or perspective may offer valuable insights; each person needs to feel that there is no *us* and *them*, but only a community seeking to identify itself inclusively as *we*. As Rudy Wiebe expressed it, "you repent, not by feeling bad but by thinking different[ly]."[5] But this is considerably more difficult than simply feeling bad; it is relatively easy to do the latter, but after a lifetime of learning how to think, and to think that our thinking is right thinking, we become rather resistant to thinking differently.

Members of international religious communities today need to face the urgent task of learning the skills and virtues required of each person, though the challenge is formidable, especially perhaps (but not inevitably) for some older members. After all, the gospel calls everyone to ongoing conversion. And in today's multicultural, globalized world, new challenges have arisen and will not disappear.

From Monocultural to Intercultural: The Terminology

Without a common understanding of major ideas, communication is impossible. We need a common vocabulary for discussing intercultural living, partly theological but much of it sociological. Precision of language is critical.

---

4. Jonathan Sacks, *The Dignity of Difference: How to Avoid the Clash of Civilizations* (New York: Continuum, 2002), 8.

5. Rudy Wiebe, *The Blue Mountains of China* (Toronto: McClelland and Stewart, 1970), 215–16.

Monocultural and Bicultural

Historically, most people other than nomads have lived and died within a world with a radius of perhaps no more than ten miles. Very few human beings are truly bicultural. Exceptionally, climate or access to food dictates a move, but usually a significant number will be involved; "people like us" describes a monocultural group. Beyond the arena of "people like us" are "people not like us," mostly encountered by individuals, explorers, or traders. Most people live and die within their own social group or culture.

True biculturalism develops in those growing up within a stable domestic arena in which each parent speaks a different native language. A child is socialized in a bilingual context, perhaps benefitting from moving physically between the territories in which each parent was raised, finding it perfectly natural to shift between two languages ("code-switching") and two geographical territories. But bicultural is also applied to someone growing up in one culture and later encountering another culture and language, learning each sufficiently to be able to pass more or less freely between two worlds. If that person is not living in the milieu in which he or she was raised, the more appropriate term would be cross-cultural. I will use bicultural to apply to a person living in two cultural and linguistic worlds simultaneously, as do many bilingual Mexican-Americans, Korean-Americans, and so on.

Cross-Cultural

A cross-cultural person belongs originally to one culture ("culture A") but later moves beyond its confines to reside for a number of years in another environment ("culture B"). The person from culture A is no longer "at home," but the people of culture B are perfectly so. The cross-cultural person is an outsider or stranger in culture B and must learn a new culture and language, the former being every bit as challenging as the latter. Some people naively think that if they commit to the formal learning of a new language, learning the culture will happen naturally. This is a dangerous simplification: adults must learn a new culture with as much care, attention, and trial-and-error as they would learn a new language.

The cross-cultural person remains an outsider, since an adult cannot simply be assimilated into a new culture. But outsiders come in many shapes and forms, typically "participating" or "nonparticipating." The former can be of great value to the insiders, while the latter are at best irrelevant (like tourists, whose value is not in their intentional contribution to the community), and at worst destructive (like an invading army). Unsurprisingly, the host population will take time and carefully scrutinize well-intentioned incomers before giving them the kind of welcome they seek.

Becoming a cross-cultural person evidently depends as much on the response of the indigenous population as it does on the *bona fides* of the would-be cross-cultural person. A transitional "testing time," often lasting months or years and not without pain and frustration, will precede wholehearted acceptance; it is a necessary form of self-protection for local communities that often carry bad memories of previous ungracious and threatening strangers. During this time, the incomer is expected to be learning the cultural rules, responsibilities and sanctions necessary for smooth day to day living.

Multicultural

Any neighborhood, country (or parish) comprised of people of many cultures is *de facto* a multicultural community; but this says nothing about how people of one culture relate to people of another. (The *how* pertains specifically to *intercultural* living). Multiculturalism can be dealt with in many ways, from indifference to hostility, tolerance to friendship, or civility to collaboration. Differences can be eliminated by anything from genocide to assimilation, tolerated by indifference or unconcern, or managed: negatively by "separate development" (*chacun pour soi*) or mutual apathy leaving everyone in a state of enduring *liminality*; or positively by mutual cooperation and the encouragement of diversity, as one might create an orchestra or chorus. Awareness of the features of a multicultural society provides a good stepping-stone to intercultural community.

Intercultural

From the 1950s when the discipline that studied the effects of cross-cultural contact was being developed and the vocabulary was unstable, multicultural and intercultural were often used synonymously. This fledgling discipline arose from the social sciences, including cultural anthropology, sociology, and psychology. But gradually, theology, specifically mission studies, became aware of the cultural dynamics at work in situations of mission *ad extra*. When theological language is employed, standard usage now distinguishes multicultural (sociological) and intercultural (theological). The former identifies a social reality within neighborhoods or voluntary associations; the latter carries specific theological overtones. An intercultural community shares intentional commitment to the common life, motivated not by pragmatic considerations alone, but by a shared religious conviction and common purpose.

Multinationals hire people who travel internationally and extensively. They need skills for communicating with a wide variety of business partners. For decades, such skills have been identified, taught, and acquired across the business world. Meanwhile, many religiously-based communities have encountered the challenges posed by their increasingly multicultural membership and the awareness of the near-bankruptcy of the standard assimilation model of recruitment ("Come join us, and we will teach you to do things our way"). Over the years, the contours of intercultural living and ministry have become increasingly clear. But partly because they have been shaped by previously-gained insights from the social sciences, the majority of people in today's international religious communities have been unaware of, struggled with, or resisted the challenge (which is fast becoming a real imperative) of intercultural living.

Intercultural living is a faith-based and lifelong process of conversion, emerging in recent decades as a requirement of members of intentional, international religious communities. Healthy intercultural living depends on the level of commitment and support generated by *every* member of the community. Individuals vary in their adaptability and learning-levels, but each one generates positive or negative energy, and the quality of intercultural living depends significantly on the aggregate of positive energy generated by the whole group. A small, resistant group can generate enough negative energy to thwart the wider community. The future of international religious life depends significantly on the ability of each community (local and institutional) to live interculturally; those that fail to do so will fragment or die.

Before identifying the dynamics of intercultural living, we need to address culture, since this is the context for lived faith; there is no person without culture, and faith can only be lived culturally. We live our Christian faith not in a vacuum and not without a specific cultural context; but intercultural living happens in multicultural contexts, since lives unfold in varied contexts. So culture is of paramount significance.

Culture

Most people assume they can identify and understand culture, but it is the topic that needs the most clarification. It is recognizable under many forms, and every human person, raised in a social environment, has culture. But no one is *born* with culture, and, given different social circumstances, any individual might have become socialized or *acculturated* differently. A baby boy born and raised in Shanghai by Chinese parents will become culturally Chinese, all things being equal. But that very same child, flown to Chicago soon after birth, and adopted by Euro-American parents, will become acculturated as a Euro-American. Environment and socialization are critically important.

Descriptively, we can identify culture in a number of ways. Each merits a much deeper treatment than we can offer here. Culture is,

- *The [hu]man-made part of the environment:* It includes *materials* (artifacts, buildings), *institutional elements* (politics, kinship, economics, belief, and thought/religion), *symbolic elements* (writing, orality, and words-objects-gestures to "say the unsayable"), and *moral* components (values, virtues, and their opposites, vices).

- *The form of social life:* Identified in the actual ("normal," habitual and approved, or "deviant," acknowledged and disapproved) behavior of a social group, it can be interpreted through the underlying belief-and-thought system. But there will always be a discrepancy between what people *say* they believe, approve, or disapprove of, and actual observed behavior. Social life is not always harmonious, virtuous, or lawful. But insiders (and outsiders with appropriate knowledge) can identify ignoble and heroic behavior. Social pathology and virtue can be found within any social system. Culture is expressed in "customary" (not simply individual) behavior, backed by sanctions.
- *A meaning-making system:* A system pervades a whole society and makes intelligible communication possible, given certain standards and rules. Communication can work at several levels, and a meaning-making system need not be technically perfect. So with culture. Linguistics distinguishes *grammaticality* (strict rule conformity), *acceptability* (appropriate information transfer), and *meaningfulness* (adequate information transfer) as three criteria by which to judge the effectiveness of communication. *Rule-governed creativity* allows a virtually infinite number of utterances to be generated *and understood* with a limited core of grammatical rules (about fifty). Natural to the native speaker, it is a very difficult acquisition for those struggling with a second language. The rules of chess are few yet the moves are limitless; it will be years before members of intercultural communities become as proficient as chess players.
- *Culture as skin:* The skin is the human body's largest organ. Grafting it is difficult and sometimes impossible. If it is severely burned, death may be inevitable. And yet skin can tolerate scars, blemishes, wrinkles, and many dermatological conditions. We cannot be "in someone else's skin"; and if ours were to be stripped or "flayed," we would certainly die. Cultures, like skin, need not be perfect and can tolerate wear and tear as well as trauma, but the integrity of the skin is as necessary for life as is the integrity of a culture.
- *An enduring social reality:* Cultures rise and fall, flourish and die, and no culture appears to be immortal; here are features to provide food for thought and discussion for anyone attempting to live interculturally. Culture is transmitted over time, through the generations; it is an ongoing process rather than a simple social fact. Although some cultures (termed "traditional") may appear to be in stasis or equilibrium, every culture is in process of change, whether relatively slow or very fast. Some cultures adapt better to change than others. Reality (what people consider to be real) is socially constructed: people are born into a preexisting community that has already interpreted the world and determined the meaning of things, events, and relationships. The process of socialization or encultura-

tion extends through the first decades of life, when an individual is aggregated to the preexisting world of meaning. Once adequately socialized, it becomes increasingly difficult to think that our thought or ways are wrong.

Spirituality and Intercultural Living

Faith can be lived only within a cultural context, because to be an integrated human person is to be a person of culture. Having identified some of culture's features, we must consider how faith and culture coexist. Christian spirituality is essentially the (new) life given at baptism by the Holy Spirit to guide our faith journey through life. It might be described as *a way of being in the world with God*, when each variable—way, being, world, God—is shaped according to an individual's experience. Through a single lifetime, a person may embrace a number of possible ways (single, married, celibate; having a profession, trade, or employment), experience different states of being (from youth to age and health to sickness), live in a number of different worlds (from rural to urban, tropical to temperate), and relate in different ways to God (Jesus, Spirit, Father; Lord, King, Warrior; Creator, Redeemer, Wisdom).

Spirituality is far more than beliefs. It shapes and is shaped by our attitude to Creator and creation, how we pray or express our embodied selves, how we respond to suffering, disaster, and tragedy, and our life choices. From our perspective, it is critically important to acknowledge the many legitimate cultural and personal expressions of Christian spirituality, realizing that these will create challenges when we discuss liturgy, prayer, ritual, music, dance, language, silence, privacy, conformity, and so on. We must discover ways to approach our cultural differences, with a view to forging an enduring intercultural community. Some of the most contentious issues within a community are also, if approached sympathetically and creatively, enriching for all. Here we can itemize only the following four as among the most worthy of serious consideration.

Social Location

Everyone lives within a *microcosm* or enclosed world: the individual body, a room within a house, a neighborhood within a city, or a nation within the world. Beyond the *microcosm* is a *macrocosm*: a larger world, a community beyond the individual, a school beyond a classroom, a country beyond one's border, or a universe beyond one's world. All creation can be seen as consisting of worlds within worlds and worlds beyond worlds. In community building, the *relationship* between *microcosm* and *macrocosm* is critically important. A particular *microcosm* may be closed (strong) or open (weak) in relation to the *macrocosm* beyond; the more closed it is, the more resistant to extraneous contact or interference, while the more open it is, the more accommodating or welcoming to outside communication will people be.

More interesting than individuals' greater or lesser openness to external forces or relationships is the social fact that whole groups of people (different cultures) exhibit the same dynamic. Some individuals welcome "otherness," in the form of other people, technology, or ways of living, while some appear almost programmed to be suspicious or wary of otherness, in other people, technology, or ways. But when a whole culture exhibits such trends, social facts cannot be reduced to individuals' whims or prejudices.

Intercultural community building requires that serious consideration be given to how members were shaped by their social location, and how tolerant a community can be of individual variation that cannot simply be reduced to personal choice or comfort, or handled by diktat. Conversation about the social geography, the place where individuals were born, the circumstances of their socialization, the climate, the amount of contact with outsiders, or the degree of social mobility will create an informed community and should lead to greater mutual understanding and empathy.

Body Tolerance

Culture and temperament shape attitudes to one's own body, and all must be sensitive to cultural differences. "Body tolerance" is one's comfort level regarding bodily display or reserve, not itself correlated with immodesty or modesty. Every society has norms of modesty, but there is a range of cultural difference; sensitivity and enquiry are required if people are to learn mutual respect.

We can visualize a continuum ranging from "low body tolerance" (Apollonian) to "high body tolerance" (Dionysian). "Apollonian" (after the god Apollo) designates a serene, ordered, disciplined demeanor, and bodily display that is poised and controlled. "Dionysian" (after the god Dionysus) refers to a more relaxed, spontaneous, uninhibited person or style. Some individual differences exist, and there is some correlation between colder or more temperate regions (Apollonian), where bodies are swathed in heavy, uniform clothing, and the warmer, more tropical regions (Dionysian), where people are less constrained and more flamboyant in dress and demeanor.

Official documents of the Catholic Church refer to "the noble simplicity of the Roman Rite": this describes an Apollonian style adopted—indeed imposed—universally. Recently, some things have changed, yet for many communities the Roman Rite remains overchoreographed and too predictable and controlled. Generally, African Americans and others are much more Dionysian than German or British people. But the style of many Asian cultures tends toward the Apollonian. Communities seeking liturgical renewal often find that rules and rubrics range from the awkward to the irksome.

Within intercultural communities, cultural and individual behaviors relating to body tolerance can be very difficult to reconcile, and community members can find that liturgy and prayer, designed to gather, unite, and lead to God, are the major occasions for tension, disharmony, and frustration in the community. Open conversation and true dialogue are needed if community members are to appreciate that the significant differences between individuals are not simply a matter of whim or preference, but coded in their cultural makeup. Topics might include: What was your usual mode of dress: formal or casual, "up" or "down," loose- or tight-fitting, uniform or varied? How much did you wear: a lot or a little; seasonally varied or perennial? How did you present your body: (mostly) concealed or revealed; overdressed or underdressed? What was your attitude to personal and communal nakedness? How would you describe personal modesty? During childhood, and in initial formation in religious life, were most people's attitudes to bodily display and concealment similar to or different from your own?

Health and Sickness

People have very different cultural attitudes to sickness and death. In a highly medicalized society, serious sickness is often presented as a temporary irritant to be cured with maximum speed and minimum pain; and death as something to be postponed almost indefinitely. Even during the dying process, the prospect of recovery is routinely advertised by medical professionals, so death comes as a surprise. Before death, the terminally ill are routinely removed from home and institutionalized, thus minimizing people's encounters with death; to a significant degree, it takes place beyond the ordinary daily routine and away from the domestic sphere.

But in societies where expensive and extreme medical expertise is not widely available, sickness is much more frequently encountered by almost everyone, and a person who is evidently ailing is very often cared for and surrounded by family, until death. Even when someone is hospitalized, many family members cook, tend for, and support the dying person. Few mothers have not experienced the death of an infant or small child, and few children have not seen a number of dead persons immediately prior to their burial. Death is part of life; so much so that in many traditions the deceased person will be buried at the threshold of the door or adjacent to the family home.

Cultural attitudes to health and sickness, death and dying, will inevitably show up on the occasion of the dying or death of a member of an intercultural community, or of a parent or sibling. Talking about such attitudes, the better to prepare the whole community, is highly advisable, though a delicate topic to raise dispassionately.

Time and Space

Cultural attitudes to time (chronemics) are notoriously varied, as are attitudes to space and privacy. Linear or chronological time marks time's regular passage as measured by a clock—or the sun. But some people rarely see the sun, and others rarely tell time by a clock or watch. Not by chance do "clock-watchers" speak of time using verbs associated with economics: saving, wasting, losing, using, or spending time. Nor is it coincidental that in such societies, where people worked long hours for a company or institution, they received a gold watch if they reached retirement age. Up to this moment their time had been largely governed by their employers; the phrase was "time is money," or "your time is not your own." Now their time is finally their own again—a fact symbolized by the gold watch: now, finally, their time is their own.

In rural or nonindustrialized society, the sun is the primary measure of time. People rise and sleep with sunrise and sunset. If electricity is expensive, intermittent, or nonexistent and people have little of what others call "leisure time," they seem less driven and freer to do what they choose. Time is not a commodity to save or waste but the backdrop to daily life. If "clock-watchers" complain of having too little time, people elsewhere usually find that they can make their own priorities and accomplish what is needed. Their attitude is determined as much by culture as by personal whim.

Likewise, attitudes to space (proxemics) can be considered. How people relate physically to others is partly a matter of temperament and appropriateness. Some people like to get close, while others maintain a certain distance. But culture and context also determine appropriate distance and closeness between specific people. People of different cultures need to adjust, and this can be a delicate and even embarrassing process.

Questions arise and might be discussed profitably in a community setting: Did you unconsciously relate to time as a scarce commodity (did you "save, waste, spend, keep, lose" time)? Do you sometimes or often wish you were somewhere else and doing something else? Would you rather be younger? And in relation to ideas about space: How highly do you value personal privacy? Can you live alone? Are you afraid of enclosed/open spaces? Do you favor prayer and liturgy that is more interiorized and private or more social and public?

Living Interculturally

So much remains unsaid. We have not explored "cultural profiles" that contrast egocentric and sociocentric societies, identify different cultural and individual emphases, and show likely tension points for communities. Nor did we identify the shift that can move a community from assimilation to inclusion and welcome. But we can conclude with some features that mark intercultural communities.

The most important focus is a common project, but not just some practical task. A community may repair property after a storm or undertake a fundraising drive; these are not a "common project." For a faith-based religious community, the common project that would be the community's best understanding of and response to what God is asking would be what draws the attention and stimulates the vitality of each member. It may be the "mission statement," founding charism, or raison d'être; and it needs to live not in documents or nostalgic memories but in each and every one. As a plant or animal will die without water, so a community's zeal and focus will atrophy unless its common project is nurtured and tended. And this requires a number of corollary features or qualities.

First, a common project is only common if everyone's contribution is sought and acknowledged; exclusion of any, or disrespect for individual efforts, will undermine their commitment, leave too much to specialists, or become an ideological preoccupation. Second, the atmosphere within the community must be such that people will take appropriate risks and sometimes fail, but mistakes and immaturity will not be so strongly sanctioned as to stifle future effort. Third, because of inevitable misunderstandings and frustrations built in to the community, life must be a forum or procedure allowing people to vent their frustrations publicly, without feeling intimidated, inhibited, or accused of cultivating personal animosity. If one person's frustration is allowed to surface, others can identify with it and move to take constructive rather than destructive measures.

A fourth, complementary, feature is that appropriate correction is sometimes necessary, and leadership is responsible for finding appropriate action. Vindictiveness is unjustifiable, but attentive listening, perhaps mediation, and flexibility are required, as well as sincere attempts at fence mending and an ongoing commitment to dialogue and development. Fifth, attention must be given to stress or depression and differences that can harden unless individuals' psychological well-being is supported and misunderstandings (arising as much from overload as from language differences or bad will) resolved. Finally, members of an intercultural community need to feel that they are all on the same side, working for common goals and the implementation of a common vision. This requires compassion and concern, and sometimes explicit encouragement rather than simply a lack of criticism. Each of these incidences and responses may occur in any human interaction, but in the case of a developing intercultural community, they will require more careful diagnosis and response than they would if all the parties shared a common culture and language.

2

Prophetic Leadership and Intercultural Communities
Partners in Peace Building

Maria Cimperman, RSCJ

Why write an essay on prophetic leadership and interculturality? What difference does this make? What does each bring, and why do we need this combination at this time? Why? What? How? Prophetic leaders see the necessity of intercultural living and ministry if we are to build peace, reconciliation, and new structures for our time. Efforts to deepen and widen our bonds through intercultural living (community, ministry, and prayer) offer a way forward beyond the fault lines of so much conflict today. Prophetic leadership calls forth the intercultural dimensions to help us find a way forward to God's vision of peace, justice, and love. Engaging interculturality is a way of engaging conflicts and transforming structures, as God transforms all.

I write this in the wake of the massacre and terrorist attack at Charlie Hebdo in Paris, a car bombing outside a police college in Yemen (January 7, 2015), and reports of well over one hundred people killed and a town burned down by Boko Haram militants in the northeastern Nigerian town of Baga, a continuing crisis of escalating violence. This all happened on the same day! Weighing equally heavily is the turmoil in the United States, still reeling and not yet free enough to respond beyond platitudes to the cries of racial injustice raised by the death of Eric Garner due to a chokehold and chest compression by police in Staten Island, New York (July 17, 2014), and the

Maria Cimperman, RSCJ, is a religious of the Sacred Heart of Jesus. She is associate professor of theological ethics at Catholic Theological Union (CTU) in Chicago. Her work is at the intersection of moral theology, social ethics, and spirituality. She is author of *When God's People Have HIV/AIDS: An Approach to Ethics* (Maryknoll, NY: Orbis Books, 2005) and *Social Analysis for the 21st Century: How Faith Becomes Action* (Maryknoll, NY: Orbis Books, 2015). She is also the director of the Center for the Study of Consecrated Life, also at CTU.

shooting of Michael Brown, a black man in Ferguson, Missouri (August 9, 2014), followed only a few months later by the targeted revenge shooting of two police officers in New York City (December 20, 2014). In the midst of the police officers' funerals, we have police and the mayor unable to dialogue (to the point that some police officers turned their backs on the mayor when he spoke at the funerals of the murdered officers). T-shirts with the words "I can't breathe" and placards with "We love our NYPD" (New York Police Department) come to mind as I see photos of public gatherings of France and beyond with people holding up pens and signs with "*Je suis Charlie*" (I am Charlie), in solidarity with the people of France and supporting freedom of expression.[1] So much is in motion. Prophets and leaders, reluctantly or not, know this terrain.

At the same time, while not making headlines, inroads with great potential are happening. We are gradually moving from cross-cultural to intercultural ways of being. My own context and experience remind me of this. As a member of an international congregation (Religious of the Sacred Heart of Jesus) teaching in an international school of theology (Catholic Theological Union) and living in an international community in Chicago, Illinois, all of which are putting significant effort into becoming intercultural communities, I am keenly aware of both the formative gifts and challenges of interculturality. The gifts and challenges hold great potential for conflict resolution and peace building, for church and the world.

Toward Understanding Interculturality

Prophetic leadership engages interculturality to assist in transformation of persons and systems. The description of interculturality I rely on is found in the introduction to this volume, with particular appreciation for the following:[2]

> Intercultural refers to the sustained interaction of people raised in different cultural backgrounds. In contrast to multicultural or cross-cultural settings, it denotes mutual exchange between cultures that can lead to transformation and enrichment of all involved.
>
> It also means that there are mutually reciprocal relationships among and between cultures; people from different cultural groups interact with one another, learn and grow together; build relationships and become transformed, shaped, and molded from one another's experiences. The

---

1. There is a discussion that needs to occur about the freedom of expression and how we use satire about revered figures and the Divine; nevertheless, violent responses are unacceptable.

2. See "Introduction" in this volume, xv.

focus is on relationship building (not survival), deep connections, inter-actions, mutual gifting, respect, and learning from one another. Here, the racial and cultural power imbalances are addressed, the common-ness is more highlighted than the differences, people are enabled to learn from each other, people appreciate and work together for a common cause, and this leads toward the transformation of all peoples.

We are always on this journey, gradually moving toward intercultural ways of being. This is a powerfully transformative ongoing reality and desired (begged for) grace. I see both amazing potential and significant challenge in becoming intercultural communities. The work is ongoing, and the end is not yet even closely in sight, but as "language shapes thought," so does walk-ing this path daily create habits and virtues toward becoming the people of God, with unity in our diversity, contributing further to the building of the reign of God that is here and not yet. Thus, this end, our telos, is here in sight and must remain so for our efforts to bear transformative fruit.

My desire in this essay is to illuminate and galvanize the transforma-tive potential of interculturality through the pastoral spiral, a tool for social transformation. The pastoral spiral uses the elements of experience, social analysis, faith reflection, and action in order to resolve conflicts and create new ways of relating and new structures.[3]

Because this is not easy, we particularly need prophetic leadership. Our time desperately needs prophetic leadership, and the only assurances we have is that (1) this will not be easy; (2) this is necessary; (3) we must do this together; and (4) God is with us, moving far more than we imagine. For people of faith, this must be and is enough. The promise of more is here, though we may see only wisps of exterior movement on the global scale we seek. Neither prophets nor leaders necessarily see the results of their efforts, so God's promise of Emman-uel is enough for us as well. While this makes prophetic leadership daring, it is also joyful; the joy is grounded in a hope that sees even slivers of movement and announces them in order to regularly remind the wider community of God's movements in our midst. Such is the nature of prophetic leadership. Interculturality offers us a way as we walk our path.

The possibilities that intercultural encounters offer in dealing with con-flicts and ethical issues that need structural transformation can be found in another paragraph from this volume's introduction:

Interculturality stands for movement from toleration of differences to appreciation and celebration of difference in the cultures. Therefore,

---

3. For more on the pastoral spiral, see Cimperman, *Social Analysis for the 21st Century*; Frans Jozef Servaas Wijsen, Peter Henriot, and Rodrigo Mejia, eds., *The Pastoral Circle Revisited: A Critical Quest for Truth and Transformation* (Maryknoll, NY: Orbis Books, 2005).

acceptance and joining with the other cultures in celebration are some signs of integration. Imbibing the values of other cultures and living joyfully become a sign of growth. Interculturality can be nurtured when one enters the sphere of spirituality with the concept that everyone is created in the image of God, and that cultural diversity is part of God's plan. Therefore, living and interaction with other cultures are participation in God's plan, and transforming cultures takes a person to another level.[4]

The challenge of intercultural living and ministry is that it continually reminds us of our need for transformation. We are continually asking forgiveness, awareness, and the grace of reimagining, realizing we are always guests in another's abode. Indeed, it is part of God's ongoing revelation to us.

In what follows, I will sketch a way in which prophetic leadership can utilize the gifts of interculturality and move toward not only resolving conflicts but also finding a way beyond the conflict to the underlying structural issues that are at stake. This method can be used in formation communities, religious orders, classrooms, parishes, social ministries, and civic centers and adapted according to the circumstances. In this essay, I will focus on how an intercultural religious community might utilize the pastoral spiral (a method toward personal and social transformation using experience, social analysis, faith reflection, and action) with a conflict or social issue. In order to do so, we need qualities consistent with prophetic leadership.

In looking at our world and the many conflicts we can be embroiled in at any moment, and for a way forward in hope, prophetic leadership must also utilize the gifts of interculturality more and more in conflicts and areas that require discernment. To the extent that we seek to live and minister as intercultural communities, however imperfectly, we are being formed for prophetic leadership and ongoing transformation.

As we briefly look at the steps of the pastoral spiral, I will include characteristics of prophetic leadership pertinent to each stage. In doing so we will see how such a leader (or, more accurately, community of leaders) might invite the gift of our diversity into the process of conflict resolution, and even into creative decision making. But first a few introductory words about prophetic leaders.

Emerging Prophetic Leadership

Not all prophets are leaders. Not all leaders are prophetic. We bring the two together in order to highlight characteristics about each which, together, can

---

4. See "Introduction," xvi.

serve our world today. We bring them together not so much to create a particular kind of person but to offer some ideas of virtues (practices and dispositions toward becoming a particular kind of good person) to cultivate for the world today and for God's mission of justice and peace in the world today.

Now a proviso about the word prophetic. I urge great restraint in ever calling oneself a prophet or prophetic. Let others call you a prophet if they wish, but do not declare yourself a prophet. Prophets are the ones who hear the word of God and proclaim it. Historically, prophets suffered much. Persons called to be such did not want to be prophets; they could anticipate the difficulties that would arise in this vocation. What I do here, though, is to look at some of the characteristics of prophets that are particularly helpful to our efforts to be intercultural communities that can respond to conflicts, can see things clearly together, and can serve social change. There are characteristics of prophets that are useful for looking at how to respond to conflicts and to find answers for harmonious living. These are the ones I will use.

Leadership. Much is said about leadership at many interdisciplinary levels. I will use the analogy of a web weaver as the attribute of a leader who could help us create reconciliation and social change. John Paul Lederach's seminal work *The Moral Imagination*[5] offers many ways that this vision of a leader, who invites the leadership of all, is an essential image for us today. Peter Senge, Otto Scharmer, and others who work with Theory U[6] models of leadership see that transformative leadership calls forth the leadership of all members of the community, ultimately convoking global leadership. Images of weaving and webs of relationship lead us to see how efforts for intercultural living have global and local implications. Inviting gifts that emanate from interculturality is natural to the web weaver.

In what follows, I will examine how prophetic leadership and intercultural communities, as they proceed through the steps of the pastoral spiral, can offer a significant contribution to conflict resolution and social transformation. Prophetic leadership, at each stage in the pastoral spiral (our tool for social transformation), engages the attributes of interculturality (living and ministering). I briefly explain each step as we enter into it.

Listening to Experiences

The first step in dealing with any conflict or social issue is listening to a person's experience, hearing what happened from the point of view of persons closest to the event. Here we begin prophetic listening, the discipline of lis-

---

5. John Paul Lederach, *The Moral Imagination: The Art and Soul of Building Peace* (Oxford: Oxford University Press, 2005).

6. See C. Otto Scharmer, *Theory U: Leading from the Future as It Emerges* (Oakland: Berrett-Koehler Publishers, 2009); Peter Senge, C. Otto Scharmer, Joseph Jaworski, and Betty Sue Flowers, *Presence: Human Purpose and the Field of the Future* (New York: Crown, 2008).

tening with others in such a way that it helps them get in touch with "what God is telling them" (see 1 Cor 14:29; 1 Thess 5:20–21).[7] Lederach writes, "Prophetic listening is like going on a journey alongside the person to whom we are listening. This kind of listening does what few other things can do. It helps us feel the presence in direction of God's truth."[8]

The crucial task of the leader here is to create a safe social space that brings all the voices together, including truth, mercy, justice, and peace. Experiences of interculturality serve this space well ("The focus is on relationship building [not survival], deep connections, interactions, mutual gifting, respect, and learning from one another."[9]) and build upon them. However, in this space, while on one level it is true that interculturality's focus is not on survival, on a larger level this is about survival of groups in the midst of conflict and after conflict.

This stage is absolutely crucial. If there are safe spaces, the narratives have a place and truth telling can begin. The prophetic leader invites and gathers people to share their stories. The prophet here is listening to the realities narrated and to God's voice heard in the narratives. The image I use is that of listening to the heartbeat of God's people experiencing conflicts and to God's heartbeat in the world.

The shared narratives name the conflict, pain, or injustice loudly, visibly. Intercultural living allows the narratives a deep richness. Images from around the world can be offered, shaping meanings to the realities heard in the stories. The narratives will give color, sound, visual images to explain the experience and the cries. Prophets are very attentive to narratives, and often prophets name injustices very vividly. Scripture scholar John Donahue reminds us of the "vivid descriptions and imaginative language of the prophets that challenge both our imaginations and our values."[10] The images raise up the seriousness of the issues so that none may think otherwise. It is precisely because one has hope for better than the current reality that one can name the issues honestly. Hope is bold and names the reality, yet sees possibility in even the slightest glimmer of movement.

Sharing narratives together creates interlocking narratives, even if others have not experienced the same event. The narratives begin to connect people. The process has begun. Prophetic leaders are connected to the experience of suffering, though not necessarily as directly as those suffering most. Some proximity offers both a perspective and an empathy for the other.

---

7. See John Paul Lederach, *Reconcile: Conflict Transformation for Ordinary Christians* (Ontario: Herald Press, 2014), 122.

8. Lederach, *Reconcile*, 122.

9. See "Introduction" in this volume, xv.

10. John R. Donahue, *Seek Justice That You May Live: Reflections and Resources on the Bible and Social Justice* (New York: Paulist, 2014), 73.

Within intercultural gatherings, as people share similar realities from their contexts, it is important to note (overtly even) how the different images and explanations can illuminate other similar experiences or the distinctiveness of the event. As sharing experience opens up realities, personal narratives can evoke relational understanding and empathy. When people have had sufficient opportunity to share their narratives, the next step flows. Sharing experience offers a beginning, and then social analysis gathers data to support the narratives and to further illuminate and underscore the reality.

Social Analysis

Social analysis begins data collection that further informs. Narratives illuminate the particularities of a person's experiences. Social analysis now widens and deepens our areas of understanding. Social analysis looks at the details in order to see how the conflict had been created and how it works. Both narratives and statistics are necessary to resolve issues. Here again, intercultural living and ministering can further highlight various areas and offer perspectives coming from different communities.

While narratives are offered from one's own experience, here the details that precipitated the dimensions of the conflict are offered, with painstaking detail. Experience needs the support of data, and data have to engage the experience. At the same time, neither is limited by the other, even as there must be some proximity of reality to both.

In this step research tests the narratives. This begins by naming all involved in the issue. Intercultural communities are particularly helpful here because the different views offer a wider spectrum of possible insights. A wide spectrum of naming is often a good indication of how well narratives have been received, how one's voice was heard, and how free and safe the space is for deeper uncovering and discovering of truths.

In the first part of social analysis, good dialogue can identify what/who is missing from a conversation, and steps can be taken to bring other voices to the table. For example, in September 2014 in my medical ethics course, I asked the twenty-seven students what was happening in medicine or health care in their countries of origin or where they had recently lived and served. A number of issues were named. Interestingly, no one brought up Ebola, so I, living in the United States, mentioned it and said we must be attuned to this because it is a pandemic. Once I mentioned it, a student from Nigeria nodded and spoke. He said that, while only a few cases had at that point been located in Nigeria, because of the way power and economics worked he was aware that, if he contracted the Ebola virus, he would never be evacuated to the United States for treatment, and he would have a slim chance of surviving. There was silence for a moment, and then another student, a nurse working in intensive care in the United States, nodded and said, "I know.

I work with some of the highest levels of technology in my hospital, and I keep wondering how we in the United States might offer more." Two voices are present here, and while they came from vastly different continents, in the same room, and willing to trust one another, they each spoke of the role of economics, its impact and its potential.

Later in the semester the entire class read *In the Company of the Poor*,[11] and encountered the authors, Dr. Paul Farmer and Fr. Gustavo Gutiérrez, OP. Both advocated changing the use of the expression of first, second, third, or fourth worlds into a working reality of "one world." They were finding experts in both medicine and theology to engage their realities and issues, helping them see one another not as "have nots" and "haves" but as one community. This helped a very international group talk to one another and move toward becoming an intercultural group. This also gave the group resources for further information. Farmer and the group he cofounded, Partners In Health (PIH), were also advising the countries hardest hit by Ebola: Liberia, Sierra Leone, and Guinea. PIH began offering new data and new suggestions from their expertise. One assertion of Farmer that gave hope and a lens for the students' values was that it is possible to have the same recovery rate from Ebola in these countries as in the United States, which is 90 percent. While it is delicate terrain, it is essential for leadership to create the spaces for many voices to speak and also find social data for analysis. From this type of connection and work comes a sense of responsibility and creative possibility.

Once the various actors or people involved have been named, their involvement is delineated in areas that include, but are not limited to, economics, politics, culture, religion, and the environment. The prophetic leader is here listening, keenly attentive to the cries of injustice and to the voices offering information to help understand what happened, in simplicity and complexity. If any voices are absent, prophets speak loudly, naming what is happening and asking, even demanding, a response. This is part of prophetic listening, listening for God speaking among the people. This is where leadership is essential, creating a space where different perspectives can be shared, and seeking out voices to invite and participate in the dialogue.

Because social analysis often confirms with challenging details the conflict already present, prophetic leadership helps the community face God's horizon, the reign of God, as it searches, researches, and shares. An intercultural community can help our wider communities look at the genocide in Rwanda, and dialogue about how to ensure now, twenty years later, the generation coming of age will not solve conflicts through further violence. Trust and truth telling are called forth and welcomed. Prophetic leadership can then widen from individuals and the group, and examining the data can

---

11. Michael Griffin and Jennie Weiss Block, eds., *In the Company of the Poor: Conversations with Dr. Paul Farmer and Fr. Gustavo Gutierrez* (Maryknoll, NY: Orbis Books, 2013).

lead to insights that together name the conflict's dimensions and leave space for new responses.

This will mean learning to respond as a community in process, with some slip ups on the road to more sure-footed responses. The good response and not so appropriate response, both are part of the process. For example, some years ago I taught a course in which I put much effort into building a community of prophetic dialogue, one that could together look at conflicts with the eyes of a community seeking God's ways. Throughout the process of the pastoral spiral, all the participants, in small groups and in the larger group, engaged one another's social issues. We were a diverse community, international, but not yet, I found, intercultural. Near the end of the course, each person presented a paper on the area of conflict of injustice that the person had worked on throughout the semester. During the presentation on a social justice issue in the Democratic Republic of Congo, one student looked at the political and economic influences subverting the resolution of the problem, and named the role of Rwandans in the eastern part of the Congo holding back a peaceful resolution. Never before in the class, neither in small groups nor in large group, did the student mention this. The comment took most of us by surprise, including the student from Rwanda in the class! I missed the conflict. So did everyone else in the room. What I learned here is that surprises will happen, even as we do our best to communicate, and that is also part of the learning curve of all cultures and communities, as all of our stories include histories and ongoing conflicts. It was later, while sharing this story with a colleague, that I heard, "Yes, that would have come up, directly or indirectly, but unless you knew that history well enough, you may not have seen this coming." In a later conversation with the student, I found out that it was only in preparing the presentation that the student sensed a significant lacuna that needed to be added to the presentation; she did so just before the presentation. We are all learners.

The same happens at various times in community living. As there is always more to each of us than at times we ourselves realize, so is the process of sharing intercultural living. This is not a point for discouragement but a point of humility (truth). The more we grow into intercultural communities, the more the conversations can be had earlier.

Movement does happen. It was in this same group that when we engaged culture, significant insights emerged. One student was looking at her research topic, a corrupt government leadership attempting to change the constitution, which in that country limited the term of the highest levels of leadership. The general population, while at times questioning what was happening, had not galvanized, and the student researching could not understand why the people were not mobilizing to prevent the change in the constitution. However, during the large-group discussion, someone asked how leadership was portrayed in that country. "The president is like the chief," the student explained. And in elucidating further, it was as if the scales on her eyes were removed. In utter astonishment, the student continued, "A chief is a chief for life. That is how many understand the president's role. Yet if a president rules for life, then there will be no accountability. A chief has responsibility and an honorable role in the community. We have not yet seen this sense of responsibility with any consistency in the role of president." It was in looking at culture through different eyes and asking a question from that lens that the insight emerged that now gave the student a deeper understanding of underlying areas to be addressed for the transformation of systems and persons.

At another moment, a group looking at the migration of peoples saw how the group's consideration of the religion of persons migrating had impacted the group's capacity to be welcoming and creative. The person offering this insight was one whose parents' religion had prevented them from migrating to another country. He was now in another country, and he knew the experience of being a member of a religious minority. Because of this experience, while he did not initially share this narrative since it was not directly related to the topic of migration, his story came forth when the data in the group's research showed other minority religion groups. Here we see again the importance of communities, at whatever step in the process, to show prophetic leadership by opening up spaces for this sharing.

This step in the pastoral spiral offers both information and opportunity to acknowledge any part of one's involvement or participation in the injustice. This is the section that closely engages our earlier description of interculturality: "Here, the racial and cultural power imbalances are addressed . . . people are enabled to learn from each other . . . and this leads toward the transformation of all peoples." Understood here also is that this is not limited to racial and cultural imbalances but to all the areas of relationship that need to be addressed and, ultimately, reconciled.

The leader continues to find ways to invite all and to show how the entire community, with its many gifts, is called to participation of not only naming the issues but also lamenting, contemplating, and creatively responding. When we see our involvement (or lack thereof) in any of the areas, we lament. This step in the pastoral process includes naming the realities, and acknowledging our own sinfulness, our own failure to bother to love.[12] We lament because we hope. We are people of hope, who acknowledge the reality before us but believe we are created for so much more, and that so much more is possible. Our lament here is both an act of humility and of hope. Good leadership keeps open safe spaces that give us room to see where we too are responsible for what is happening.

---

12. I am grateful to James Keenan, SJ, for this definition of sin.

Faith Reflection

When we are able to see our role in a situation, often we are moved to remedy this with immediate action. However, the response with the most potential is that of silence, stillness, of prayerful reflection.[13] Just as prophets listen to God's cries and hear the cries of the people in pain, prophetic leadership must here urge an attentively quiet listening and an open-hands (consider the image of the risen Christ with arms open) approach to the reality. This is a most creative space, if only we let it be so. Here the leader gathers the voices together, acknowledges the wounds, the concerns, the desires for another world that can live in peace, with justice and love. The weaving of relationships toward a new reality is happening here, interweaving the diverse pieces with creative potential. Quieting, while difficult in many of our cultures today, is a space pregnant with possibility. Prophetic leadership keeps the community close to the sacred scriptures and stories of God that offer a landscape of hope and possibility, reminding people of God's desires and love. Intercultural communities also offer ways of praying together that may include begging Sophia's wisdom. Leaders must continue to ask the questions that quietly evoke the depth and breadth of imagination and creativity that the members possess, individually and collectively. "I wonder, How am I being called to respond here and now? How are we as a community being called to respond?"

Trust in God holds the group together at this time. Prophets again remind people of their inherent identity in God. As the webs of relationship do their work, intercultural groups imagine with the diversity of images, sounds, and words available; much is possible. New ways do emerge, and intercultural communities have immense potential to not only illuminate the problems but point to new directions. The same gifts that allow us to see where a structure is unjust help us reimagine new ways of relating. If new structures emerge, they will probably be significantly different, for what held the previous structures up needs to be dismantled. Some will also resist structures, discerning that for a time at least, the webs of relationship can create the new that seeks to emerge more fully. As energy steeps in the quiet spaces of faith reflection, the energy is rekindled as new directions begin to emerge. The energy of action ultimately comes from a calm, focused space. It is helpful to note that if we give time to reflective space, when the insights come, they come quickly and with clarity. These are the spaces that hold and move transformative action, in persons and in systems (created by persons).

---

13. Depending on one's spiritual background, the response could be named meditation, contemplation, prayerful reflection. The point is that we listen to hear where the Spirit is moving us to act, where insight will emerge from our deepest sense of understanding, and perhaps beyond our understanding.

Action

Here we find ourselves in the next step of the pastoral spiral. If action flows from the faith reflection and doesn't jump over it after social analysis, prophetic leadership has now moved more fully to the wider community. (This is, after all, a hope of prophetic leadership. Intercultural communities become communities of prophetic leadership and the webs of relationship grow ever more widely.) The actions considered do not necessarily take on all the areas in the analysis; there is usually a prioritizing of the most essential steps. Here again, the intercultural community offers its collective wisdom. A plan is then made, and one can first try some possibilities out (prototype) or begin the response. The key here is making sure that somehow each member of the community is involved, directly or indirectly. Important in action is a strong web of coresponsibility so that all feel responsible (able to respond), connected, and willing to create the new, emerging with the gifts each has. This step connects and deepens the communities involved and opens spaces for welcoming new relationships as change is enacted.

Leadership continues to emerge in the wider community as more see how all are welcome and necessary in responding to conflict and creating new relationships. Intercultural living and ministering remind us of the necessity of all. Because this is a pastoral *spiral* rather than a circle, the reminder is that as change and conflicts require new ways of relating, some steps will need to be repeated and adapted as efforts for change begin. This is part of change, and intercultural communities of practice work with this all the time. This effort goes with the pastoral spiral.

Conclusion

Prophetic leadership and intercultural living and ministry together serve social transformation. The necessity of both is clear from the introduction to this essay. Both interculturality and prophetic leadership are essential for creatively participating in the reign of God. The pastoral spiral offers one way of utilizing and highlighting how intercultural living and prophetic leadership offer much in contributing to the building of God's kingdom, one that is rooted in love, grounded in peace building, and lived justly. This is our gift and this is our call.

3

The Mission of Money
Toward a Theology of the Righteous Rich

Jonathan J. Bonk

This essay argues that the integrity and the credibility of Christians—not just clergy or missionaries—are compromised when their relatively affluent lifestyles are conspicuously at odds with what is taught and modeled by biblical authors and exemplars such as Moses, the prophets, Jesus, and the apostles.

Greed Is Idolatry: What Is Greed, and Why Does It Matter?

Among those who make their living by speaking *for* God and *about* God, cross-cultural Christian missionaries—perhaps more than any other professional religious group—are acutely conscious of the need for consistency between *what they say they believe* and *how they actually live*. The professionally pious are in constant peril of our Lord's scathing indictment of the religious leaders of his day, recorded in Matthew 23. It seems to have been this awareness that lay behind St. Paul's personal lifestyle choices, summarized in his final farewell to the Ephesians: "I coveted no one's silver or gold or clothing. You know for yourselves that I worked with my own hands to support myself and my companions. In all this, I have given you an example that by such work we must support the weak, remembering the words of the Lord Jesus, for he himself said, 'It is more blessed to give than to receive.'" (Acts 20:33–35; cf. 1 Tim 6:6–11, 17–19).[1]

Canadian-born **Jonathan J. Bonk** is the executive director emeritus of Overseas Ministries Study Center, New Haven, CT, USA, and senior contributing editor to the journal *International Bulletin of Missionary Research*. He serves as research professor of mission at Boston University School of Theology and is director of Dictionary of African Christian Biography at Boston University.

1. All scriptural quotations are from the New Revised Standard Version Catholic Edition (NRSVCE), copyright © 1989, 1993 the Division of Christian Education of the National Council of the Churches of Christ in the United States of America.

Our scriptures do not advocate a double standard—one for those who make their living from professional piety and another for everyone else. What the Bible says *to* and *about* the rich, it says to and about *anyone*—clergy or layperson—who professes belief in gospel, identifies with the church, and is relatively affluent within their social context.

As surprising as it may seem to some Christians, only one subject—*idolatry*—receives more attention in the Bible than the recurring theme of *economic justice* and *equity*.[2] And the two subjects are often related. Since *greed* is *idolatry*, any society or smaller community characterized by social and material inequities will not long survive and can never thrive. That was the deeply unpopular message of the Hebrew prophets in biblical times. It is a message repeatedly confirmed in the fate of societies since then, a message whose truth is resoundingly supported by recent research.[3]

The Jewish scriptures record a people's perennial but ultimately futile quest for national security. Failure to create and adhere to the spirit of Mosaic law—practices ensuring economic and social equity—spelled the doom of the Jewish nation, successively vanquished, occupied, and exiled by the Assyrians, the Babylonians, the Medes, the Persians, and the Romans. And such inequities, if allowed to evolve unchecked within modern-day communities of Christians, will produce similar results. We reap not only what we sow, but more than we sow. That is the timeless and universal law of all harvests.

No believing Jew or Christian can avoid the uncomfortable truth that national or ecclesiastical insecurity is almost inevitably a function of ethical failure and theological lapse, manifest in the steady erosion of what their scriptures refer to as *justice*. It should not be lost on Bible readers that those most in tune with the ethical/theological roots of insecurity—the prophets—were typically viewed by their contemporaries with deep hostility. Those who by heeding the prophets had much to lose politically and economically could not tolerate God's invasion of their comfortably established social and economic status quo.

In the Hebrew scriptures, *justice* is always associated with *equity* . . . with a society's or a family's prioritization of care for the most marginal and vulnerable, including strangers and sojourners. This emphasis becomes even more emphatic in the Christian scriptures, in which Jesus declares that the Spirit of the Lord has anointed him "to bring good news to the poor. . . . To proclaim release to the captives and recovery of sight to the blind, to let the oppressed go free, to proclaim the year of the Lord's favor" (Luke 4:18–19). As Jesus approaches the end of his earthly ministry, he reminds his followers that it is

---

2. See Jim Wallis, "A Bible Full of Holes," *The Mennonite* (November 21, 2000): 6–7.

3. Particularly useful is the published report by Richard Wilkinson and Kate Pickett based on thirty years of research, *The Spirit Level: Why Greater Equality Makes Societies Stronger* (London: Bloomsbury Press, 2009).

their relationship to the poor in this life that will determine their fate in the next: ". . . the king will say to those at his right hand, 'Come, you that are blessed by my Father, inherit the kingdom prepared for you from the foundation of the world; for I was hungry and you gave me food, I was thirsty and you gave me something to drink, I was a stranger and you welcomed me, I was naked and you gave me clothing, I was sick and you took care of me, I was in prison and you visited me'" (Matt 25:34–36).

While economic and social inequity within communities pose profound relational and communicatory challenges, equally serious are complex issues of integrity and credibility that confront wealthy followers of Jesus living and ministering in contexts of profound poverty. If *greed* be understood as *the insistence on more than enough in contexts where neighbors have less than enough*, even the best intentioned among us can be regarded as greedy. And *greed*, in St. Paul's undiplomatic words, *is idolatry* (Col 3:5).[4] A missionary or a minister of even modest means might, in the minds of those who are poorer, be simply *peddling the word of God for profit* (2 Cor 2:17). Who among the poor would not like to trade places with them, earning a comfortably secure living from professional piety? Who would not want to do well by doing good, if given the option?

Following the lead of affluent Western societies and their concomitant notions of "development," a growing proportion of people in our globalized world are shaped and defined by a way of life known as "consumerism," which St. Peter characterized as "the futile way of life inherited from [our] ancestors" (1 Pet 1:18). Consumer societies rely for their survival on the escalation of each successive generation's sense of material entitlement. One generation's luxuries must evolve into the next generation's needs if the complex economic system is to survive.[5]

Among the most theologically disturbing effects of gross material inequity within community and church is the social isolation of the rich from the poor—an isolation that dilutes or even eliminates empathy and its essential implications for family, community, and nation.[6] Possession of wealth virtually ensures social insulation. Wealth serves as a buffer from the harsh realities of everyday life. The word *insulate* is thought to have derived from the

---

4. Brian S. Rosner, *Greed as Idolatry: The Origin and Meaning of a Pauline Metaphor* (Grand Rapids, MI: Eerdmans, 2007).

5. Peter C. Whybrow observes, "As America's commercial hegemony has increased and our social networks have eroded, we have lost any meaningful reference as to how rich we really are, especially in comparison to other nations." See Peter C. Whybrow, *American Mania: When More Is Not Enough* (New York: W. W. Norton, 2005), 38–39. Whybrow is the Judson Braun Professor of Psychiatry and Bio-behavioral Science and the director of the Jane and Terry Semel Institute of Neuroscience and Behavior at the University of California in Los Angeles.

6. See J. D. Trout, *The Empathy Gap: Building Bridges to the Good Life and the Good Society*, (New York: Viking, 2009).

Latin *insulatus*—meaning to make into an island. In its common use, "to insulate" means "to prevent or reduce the transmission of electricity, heat, or sound to (or from) a body, device, or region by surrounding it with a non-conducting material."[7]

Both the etymology and the definition of this word are instructive in the context of this essay, since affluent Christians can be commonly observed inhabiting "islands" in the seas of poverty around them. Even modest wealth serves as "nonconducting material" that protects the affluent from the "heat" and "sound" of poverty.

Since biblical faith is not primarily doctrinal but *relational* (lived out in relationship to God and neighbor), for one Christian's relative affluence to prevent, distort, or even destroy relationships within the community of faith is a matter of grave and even ultimate concern. As the apostles and church fathers rightly understood, just how inequity within the church is handled either demonstrates the church's deepest hypocrisies or manifests its extraordinarily unique character (1 John 3:10–24).

In both the Old and the New Testaments, there is a modest stream of teaching that soothes the rich: the sanctity of private property, the association of wealth with happiness, prosperity as a reward for righteousness, and the frequently close link between personal behavior and poverty. Such teaching reassures those who, by whatever means, find themselves in the happy state of relative comfort and affluence. But in counterpoint to this thin strand of teaching is the relentlessly unflattering portrayal of the rich that suffuses both the Old and the New Testaments. Only the sketchiest outline of what I have discussed more fully elsewhere is possible here.[8] Consider the following:

Rights Associated with Acquiring, Using, or Disposing of Personal Wealth Were—for the People of God—Subordinated to an Obligation to Care for Poorer, Weaker Members of Society

The divinely sanctioned guidelines outlined below seem to have been intended to prevent the permanent division of God's human community between those who enjoyed economic advantage and those who endured economic hardship. Hence we have these examples.

- *In recurring Jubilee years* all land was to revert to its original owners (Lev 25:8–28); *The Jubilee* seems to have been designed to have a leveling effect.

---

7. *Collins English Dictionary of the English Language*, 1979.

8. I have written on this subject on numerous occasions elsewhere. See, e.g., "Money, Wealth," in William A. Dyrness and Veli-Matti Kärkkäinen, eds., with Juan Francisco Martinez and Simon Chan, *Global Dictionary of Theology: A Resource for the Global Church* (Downers Grove, IL: IVP Academic, 2008), 576–82.

Its practice meant that whatever economic advantage, momentum, or mass that might for any reason—luck, good management or mismanagement, ability or lack of ability—have been gained by one person over another, could not be legitimately sustained indefinitely. Jubilee was a time of fresh beginnings for the land and for the economic prospects of the unfortunate. Compliance with Jubilee made the exponential and permanent accumulation of properties impossible (Lev 25:8–43). Unfortunately, in Jewish Biblical history compliance seems to have been the exception, rather than the rule.

- Regular *sabbatical years,* called for the forgiveness of all debts (Deut 15:1–6; 2 Chron 36:15–21), were clearly intended for the well-being of the poor, wild animals, and the land itself. Debts were to be canceled, giving those who had suffered catastrophic economic misfortune opportunity for a fresh beginning. It was as though life was a game, played in seven-year segments. At the end of the game, the pieces were redistributed and everyone began to play again (Deut 15:1–11). What one might consider a sound business principle—refusal to lend money to someone unlikely to repay it—God calls a "wicked thought" in Deuteronomy 15:9 (see also Ex 23:10–11; Lev 25:1–7).

- *Annual tithing* was mandated, with aliens, orphans, widows, and the landless as primary beneficiaries every third year (Deut 14:22–29). Most of the practical provisions of Mosaic Law governing property and possessions had the poor in mind, perhaps anticipating the instability and unviability of any community characterized by gross economic inequity among its members. Tithes were emphatically not designed to enrich the religious establishment, the equivalent then of today's clergy (Deut 26:1–15).

- *Guidelines for loans, interest, and collateral* were deliberately crafted and interpreted with poor borrowers in view—widows, orphans, aliens—rather than lenders (Exod 22:25–27; Lev 25:35–38; Deut 23:19–20; 24:6, 10–13, 17–18).

- *There should be no poor among you,* said the Law (Deut 15:4). An entire complex of laws was meant to preserve society from reified, intergenerational inequity. Employers were likewise strictly prohibited from taking advantage of poor employees (Deut 24:14–15; see also Lev 25:35–43; Deut 15:12–18; Pro 14:31; 19:17).

- *Gleaning regulations were designed to sustain the poor* (Deut 24:19–20).
- *Debt repayment guidelines favored the poor* (Deut 15:1–11).
- *Guidelines for employers favored employees* (Deut 24:14–15).

While much more could be said, it is obvious that God not only intended the poor to be protected from exploitation, but that they were to be the law's chief beneficiaries.

Wealth Is Seen as Inherently Dangerous and Is Frequently Associated with Fatally Destructive Behaviors of Persons and Nations Alike

- *The prosperous tend to marginalize God* (Deut 8:10–20).
- *Wealth is the natural culture in which pride and the delusion of the self-made man or nation flourish* (Ezek 28:4–5; Jer 6:13–15; 12:1–4; 17:11; 1 Tim 6:6–19).
- *Wealth is usually associated with overindulgence, gluttony, and greed, which is idolatry* (1 Kgs 6–7; 10:14–29; 11:1–6; 1 Cor 5:9–11; Col 3:5).
- *The wealthy frequently abuse personal power by their mistreatment of the weak and their contempt for the poor* (1 Kgs 10:14–29; cf. 1 Kgs 12:1–24; Jer 22:13–17; Ezek 16:49; 22:25–29; Job 12:5).
- *The priorities and orientations of the rich are often fatally misguided* (Isa 5:7–8, 20–23).
- *Personal overindulgence and servile catering to the wealthy compromise the integrity of those who claim to speak for God* (Jer 6:13–15; 8:10–11; Mic 2:6–11; 3:5, 10–11). Religious leaders and missionaries in the early days of the church who "loved money" warranted especially harsh criticism (Matt 23:23–26; Luke 11:39–42; cf. Matt 7:21–27; Luke 6:46; 11:28; 2 Cor 2:17).
- *Our Lord pronounced woes on the rich*, declaring that it was almost impossible for a rich man to inherit eternal life, and that to be a "wealthy disciple" is almost an oxymoron (Matt 19:16–24; Jas 5:1–6).
- *Preoccupation with self, money, and pleasure are signs of the doomed "last days" way of life* (2 Tim 3:1–5).
- *Personal wealth demands absorption in mammon, deadening a person's or a nation's sense of their spiritual destitution* (Matt 13:22; 22:5; Luke 12:13–21; Rev 3:14–21).
- *Wealth is never sufficient, breeding greed . . . a continual desire for more* (Eph 4:17–19; 5:3–11).

Wealth and Prosperity Were Usually Proof of Self-Indulgence, Greed, and Exploitation of the Poor (Prov 13:23; Isa 32:7; Job 21:7–16)

- *Faithfulness to God is no guarantee of either prosperity or security* (Jer 44:15–18).
- *It is possible to have too much* (Prov 30:8–9).
- *Passive neglect of the poor leads to judgment* (Deut 8:19–20; 28:15; 2 Chron 36:15–21).
- *Religious orthodoxy without practical concern for the poor is a hollow sham* (Isa 1:10–23).

God Actively Identifies with the Poor and
the Socially Marginalized (Exod 22:21–27).

- *The promised messiah would identify with the poor and the oppressed* (Ps 22; Isa 53). Jesus was born in a stable and his parents were far from rich (Luke 1:46–56; 2:1–20, 21–24; cf. Lev 12:8). His Nazareth manifesto focused explicitly on the poor (Luke 4:16–30; Matt 15:31–46).
- *God's children are marked by their proactive concern for the poor and the oppressed* (Job 30:24–25; 31:16–28; Amos 5:4–24; 6:4–7; 8:4–7).
- *God meets the needs of the poor through the actions and interventions of his obedient people.* This was the intent of the laws dealing with the treatment of the poor by the rich (Neh 5:1–13).
- *Christ's true followers proactively identify with the poor in practical, costly ways* (Matt 23:1–39; 25:31–46).

With biblical history and teaching informing and guiding the church's understanding of itself, its mission, and its *modus operandi*, we now return to the question posed in the title of this essay: in an age of dwindling resources and unique difficulties, where do the opportunities for faithfulness lie?

Economic Dimensions of Christian Conversion:
Essential but Complicated

As unprecedented as contemporary challenges facing the church may seem, they are not as unique as our parochialism may lead us to assume. In the earlier centuries of the church, Rome—an imperial civilization based on military expansion and slave labor—was the predominant political, military, and economic force, bending much of the then-known world to its will. It was a system that entrenched opulence for an elite few, relative social stability for Roman citizens, and an uneasy "peace" for the subjugated. Its global reach and influence foreshadowed that of Victorian Great Britain two hundred years ago and the United States today, with its vast, far-flung military presence and global economic reach. Although accurate figures are difficult to confirm, credible sources say that in 2011 there were up to 900 American military bases in 148 countries around the world.[9] American influence is also wielded through the International Monetary Fund (IMF), the World Bank, and scores of mammoth multinational corporations, financial institutions

---

9. See "Ron Paul Says US Has Military Personnel in 130 Nations," http://www.politifact.com. See also "The Worldwide Network of US Military Bases," on Globalization website, http://www.globalresearch.ca. For information on the lucrative and utterly corrupt global weapons trade, in which the United States enjoys a 44 percent share, see the U.S. Congressional Research Service's Grimmett Report, "The Arms Trade Is Big Business," http://www.globalissues.org.

and communications systems affecting a large proportion of the planet's inhabitants, directly or indirectly.

When Rome was the dominant global force, wealth derived chiefly from the possession of inherited or expropriated agricultural estates, controlled by the Roman plutocracy. It could be a brutal system. As Peter Brown explains, "The super-rich had always been absentee landowners on a massive scale; they felt little responsibility toward their dependents. Distance and the complex administrative systems needed to extract and pass on rents attenuated their presence on the land. An entire hierarchy of little lords stood between the super-rich and their slaves and tenants."[10]

At that time great debates concerning the Bible's teaching on mammon raged within the church. What should be the church's relationship to the wealthy? On one side of the theological/ethical divide, the wealthy landowners of Milan were portrayed as Ahab in the story of Naboth: "The story of Naboth is an ancient tale," Ambrose (ca. 340–397 CE) wrote, "But today it is an everyday occurrence."[11] To Christian theologians espousing this perspective, avarice was the root of all evil, and Elijah's curse must necessarily apply to the rich landowners of their day: "You have slain, and you have taken possession of the inheritance. Therefore, in the place where dogs licked up the blood of Naboth, dogs shall lick up your blood" (1 Kgs 21:19). As far as Ambrose, the Bishop of Milan, was concerned, only the repentant rich could hope to find a place in the church. For the rich, the church was a profoundly uncomfortable place.[12]

But renunciation of wealth could have disastrous consequences for the very people it was ostensibly calculated to help. Procurement of grain for the teeming populations of cities was a principle concern for officials, since drought or crop failure in one or more of the empire's far-flung bread baskets presented the specter of famine and all of its attendant social disorders.[13]

Thus, when in 408 CE Pinianus and Melanian—a super-rich young couple—began to divest themselves of the vast estates and luxurious villas that were theirs by inheritance, there was a backlash by the eight thousand slaves who had been instantly manumitted by their pious sacrifice. The slaves refused their freedom. Neither they nor those who lived on these vast properties wished to be handed over to new owners, whoever they might happen to be. The seemingly principled and heroic renunciation of wealth by the young couple constituted an abandonment of their obligations to maintain

---

10. Peter Brown, *Through the Eye of a Needle: Wealth, the Fall of Rome, and the Making of Christianity in the West, 350–550 AD* (Princeton, NJ: Princeton University Press, 2012), 296.

11. Ibid., 138ff.

12. See Brown's chapter on "The Pelagian Criticism of Wealth," in ibid., 308–21.

13. Brown, *Through the Eye of a Needle*, passim.

social stability and secure the well-being of their dependents.[14] In the modern world of multinational corporations, it takes little imagination to realize that similar divestment of wealth by the super-rich would likewise wreak havoc on the most vulnerable. Whatever we deem as "evil" has no pure existence but is inevitably so thoroughly infused with "good" as to make goodness the first casualty when "evil" is abandoned or purged.

On the other side of the converted rich debate was the more nuanced and accommodating approach represented by Augustine (354–430 CE). He did not regard wealth itself as intrinsically problematic, since it, like all of life, lay within the providence of God.[15] This being so, the question was one of management. A righteous manager would steward wealth to the glory of God and in the service of God's agenda in his world. Both the wealth itself and the *modus operandi* of those to whom it had been providentially entrusted lay within the purposes and mission of God. Not only was it possible for rich people to be welcomed into the church, it was essential that they be welcomed, for they were a crucial means for the accomplishment of God's mission through the church on earth. This mission included not merely salvation in the sweet by and by, but generosity, justice, care for the needy, and investment in the common social good in the here and now. The righteous rich were not to be regarded as a grudgingly permitted, embarrassing aberration in the community of faith; they could and should be welcomed as an integral part in the church's contribution to the common good.

Similarities between the Roman Empire and the present world order, long dominated by the United States, and before that by Great Britain, while differing in the details, are apparent.[16] The West is an essentially "extractionist" society—extracting forests, water, minerals, clean air, and the environment in exchange for a comfortable way of life. Our way of life depends on increasing volumes of extraction since we have defined success and happiness in terms of more. This pernicious but deeply alluring gospel has been an implicit, and even explicit, part of the message that Westerners, including its missionaries, have carried to the uttermost parts of the earth. Thanks to the success of this gospel's emissaries, the planet is now on an apparently irreversible trajectory to environmental doom and climatic disaster. We live in an age of starkly dwindling resources.[17]

---

14. Ibid., 294–97.

15. Ibid., 376–84.

16. See Indur John Mohan Razu, *Global Capitalism as Hydra: A New Look at Market, Money and MNC's. Ethical Dilemmas Between the Idols of Death and the God of Life* (Delhi: ISPCK under Bombay Urban Industrial League for Development [BUILD], 2010). See also Madelaine Drohan, *Making a Killing: How and Why Corporations Use Armed Force to Do Business* (Toronto: Vintage Canada, 2003).

17. The Living Planet Report for 2014 makes sobering reading. Issued every two years for the last forty years, the gloomy but unsurprising report indicates that "population sizes

As in the days of the early church, so we too must wrestle with what it means to be a wealthy person, a privileged community, or a business enterprise aspiring to practicing biblical righteousness in our contexts. Reminiscent of Joseph in the service of Pharaoh, or Queen Esther in the courts of Xerxes, we find ourselves immersed in the complex world of powerful multinational corporations—financial, pharmaceutical, telecommunications, electronics, media, manufacturing, shipping, transportation. We are in many ways severely curtailed in our ability to wield influence for good. But we must try. We take as a hopeful sign the business enterprises, sometimes large ones, for which constructive social engagement is the paramount concern, over profits. One thinks of the Guinness family business in Ireland, brewers of one of the most iconic beers in the world. For the first 250 years of its existence, the primary mission of this company was to be a force for social good in the lives of its employees, across the length and breadth of Great Britain, through its financing of evangelical and Quaker driven social reforms, and around the world through Protestant missions. Guinness beer was a means to greater ends.[18] There are businesses today in my own (Mennonite) circles whose goals are infused with proactive, creative, active service to "the least of these."[19]

But in the end, each of us is parochial. Our spheres of influence are limited, even if we are relatively affluent. Like our Lord, the key to authentic mission for any of us always entails incarnation—immersion in a specific place, time, and culture, and domination by powerful political and economic interests at odds with what we are doing, and at times even to who we are. Jesus, after all, was a laughably parochial figure, even for his own time. Living, ministering, and dying in an occupied back eddy of a powerful empire, with no influence on the political powers of his day; at the behest of curious crowds and insignificant men and women, many of them on the margins of their own Jewish society; attending to the wrenchingly personal agendas of the sick, the blind, the crippled, the diseased, and the disreputable; tried,

---

of vertebrate species—mammals, birds, reptiles, amphibians, and fish—have declined by 52 percent over the last 40 years." It goes on to point out that our finite planet cannot sustain steadily increasing human demands on nature. Even if the world's population were to remain what it is, and human demand on resources were to remain what they are, we would require a planet with almost twice as many resources—trees, fish, animals, oceans—in order to assure survival. See http://www.worldwildlife.org.

18. See Stephen Mansfield, *The Search for God and Guinness: A Biography of the Beer That Changed the World* (Nashville, TN: Thomas Nelson, 2009).

19. I mention only one umbrella organization, the Mennonite Economic Development Associates (MEDA), "an international economic development organization whose mission is to create business solutions to poverty. Founded in 1953 by a group of Mennonite business professionals, we partner with the poor to start or grow small and medium-sized businesses in developing regions around the world." See http://www.meda.org.

condemned, and crucified on the basis of charges trumped up by a corrupt religious establishment. It is *this* Jesus who is our resurrected and living Lord. It is *this* Jesus whose Spirit infuses and animates the church. It is *this* Jesus whose humble followers turned the world upside down. It is *this* "five-loaves-and-two-fishes" Jesus who calls and equips his people with the gifts of apparent insufficiency and inefficiency . . . mere grains of wheat, falling into the ground and dying, to produce the fruit of righteousness. If we are among those who seem affluent by the comparative measure of those around us, what does this righteousness look like?

Toward a Theology of the Righteous Rich

In the biblical narrative, economic repentance is rare. A reading of the prophets makes one quickly aware that those with power found ingenious ways to annul or circumvent divinely mandated moral obligations that impinged on their entitlements. According to the prophets, the Jewish nations collapsed and their peoples were forced into exile precisely because they broke both the spirit and the letter of the Law, with its heavy bias toward the poor: "This was the guilt of your sister Sodom," Ezekiel reminded his nation's doomed but smugly complacent leaders; "she and her daughters had pride, excess of food, and prosperous ease, but did not aid the poor and needy" (Ezek 16:49).

Scriptural teaching on wealth and poverty is disquieting to those of us shaped by cultures that foster, laud, and rely on ever-increasing levels of material consumption. Of course, we North Americans are well aware that our shared planet is home to vast numbers of impoverished and destitute peoples, and that some of these are found in our own cities. But our niggling discomfort is easily quelled. What, after all, do such people have to do with *us*? Our very helplessness in the face of endemic human tragedy is, in its own way, reassuring, because it lets us off the hook. Meaningful ministry does not begin with solutions, but with incarnation. Jesus is our model.

For incarnational ministry to be effective, personal behavior must correspond with professed belief. As the old adage says, "what you are speaks so loud that I can't hear what you say." I propose that missionaries serving in contexts of urban poverty accept the status of "*righteous rich*" and learn to play its associated roles in ways that are *biblically informed* and *contextually appropriate*. This recommendation is predicated on the assumption that the missionary understands Jesus to be both the message itself and the exemplar of all those who minister in his name.

It is clear that the Christian scriptures draw a sharp distinction between the *righteous who are prosperous* and the *rich who are unrighteous*, and that the distinction between the two is determined chiefly on the basis of their respective dealings with the poor.[20]

Job is the most ancient and probably the best-known biblical character to be characterized as both *rich* and *righteous*. This being the case, it is appropriate to bring this brief article to a conclusion by listening to his views on the subject. A laudable goal for any modern righteous person of means, whether missionary or corporate tycoon, would be to truthfully repeat Job's words to God, and to then hear an echoing "Amen" from the poor among whom he or she resides.

> [16] If I have withheld anything that the poor desired,
>   or have caused the eyes of the widow to fail,
> [17] or have eaten my morsel alone,
>   and the orphan has not eaten from it—
> [18] for from my youth I reared the orphan like a father,
>   and from my mother's womb I guided the widow—
> [19] if I have seen anyone perish for lack of clothing,
>   or a poor person without covering,
> [20] whose loins have not blessed me,
>   and who was not warmed with the fleece of my sheep;
> [21] if I have raised my hand against the orphan,
>   because I saw I had supporters at the gate;
> [22] then let my shoulder blade fall from my shoulder,
>   and let my arm be broken from its socket.
> [23] For I was in terror of calamity from God,
>   and I could not have faced his majesty.
> [24] If I have made gold my trust,
>   or called fine gold my confidence;
> [25] if I have rejoiced because my wealth was great,
>   or because my hand had gotten much;...
> [27] and my heart has been secretly enticed,
>   and my mouth has kissed my hand;
> [28] this also would be an iniquity to be punished by the judges,
>   for I should have been false to God above.
>   (Job 31:16–28; cf. 29:11–17)

Whether one subscribes to the "hidden hand of the market" as the source of all good things, or whether one detects in the regional, national, and global marketplace the not-so-hidden hand of the economically and politically powerful, it is clear that Job understood himself to be personally responsible

---

20. See Christopher Wright's masterful summary of Old Testament teaching on the righteous rich in the appendix to this paper.

for playing a proactive role in the material well-being of poor people in his orbit, and that this is the way God wanted him to be. And we can be certain that this is the way Jesus wants his contemporary followers to be as well.

Jesus' own life was bracketed between the Nazareth manifesto and his portrayal of the final judgment. In neither case was speculative doctrine or fine-tuned theology on the agenda . . . as the incarnate son of God he lived correct doctrine; as the judge on the final judgment day he does not inquire about degrees of orthodox understanding, assigning a grade of pass or fail depending on our familiarity with a particular religion's insider knowledge. The playing field is completely level . . . we are judged by our kindness and open handedness in everyday parochial circumstances.

That is the message captured by Indonesian artist Wisnu Sasongko in his 2004 painting inspired by Acts 4:34: "There was not a needy person among them. . . ."

Appendix: *The Righteous Rich in the Old Testament*

Christopher Wright observes that "God may choose (but is not obliged) to make a righteous person rich." It is fitting that I should conclude this brief essay with Wright's simple characterization of the righteous rich.[21]

1. [They] remember the source of their riches—namely the grace and gift of God himself—and are, therefore, not boastingly inclined to take the credit for achieving them through their own skill, strength, or effort (even if these things have been legitimately deployed) (Deut 8:17–18; 1 Chron 29:11–12; Jer 9:23–24).
2. Do not idolize their wealth by putting inordinate trust in it, nor get anxious about losing it. For ultimately, it is one's relationship with God that matters more and can survive (and even be deepened by) the absence or loss of wealth (Job 31:24–25).

---

21. Christopher Wright, "The Righteous Rich in the Old Testament," in Jonathan J. Bonk, *Missions and Money: Affluence as a Missionary Problem . . . Revisited*, rev. and exp. ed. (Maryknoll, NY: Orbis Books, 2006), 199–200.

3. Recognize that wealth is, thus, secondary to many things, including wisdom, but especially personal integrity, humility, and righteousness (1 Chron 29:17; Prov 8:10–11; 1 Kgs 3; Prov 16:8; 28:6).
4. Set their wealth in the context of God's blessing, recognizing that being blessed is not a privilege but a responsibility—the Abrahamic responsibility of being a blessing to others (Gen 12:1–3). Wealth in righteous hands is, thus, a servant of that mission that flows from God's commitment to bless the nations through the seed of Abraham.
5. Use their wealth with justice; this includes refusing to extract personal benefit by using wealth for corrupt ends (e.g., through bribery), and ensuring that all one's financial dealings are nonexploitative of the needs of others (e.g., through interest) (Ps 15:5; Ezek 18:7–8).
6. Make their wealth available to the wider community through responsible lending that is both practical (Lev 25) and respectful for the dignity of the debtor (Deut 24:6, 10–13).
7. See wealth as an opportunity for generosity—even when it is risky, and even when it hurts, thereby both blessing the poor and needy, and at the same time reflecting the character of God (Deut 15; Ps 112:3; Prov 14:31; 19:17; Ruth).
8. Use wealth in the service of God, whether by contributing to the practical needs that are involved in corporate worship of God (1 Chron 28–9) or by providing for God's servants who particularly need material support (2 Chron 31; Ruth).
9. Set an example by limiting personal consumption and declining to maximize private gain from public office that affords access to wealth and resources (Neh 5:14–19).

Other References

Bonk, Jonathan J., *Missions and Money: Affluence as a Missionary Problem . . . Revisited.* Revised and Expanded Edition. (Maryknoll, NY: Orbis Books, 2006).

Easterly, William, *The Elusive Quest for Growth: Economists' Adventures and Misadventures in the Tropics* (Boston: MIT Press, 2002).

———, *The Tyranny of Experts: Economists, Dictators, and the Forgotten Rights of the Poor* (New York: Basic, 2014).

———, *The White Man's Burden: Why the West's Efforts to Aid the Rest Have Done So Much Ill and So Little Good* (New York: Penguin, 2010).

Goudzwaard, Bob, *Aid for the Overdeveloped West* (Toronto: Wedge Publishing, 1975).

Greeley, Andrew M., *No Bigger Than Necessary: An Alternative to Socialism, Capitalism, and Anarchism* (New York: Meridian, 1977).

Holman, Susan R., ed., *Wealth and Poverty in Early Church and Society.* Holy Cross Studies in Patristic Theology and History (Grand Rapids, MI: Baker Academic, 2008).

Illich, Ivan, *The Church, Change and Development* (Chicago: Urban Training Center Press, 1970).

Judt, Tony, *Ill Fares the Land* (New York: Penguin Press, 2010).

Longenecker, Bruce W., *Remember the Poor: Paul, Poverty, and the Greco-Roman World* (Grand Rapids, MI: William B. Eerdmans, 2010).

Schumacher, F., *Small Is Beautiful: Economics as If People Mattered* (London: Blond & Briggs, 1973).

Stiglitz, Joseph E., *Globalization and Its Discontents* (New York: W. W. Norton, 2002).

Wuthnow, Robert, *God and Mammon in America* (New York: Free Press, 1994).

4

Technology and Postmodern Culture
Impact on Our Formation for Intercultural Mission

Bede Ukwuije, CSSp

Pope Francis, in his Message for the 48th World Communications Day,[1] while lucidly underlining the limits of modern means of communication, invited Christians to "boldly become citizens of the digital world." He proposed that the new manner of being missionary should involve going to the "digital highways" in order "to dialogue with people today and help them to encounter Christ." The formation of priests, religious, and missionaries today cannot ignore the use of the new technologies of communication, not only because they are useful for the transmission of the Good News but also because they shape and transform the mentality of the candidates who want to give themselves for the service of the gospel.

In this reflection, I want to underline the impact of what are called new technologies—smartphones, the Internet, Facebook, Skype, Twitter, Instagram, etc.—in the formation of missionaries, priests, and religious. Given that the new candidates for formation are already "digital natives," how will formation respond to the demands of this new culture?

First, I will describe some of the features of what is commonly called the postmodern culture, which includes the dominance of the new technologies of communication. Second, I will show how this postmodern culture impacts the formation of priests, religious, and missionaries. Finally, I will propose some ways through which the formation of missionaries, priests, and religious can face the challenges of the new situation.

Bede Ukwuije, CSSp, is an assistant superior general of the Congregation of the Holy Spirit (Spiritans), Rome; professor of systematic theology at the Spiritan International School of Theology, Attakwu, Enugu, and the Institut Catholique de Paris.

1. Pope Francis, Message for the 48th World Communications Day, "Communication at the Service of an Authentic Culture of Encounter," June 1, 2014.

The Postmodern Culture

It is very difficult to give an integral definition of postmodern culture. It is so blurred and difficult to distinguish between what is modern and what is postmodern. The temptation will be to talk of postmodern culture as if the world has totally moved away from modernity. I will present postmodern culture here as a continuation of modernity. The difference is that, while the modern person was convinced of the total autonomy of human reason, as opposed to the traditional conception of transcendental and eternal truth, the postmodern person experiences the fragility of his being while still sticking to the autonomy of human reason. Moreover, the high velocity of the development of new technologies has transformed modern culture, which was limited to the Western world, into a global culture, hence the designation of the world today as a "global village." I will attempt to describe only two dimensions of postmodern culture, namely, secularism/relativism and the revolution of the new technologies.

Secularism and Relativism

Secularism is a major feature of postmodern culture, which is a prolongation of modernity. Secularism is the expressed desire "to eliminate every trace of faith that is incarnate in history and society and to prevent it from exerting any moral judgment on political and social action."[2] As Patriciu Vlaïcu rightly put it, "in secularized societies, religion is often tolerated but does not play a determining role in social, moral, cultural or political life. Religion is tolerated but marginalized and thus faith becomes a private as opposed to a collective matter."[3]

Secularism goes with relativism. At the beginning of the conclave in 2005, Cardinal Joseph Ratzinger declared: "We are building a dictatorship of relativism that does not recognize anything as definitive and whose ultimate standard consists solely of one's own ego and desires." He continued this discussion as Benedict XVI in his book *Light of the World*:

> It is obvious that the concept of truth has become suspect. Of course it is correct that it has been much abused. Intolerance and cruelty have occurred in the name of truth. To that extent, people are afraid when someone says "This is the truth" or even, I have the truth. . . . The reality is in fact such that certain forms of behavior and thinking are being presented as the only reasonable ones and therefore, as the only appro-

---

2. *L'Osservatore Romano*, February 11, 2009.

3. Patriciu Vlaïcu, "The Consequences of the Enlightenment, from the Perspective of the Orthodox Communities in France," *International Review of Mission* 95 (2006): 299.

priately human ones. Christianity finds itself exposed now to intolerant pressure that at first ridicules it—as belonging to a perverse, false way of thinking and then tries to deprive it of breathing space in the name of an ostensible rationality.[4]

Relativism is at the heart of what is called the new global culture. This culture is expressed in a new language that is evident in the following concepts collected by Marguerite Peeters[5]: globalization with a human face, consensus, quality of life, gender equality, sexual reproductive health and rights, security, etc.

Some words representing traditional values tend to disappear from this new language. For example, "truth, love, charity, husband, wife, spouse, parents, father, mother, son, daughter, brother, sister, person, family, communion, heart, conscience, reason, intelligence, will, complementarity, identity, virginity, chastity, modesty, decency, happiness, growth, joy, hope, faith, good, evil, sin, suffering, sacrifice, gift, gratuitousness, service, common good, morality, law, nature, dogma, response, mystery, meaning, definition, reality, democratic representation. . . ."[6]

A deep dimension of secularism is *the eclipse of teleology*. "The idea of salvation is domiciled to the here and now. The after-life, which is ultimately what gives meaning and solace, is hardly ever remembered in normal day to day life. In real terms, therefore, the world remains a *summum bonum* to be sought by all means."[7]

Paradoxically, this eschatological deficit is accompanied by the development of a functional religion, especially in Africa and Latin America. This is evident in the idea of a *cross-less Christianity*. Pentecostal churches have made miracle, healing, and material prosperity proofs of the existence of God.[8] Some relate with God as bank customers relate with ATM machines. They insert their cards, press some buttons, and money comes out. In certain cases, when money does not come out, people get angry and break the machine. In the same manner, God is expected to perform miracles; if not, he is not worshiped.

What is common between the Western model of secularism and this new type is that the material world of things of enjoyment—technological plea-

---

4. Benedict XVI, *Light of the World* (San Francisco: Ignatius Press, 2010), 50–53.

5. Marguerite Peeters, *The Globalization of the Western Cultural Revolution* (Brussels: Institute of Intercultural Dialogue Dynamics, 2007).

6. Ibid., 24.

7. Josephat Oguejiofor, "The Resilient Paradigm: Impact of African World View on African Christianity," in Bede Ukwuije, *God, Bible and African Traditional Religion* (Enugu: SNAAP Press, 2010), 110.

8. See Bede Ukwuije, *Grace and Contradiction: Letter to an Impatient Friend* (Enugu: SAN Press, 2011), 61–65.

sures and possessions—occupy a central place in consciousness. For the former, God is not really needed to pursue the fascinations of the mind; for the latter, God is important, but only as he serves the many desires of individuals and families, and no relationship with such a God is necessary.

The secularization of the conception of life increases the anxiety before death. As Donal Dorr says, "There can be little doubt that civilized man today experiences a greater 'anguish' or 'anxiety' in regard to death than did man of other times."[9] The frenetic efforts made to gain control over death through science, what the French call *archarnement thérapeutique*, stands as a symptom of this reality. Without neglecting the complexity of the debates involved, one can also say that the increasing demand for euthanasia and assisted suicide stems from the same secularization of the meaning of life and death. Many argue that, when human suffering has become overwhelming and unbearable for the sick or the handicapped, it is better to terminate life and set the person free.

Revolution of New Technologies

At the heart of postmodern culture is the growth of new technologies that spread postmodern values, attitudes, and outlook to life. This terminology involves what scientists put together in the abbreviation NBIC, that is, Nanotechnologies, Biotechnologies, Information technologies and Cognitive sciences. I will concentrate on the domain of *information technologies,* which is most common.

I saw a computer for the first time in 1989 when I went to Lagos to book a flight for Paris. I was twenty-two years old, and had just finished the first cycle formation in philosophy. My congregation asked me to go to France to complete my priestly formation. A year later, I touched the computer for the first time in the formation community in Clamart (Paris, France). There was only one computer for the community of twelve students and three priests, and it had only one program (Word Perfect). The rector of the house insisted that we should learn to type with an electronic typewriter before qualifying to use the computer. I learned very fast because I wanted to graduate to the computer level. My counterparts in the school of philosophy, Isienu, Nigeria, told me later that a Spiritan confrere, who was studying in Canada, came back to Nigeria with what looked like a laptop. People were looking at the little box with skepticism. Some even spread the news that he was going to use it to read the consciences of the students in the formation community. Today, the majority if not all seminarians are connected through their smartphones, laptops or iPads. The formation community has a computer

---

9. Donal Dorr, "Death," in Hilary Cargas and Ann White, eds., *Death and Hope* (New York: Corpus Book, 1970), 7.

room and a cybercafé. The revolution of the new technologies has trans-formed ways of being. Some scientists even argue that they are reinventing the human being.

Simplification of Life

One of the characteristics of new technologies is the simplification of life. They simplify communication languages.[10] One needs to observe SMS exchanges to see that youths don't need to make full sentences; they write in short symbols. The problem is that most of these young ones access this symbolic communication without mastering the grammar and syntax of a particular language. Jean-Michel Besniers holds that "the new technologies not only simplify our life, they change our comportments and our mode of thinking to the extent that they reduce us to what is elementary: we become simple receivers of a local server, simple users of an automobile that has become a black box that responds to automatic commands, simple writers on programs that take more and more initiatives in the writing of our letters. We are invited to strip ourselves of elements of complexity that would make us think that we are other than machines."[11]

Beyond Human Finitude

Beyond the simplification of life, the new technologies want to reinvent the human person by putting an end to human finitude. They want to cre-ate a new humanity that would be free from passivity, suffering, and sick-nesses that are associated with the fragility of the body, aging, and undesired death.[12] This is a project proposed to societies where individuals are tired of being themselves. Addiction to the Internet is a symptom of the tiredness of being oneself, "*la fatigue d'être soi*," which is frequent in hypertechnolo-gized societies. "The more we feel impotent and depressed, the more we are tempted to turn towards machines."[13] Machines become more and more the refuge of "digital natives," uncertain of their identity.

Immediacy

Internet culture is the culture of the here and now.[14] New technologies are called "interruption technologies" because of the instant messages, e-mail alerts, SMS alerts, Skype alerts, etc. The individual is forced to be present to all these solicitations. The desire to live in the present leads to an addiction to the web. Hence, there is the situation of stress and lack.

---

10. Jean-Michel Besnier, "Les nouvelles technologies vont-elles re-inventer l'homme?," *Etudes* 4146 (June 2011): 768.

11. Ibid, 770.

12. Ibid.

13. Ibid.

14. Cf. Jean-François Fogel and Bruno Patino, *La condition numérique* (Paris: Passet, 2013).

Specialists have identified some sicknesses that are linked to addiction to the web.[15]

- Continuous partial attention, when one pays continuous and superficial attention to multiple information sources.
- Obsessive–compulsive disorder; anxiety caused by recurrent appearance of intrusive thoughts that lead to compulsive behaviors.
- Hyperattention; one moves one's attention quickly from one thing to another in order to maintain a level of excitement.
- Attention deficit hyperactivity disorder, a combination of attention deficit and hyperactivity.
- Phantom vibration syndrome: a perception problem. One feels the vibration of the smartphone on one's body while it is not vibrating and the worst is when one is not even carrying the smartphone.

Impact of Postmodern Culture on Formation

The candidates coming to the formation communities are already "digital natives." They carry with them the positive and negative influences of postmodern culture. This could be seen in the following attitudes among others: individualism, the desire to be a subject, and the crisis of long-term commitment.

Individualism

The "digital natives" in the formation communities are constantly connected to the web, television, Internet, smartphone, Facebook, Skype, Twitter. This has an influence on their concentration, both on the formation being proposed to them as well as the formation of their identity. Most messages posted on Facebook accounts are not really meaningful. They are more of self-exhibition rather than any meaningful discussion and sharing. They express the desire to show how I look this morning, how I feel at the moment, where I am, with whom I am hanging out, what I am eating, etc. Less time is given to community sharing and recreation with others. This has resulted in an increased individualism and a weakening of community life and community spirit.

The Desire to Be Subject

Traditional values are being contested. Individuals desire to be recognized as free persons, and they are deciding their own destiny. Hence, the desire for self-construction, to be the actor of one's personal development, to be free and responsible for one's destiny, which is expressed sometimes in the desire

---

15. Ibid., 31.

for auto-formation. This is not individualism *per se*, but the desire to exist personally as a subject among others. It is expressed paradoxically. The person pleading for the right to auto-formation would like all the infrastructures for formation, including qualified formators, to be provided for him/her—just like young people would like to auto-determine themselves in their families while still expecting their parents to be there for them and provide for them.

A closer look at this paradox reveals that the desire to be subject is also a desire for dialogue. The youth want dialogue. This is translated in the understanding of the credibility of authority. Before endorsing any principle or value, they scrutinize the credibility of the person representing or transmitting the value. Is he/she authentic, sincere, coherent, available, and competent? Can I entrust my destiny to him/her? This means that they expect the person handing over a tradition to them to risk his/her own personal experience while taking into consideration their own individual experiences. Pope Paul VI rightly put it: "Modern man listens more willingly to witnesses than to teachers, and if he does listen to teachers, it is because they are witnesses." (EN 41)

The Crisis of Long-Term Commitment

The culture of immediacy leads to the crisis of long-term commitment.[16] This crisis touches various traditional systems such as the family, the school, or even the military. Missionary institutes are not left out. This is one of the causes of missionary depression or demission. Many young priests and religious are finding it difficult to stay for a long time in a particular mission or apostolate. Immediately on arrival in the country of their mission appointment, they indicate the number of years they are willing to stay and begin planning for their departure.

Young missionaries are tempted to conceive mission as an activity that can be managed with ease. In their youthful exuberance they dream of converting crowds to Christ and building up churches within a short period of time. In many young indigenous congregations, little room is made for preparation for mission, especially on reflection on the "cost" of mission, and on precisely what mission requires of the missionary, in terms of self-sacrifice. Often, young missionaries break down when they encounter difficulties and failure.

Formation in the Postmodern Context

Given that the new candidates for formation are "digital natives," how will formation respond to this problem?

---

16. See Bede Ukwuije, *The Memory of Self-Donation: Meeting the Challenges of Mission* (Nairobi: Pauline Publications Africa, 2010).

Reflections on the Ethical Use of
Modern Communication Systems

Formators and religious superiors constantly face the dilemma of how to control the use of modern communication systems in formation communities. When I was the Director of Formation at the Spiritan International School of Theology, Attakwu, Enugu (Nigeria), the Nigerian Seminaries' Commission banned the use of handsets in the diocesan major seminaries in order to help the seminarians concentrate on their formation. However, the seminaries belonging to religious congregations, including ours, decided to allow the seminarians to use their handsets. First, because we believed that the ban was useless, since the seminarians used their handsets in secret and that created more headaches for the formators. Second, we thought that it was better to reflect with them on the reasonable use of such means and on the consequences for their freedom, character formation, and growth.

In the spirit of Pope Francis's Message for the 48th World Day of Communications, the formation of priests and religious should face the thrilling challenge of the new technologies. In a presentation at the Seminar for Formators at the Bigard Memorial Seminar, Enugu, on May 8, 2010, Martin Yina[17] rightly pointed out that the church has always upheld the importance of social communication in the task of evangelization (IM 14, EN 45, EA 125). What is needed is to form the consciences of the candidates in formation on the ethical use of all forms of communication. These include ethical issues like lying, misrepresentation, secrecy, disclosure, and the right to privacy, which often surface not just in organizational, mass, and computer-mediated communication but in the most informal and intimate contexts as well.[18] Formators and students have to reflect on the ethical question of whether a particular act or form of communication contributes to authentic human development and helps individuals and communities to be true to their transcendent destiny.[19] Does their participation in the digital environment help them to grow in humanity and mutual understanding? Do the new technologies really offer them opportunities for authentic encounter and solidarity?

Formation for Interiority

Formation in the present context should concentrate on the importance of interiority. Speaking on the type of evangelization that would face the chal-

---

17. Martin Yina, "Communication in Formation: The Need for a Holistic Approach in Nigeria," *The Catholic Voyage* 8 (2011): 34–46.

18. Stewart Tubbs and Sylvia Moss, *Human Communication: Principles and Contexts,* 11th ed. (New York: McGraw-Hill, 2008).

19. Pontifical Council for Social Communication (2002), *Ethics in Internet* 1, Rome, February 22, 2002, http://www.vatican.va.

lenges of our time, Pope Francis called for a "Spirit-filled evangelization." This requires the art of contemplation:

> What is needed is the ability to cultivate an interior space which can give a Christian meaning to commitment and activity. Without prolonged moments of adoration, of prayerful encounter with the word, of sincere conversation with the Lord, our work easily becomes meaningless; we lose energy as a result of weariness and difficulties, and our fervor dies out. (EG 262)

A few lines later, he added:

> The best incentive for sharing the Gospel comes from contemplating it with love, lingering over its pages and reading it with the heart. If we approach it in this way, its beauty will amaze and constantly excite us. But if this is to come about, we need to recover a contemplative spirit which can help us to realize ever anew that we have been entrusted with a treasure which makes us more human and helps us to lead a new life. There is nothing more precious which we can give to others. (EG 264)

Interiority is the space for encounter with oneself, the other, and the entire environment. Hyperattention, created by addiction to new technologies, can prevent this self-awareness. As Siro Stochetti rightly stated, the attitude of contemplation helps one to move from superficiality and alienation to self-awareness; from irresponsibility to living responsibly in the world; from individualism to witnessing in community.[20] In the light of the praxis of Jesus, who continually withdrew from the agitated world to pray (Mark 1:35), candidates in formation must learn to enter into prayer, deep conversation with God, in order to search for the will of God and gain stamina for mission. Contemplation opens the horizon for mission.

Faith as Self-Abandonment

In the postmodern context where the individual is so conscious of personal freedom and autonomy, formation should aim at self-abandonment. This is the essence of faith. The Letter to the Hebrews 11:1 defines faith as "the substance (*hypostasis*) of things hoped for; the proof of things not seen." Benedict XVI put this definition at the center of his encyclical on hope, *Spe Salvi* [SS]. He identified faith with hope and vice versa. The word "substance" here is very important in that it says that there are already in us the things that are

---

20. Siro Stochetti, "Vita contemplativa e profetica nella missione oggi," *SEDOS Bulletin* 46, nos. 7/8 (July-August 2014): 163–73.

hoped for, the whole true life. The thing hoped for is already present in us. It is not yet visible, but its presence creates certainty (SS 7). Earlier, Hebrews 10:34 reminded the persecuted Christians that it was faith that made them accept the plundering of their property: "For you had compassion for those who were in prison, and you cheerfully accepted the plundering of your possessions, knowing that you yourselves possessed something better and more lasting." Because the Christians had in them the *substance*, the basis for life, they could accept the destruction of the normal source of security (material possessions). They could give up the material basis for life because they had found a substance that endures. Hence, they have gained a new freedom.

Faith is freedom (LF 32–34). God is not jealous of human freedom. He created the human being and endowed him/her with free will. Paradoxically, a condition of access to faith is self-decentralization. Faith does not diminish the human person. On the contrary, it is through faith that the human person accesses his/her real being. Our real being is grace, given freely to us. We can only discover our true being when we renounce the illusion of being, which consists in wanting to create our present and our future. When one counts on one's capacities alone, he/she loses the ability to see beyond the failures or successes of the moment. It is when one fully trusts in God that his full capacities are enabled, and he/she can do infinitely more than what he/she thinks him/herself capable of.

The Ethics of Fragility and Vulnerability

In the postmodern context where the human person is tempted by self-mastery, formation should aim at the ethics of fragility and vulnerability. A true missionary and religious recognizes his/her fragility.[21] Being aware of our fragility does not mean that we interpret our lives negatively. The discovery of our fragility goes together with the discovery of the grace of God in us. It makes us humble and modest, while at the same time empowering us to act with God. Francis Libermann, the co-founder of the Congregation of the Holy Spirit, said to M. Briot, a young man who wanted to join his congregation but complained of moral, spiritual, and financial inadequacy: "We are a bunch of poor people living through the grace of God":

> We are all worthless people, who have been brought together by the will of the Master, in whom lies all our hope. If we thought we were worth something, we would not accomplish very much. Paradoxically, now that we are nothing, have little, and are good for less, we can dream of doing something really worthwhile. This is because we do not

---

21. Cf. Bede Ukwuije, "The God of Surprise. The Perpetual Novelty of Missio Dei," http://www.sedosmission.org.

rely on ourselves, but rather on him who is almighty. Do not be concerned about your weakness and poverty. It is when we are weak that the power and mercy of Jesus can really reveal themselves in us. The glory in anything that we achieve will thus belong to him.[22]

Pope Francis took as the motto for his coat of arms *Miserando atque eligendo* (mercy and election). He borrowed it from the commentary of St. Bede the Venerable on the vocation of Matthew: "Jesus saw a man called Matthew sitting at the tax office and he said to him: Follow me." Jesus saw Matthew, not merely in the usual sense, but more significantly with his merciful understanding of men. He saw the tax collector, and, because he saw him through the eyes of mercy and chose him, he said to him: "Follow me."[23]

God's mercy precedes our vocation. It is not because of our holiness that we are called; rather it is because God had mercy on us, called us, and that he sanctified and co-missioned us. It is not because of our intelligence that we are called; rather it is because God called us that he gave us the understanding of his mystery. It is not because we are powerful that we are called, rather it is because he gives us the capacity to do extraordinary things in his name.

Formation for Community Witnessing

In a postmodern context where the individual seeks self-construction, formation should aim at community witnessing. In his Pentecost letter 2013, addressed to professed and lay members of his congregation, John Fogarty, CSSp, the superior general of the Congregation of the Holy Spirit, wrote:

> It is the "the Spirit of Pentecost who brings us together into one large family, from different cultures, continents and nations" [Spiritan Rule of Life 37]. By coming together from so many different places and cultures, we are saying to our brothers and sisters that the unity of the human race is not just an impossible dream. In this way, our community life is an integral part of our mission and a powerful witness of the Gospel. International community living is a "response to the call of the Holy Spirit to all of us, to witness to a new quality of human solidarity, surpassing individualism, ethnocentrism and nationalism."[24]

---

22. Francis Libermann, "Lettre à M. Briot, Amiens 10 août 1843," in *Notes et Documents* IV (Paris: Maison Mère, 1935), 303–5. See also Christian de Mare, ed., *A Spiritan Anthology* (Enugu: SNAAP Press, 2011), 261–64.

23. Homilies of St. Bede the Venerable, 21, in *The Divine Office*, September 21, St. Matthew, Apostle and Evangelist.

24. John Fogarty, "Brought Together by the Spirit of Pentecost," http://www.spiritanroma. org.

Fogarty also stated: "If . . . our international and intercultural living is a call from the Holy Spirit to witness to a new quality of human solidarity in a globalized world, our circumscriptions and our communities must be 'places where the truth is spoken and lived, where domination and subjugation do not occur, where differences are acknowledged and affirmed without compromising unity.'"[25] This conviction is relevant for all religious institutes in this postmodern context.

One of the greatest challenges of formators in a multicultural context is to maintain a standard in the evaluation of students. It is difficult to know to what extent formators can go in the consideration of the cultural factor in the assessment of a student, especially in what concerns the evangelical counsels. The formators, helped by the superiors, should try to be as close as possible to the church's directives. It is necessary, therefore, to verify whether the motivations of the young candidates correspond to the demands of religious life in general and to the spirit of the religious institute concerned. Formators will verify particularly the ability of the candidates to live out the evangelical counsels in total submission to God. They will verify the suitability of the candidate's good health, absence of incompatible engagements, right intention, and readiness to allow him/herself to be guided by another in the process of formation. In missionary institutes, formators will verify whether the candidate is suitable for mission in an intercultural/international context.

Conclusion

While the new technologies, Internet, Facebook, Twitter, smartphones, iPad, etc., offer formidable opportunities of communication and solidarity with as many people as possible in the postmodern context, they also present unprecedented challenges to the formation of priests, religious, and missionaries. The candidates in formation communities, being "digital natives," present the same symptoms that are visible in postmodern culture: individualism, secularism/relativism, search for immediacy, and crisis of long-term commitment.

In order to respond to these challenges, formation should engage the candidates in a deep reflection on the ethical use of the new technologies. It should also be anchored in the rediscovery of faith as self-abandonment, as well as emphasize the importance of interiority and contemplation. Formation programs should also include reflection on the ethics of fragility and vulnerability, as well as on community witnessing.

---

25. Ibid.

5

Inserted Life
The Radical Nature of an Incarnated Spirituality

Adriana Carla Milmanda, SSpS

International community life is nothing new for the congregations of the Missionary Sisters Servants of the Holy Spirit (SSpS) and the Society of the Divine Word (SVD). What is new is the growing cultural diversity of their respective communities. This growing diversity has given rise to an awareness of a new challenge. Carlos del Valle, SVD, presents this as the challenge to pass from being *multi-* to *inter-*cultural, from taking on a dominant culture to a "com-union" in diversity of cultures.

> The change from being *multi-* to *inter-*cultural has to be an agreed and conscious decision taken at the level of community relations. Each one communicates what is theirs, and participates in the diversity. We open ourselves up to other ways of seeing, organizing, thinking, feeling, and interpreting. Communicating and meeting one another at a human level are taken as complementary. The challenge consists in creating open and free spaces where the many voices of the cultures in our communities can be heard. Imagine how our congregations might be if we allowed them to be touched by other cultures which are non-western.[1]

The questions that follow from this proposal are the following: *how* and *from where* might these open and free spaces be created that would allow for

---

Adriana Carla Milmanda, SSpS, holds an M.A. in theological research from the Catholic Theological Union in Chicago. In early 2018, she returned to South America to continue her long-term ministry in Argentina, where she has been involved in community animation and formation ministry. She was also one of the pioneering SSpS sisters on the Fiji Islands, where she lived for six years coordinating catechetical ministry in an intercultural and interreligious rural school.

1. Carlos del Valle, "La interculturalidad como llamada y horizonte de misión para la vida religiosa," *Verbum SVD* 54, no. 3 (2013): 289.

interaction and communion. Within the context of our present world, where millions of people experience the "encounter" of cultures from a position of oppression, exclusion, and exploitation of one group over another, it opens up the question as to the nature of the interaction taking place. And this cannot be ignored at the moment of examining intercultural community relations. At the deepest level, interculturality presents itself as a spiritual challenge, confronting one's motivation and convictions out of which one lives the encounter, with the "other" as a matrix of the missionary vocation.

This present article will attempt to outline the steps that will enable us to imagine *how* and *from where* spaces might be created that would lead to cultural interaction as an expression and living out of an incarnate spirituality. In the first part, I will present three challenges from my own experiences that are especially important at the moment of revising multicultural living. In the second part, I will offer, in reply to the challenges of the present world, the Latin-American experience of inserted living as a *place* out of which these spaces might be opened up according to the practice of Jesus and his kingdom.

Intercultural Living and an Incarnate Spirituality

The challenge of establishing intercultural living from the perspective of a Christian spirituality has, as its starting point, the incarnation of Jesus. From this perspective, what is human is converted into the place of a privileged encounter with God. Every human experience, with its richness and limitations, is the matrix that mediates, concretizes, challenges, and expands the experience of God. The gospel stories reflect how Jesus himself lived out this relationship with God, Father and Mother: through the experience of his own human development, community living, meeting with the "others," and during times of personal reflection and prayer. Such an incarnate spirituality demands an integrated vision that is mutually enriched by life and faith. For Christians, the experience of God is not something abstract or uprooted, but rather is called to make itself incarnate in all that is in conformity with authentic human living. This implies opening oneself up to the experience of God through healthy relationships with all that is genuinely human—body, emotions, cultural roots, context, etc. It also implies an encounter with the "others"—both at the interpersonal as well as the social level—and with a similar relationship with all of creation.

> As the religion of incarnation par excellence, Christianity should be exemplary in showing how people can embody and live the missionary dimension of faith, as Jesus did. To live deeply in our bodies, ourselves, would then be an authentic expression of spirituality: a way of being

holy; a way of conforming our lives to that of Jesus. . . . The missionary dimension of our faith calls us to reach out, whether just beyond
our comfort zone or across the invisible boundaries of race, creed or
privilege. We must be dispossessed to encounter otherness, alterity. In
so doing we discover the alterity of God who is diffracted through these
myriad human lenses, these many ways of being human, these multiple
images of God's self. . . .[2]

An incarnate spirituality roots Christianity within its own experience and
cultural context and at the same time challenges it to go out to encounter
the "others" where the radical otherness of God is opened up—the "Other"
par excellence. Paradoxically, this going out toward the "other" implies a
counter-cultural movement, given that cultures by their nature tend to mark
out their own limits to distinguish them and separate them from others. At
the same time, new distinctions and divisions delimit hierarchies and levels
of participation within each cultural group. Cultures by their nature are both
a source of unity and division, of inclusion and exclusion, providing values
that both enrich and delimit. Intercultural living, from the perspective of an
incarnate spirituality, is a challenge to intentionally take on this paradox as
modeled by Jesus himself.

Rooted as he was in his own time and culture, Jesus articulated the mystery of the incarnation through his own ministry, crossing over cultural
divisions in a double movement. One movement was descending in nature,
toward those who lived on the margins of society (the poor, women, the sick,
and children). The other was a centrifugal one, toward those who were to be
found beyond this frontier.[3]

[Jesus] seemed to be attracted by the margins of society and the marginalized people to be found there. He was forever wandering on the
borders and crossing boundaries. He crossed geographical boundaries
as they journeyed between Galilee and Samaria, the Decapolis, Judea,
or Transjordania (Mt 4:25), religious boundaries as he moved from
synagogues to graveyards, and topographical boundaries as he sailed
on lakes, climbed mountains, or was led into a desert. . . . Jesus' ministry transcended other boundaries, too, such as the invisible boundaries
that protected zones of privilege, exclusiveness, or holiness.[4]

---

2. Anthony J. Gittins, "Mission and Spirituality," in Philip Sheldrake, ed., *The New
Westminster Dictionary of Christian Spirituality* (Louisville, KY: Westminster John Knox Press,
2005), 444.

3. Anthony J. Gittins, "The Disturbing Ministry of Jesus," in Anthony J. Gittins, *A Presence
That Disturbs: A Call to Radical Discipleship* (Liguori, MO: Liguori/Triumph, 2002), 91–118.

4. Ibid., 107–8.

The following of Jesus in the missionary life challenges the Christian of today to make incarnate in his or her life this double movement: the centrifugal one that leads to crossing over cultural frontiers, and the descending one leading to the margins, where the poor and the excluded have been driven. However, we are not dealing with two separate movements, but rather, according to the radically inclusive and egalitarian project of the kingdom, with two dimensions of the same progressive movement of conversion and openness to the "other."

Contemporary intercultural studies analyze how culture and power are intertwined by both external and internal dynamic factors from which the cultures themselves need to be liberated.[5] Intercultural communities of today, which are increasingly diverse by nature, are being called upon to become places of privilege for critical reflection, and in a search for alternative ways of being. From the daily experience of living with the one who is "different," the intercultural community is being challenged to radicalize its openness to the "other," crossing over not only geographic and linguistic frontiers but also frontiers not so easily perceived, such as those of class, privilege, marginalization, or exclusion.

From this point of view, and in dialogue with my own situation and experience, I would like to outline three concrete challenges that an incarnate spirituality, taken as a centrifugal movement, poses for intercultural living.

Challenge to Live "from" the Differences

The best way to get to know and experience one's own culture is through an encounter with other cultures. When I lived on the Fiji Islands, within a situation of a great cultural variety both within the SSpS community as well as among the people of that place, one particular experience enabled me to see with great clarity, both in its simplicity and straightforwardness, how one's own culture shapes us and forms the lenses through which we perceive reality.

On one of those rare occasions when my path crossed with others who spoke Spanish on those beautiful islands, I came in contact with a married couple, Argentinian–Chilean, missionaries of the Adventist Church. If we had met each other in Argentina there would have been a long list of differences that would have made it impossible for us to share with each other (different places of worship and way of life, different cultures within our own countries, certain suspicions and competitiveness, and so on). Yet, the fact that we met in Fiji blurred all these potential boundaries. Through

---

5. For a development of this topic, see Raúl Fornet-Betancourt, "Interacción y asimetría entre las culturas en el contexto de la globalización. Una introducción," http://www.babelonline.net (2003), 1–15.

coming together for mate,[6] we spontaneously shared our reactions, our joys and obstacles toward the culture that surrounded us. Great was our surprise when we discovered how similar our reactions to shared experiences were. We reacted in a similarly negative way to certain of our hosts' customs, we shared together the same values—with which we identified—and we were frustrated in a similar way by the same attitudes. In a moment of insight I clearly noticed how we were looking through the same cultural lenses at the reality that surrounded us. These were Argentinian–Latin-American lenses that we could never have described in words but whose reality became both palpable and concrete in our sharing together, connecting us, as it did, in a very special way.

Frequently in our communities, we distinguish most easily differences due to different personality types or the generation gap. Nevertheless, that meeting with "my" people on the Fiji Islands opened my eyes to the importance of a powerful but subtle reality, less perceptible, and much more difficult to distinguish, the lenses of our cultures. The encounter with the "others" is always mediated by the culture(s) and by the contexts that have shaped us. For example, gender, social class, levels of education, previous experiences of community and the church, and even the political systems of our countries are cultural markers that influence our perceptions, fears, and expectations. They also operate at the level of practical decision making, for example, in prioritizing the criteria we use in gaining access to, use of, and distribution of resources.

The pedagogy of an incarnate spirituality is the challenge to take on from the point of view of daily living the cultural differences manifested in the encounter with "otherness." Instead of ignoring or denying the conflicts and crises that arise on account of diversity, the real challenge is to use them as raw material for a potentially enriching experience that is most useful in generating alternative models of cultural interaction.

Interculturality is an art and a process that develops with time. It needs to be intentionally worked on with patient empathy and profound compassion, as much toward oneself as toward others. The initial stage of romantic enthusiasm, generated by the novelty of different cultural expressions, usually gives way to a stage of disillusionment, and even rejection of differences—both one's own and others'. Nevertheless, often during this stage we are more

---

6. *Mate* is an infusion, like tea, inherited from the native Guaraní people. One of its special characteristics is that it is drunk together from the same container [cup] which is shared in groups for the purpose of socializing among acquaintances, family members, and friends, or companions at work or in one's place of study. The mate culture has its own rituals and vocabulary, and is very popular in Argentina, Uruguay, and Paraguay. Mate is also drunk in some regions of Chile, Bolivia, and Brazil.

influenced by our own limitations, fears, and prejudices than by knowledge and experience of the others. It is a period when one suffers misunderstanding and isolation. But it is also a time of potential creativity for the person and the community. In order to make use of their potential for transformation, intercultural communities need to find ways that allow for accompaniment, elaboration, and celebration of the cultural transitions.

At the same time the process of intercultural living requires the creation of spaces that promote critical reflection. The crossing of frontiers to "enter in the garden of another," using the image of Roger Schroeder, SVD, implies an honest and constant review of the motivations (the "why") and the attitudes (the "how") that lie behind every encounter. Other cultures cannot be judged from one's own cultural parameters. There is neither to be found in them pure darnel nor a romantic perfectionism.[7] On the other hand, the critical capacity ought to help unmask dynamics that stir up feelings of either inferiority toward or the victimization of cultures that are perceived to be, respectively, either superior or inferior to the rest. Contexts and circumstances cannot be used to justify comfortable or manipulative attitudes, or simply to switching off when confronted by an encounter with "the other."

Intercultural living today needs to be developed more from a spirituality that is nurtured and grows from an intentional openness to the plurality of "lenses" through which one may look, both at a personal and a community level, at the experience of God, daily life, and the global reality. With a compassionate and critical gaze, the spaces created through the interaction of cultures are called upon to be converted into opportunities for deepening and decentralizing one's own experience, thus giving rise to mutual transformation.

Challenge to Create Spaces

Conversion is the essential dimension of all spiritual journeys. Intercultural living as a decentralizing and counter-cultural movement is impossible without a constant and sustained journey of conversion that is taken as a way of life.

Orlando E. Costas speaks of three levels of conversion in the missionary life: to Christ, to the culture, and to the world.[8] The conversion to Christ, he explains, is the call to follow him and gradually conform to the kingdom of

---

7. Stephen B. Bevans and Roger P. Schroeder, *Prophetic Dialogue: Reflections on Christian Mission Today* (Maryknoll, NY: Orbis Books, 2011), 72–78.

8. Orlando E. Costas, "Conversion as a Complex Experience: A Personal Case Study," in John R. W. Stott and Robert Coote, eds., *Down to Earth: Studies in Christianity and Culture. The Papers of the Lausanne Consultation on Gospel and Culture* (Grand Rapids, MI: Eerdmans, 1980), 173–91.

God and its values—implying at the same time the call to be part of a community of followers. The conversion to the culture is the conversion to the social reality of the faith lived within the community and within a specific sociopolitical context. "Conversion is God's way of renewing and changing the face of his church, so as to lead it through new paths and enable it to cross new frontiers."[9] Finally, the conversion to the world is the conversion to the missionary commitment itself, and this constitutes the purpose of the missionary community in the service of the kingdom of God. These three levels are not consecutive nor completely given in unique moments. Costas compares them to the movement of a spiral that, beginning from a foundational experience, is called upon to elaborate, and in this way, through movements that constantly distance it and bring it close to the center, goes deeper into new levels.

In multicultural living this three-dimensional process is mediated through daily confrontation with the "other" and with "the different." This confrontation by its very nature intimidates and dislocates. The "different" is perceived as a potential threat. The spontaneous defense reaction is to dominate, devalue, or control, which is done by those who are strongest in number, in resources, or in personality.

> Often in religious life there is only juxtaposition and mutual tolerance, or asymmetric interaction. In our international communities what is often given is a situation of "symbolic violence": the stronger group imposes value judgments and relationship codes on the others, who react with attitudes and feelings of mistrust, threat, repulsion, rebellion or defense, withdrawal, resistance, or inferiority, exclusion, inhibition.[10]

Attitudes that oscillate between denial or undervaluing differences, and the violent reactions, abuses of power, and the stigmatization or silencing of the weaker members, result in multicultural living often being experienced as a burden. Almost unconsciously, there tends to be duplicated in the diverse intercultural microcosms the dynamics of power and oppression that operate at the level of international relations.

The current situation in the world and the church compels and urges the unmasking of culturally hegemonic and exclusive ways of living the gospel. Multicultural communities, from their own conversion and praxis, face the challenge and the prophetic responsibility to respond in an existential way to the intercultural search of our global times, to new ways of relating together in the search for justice and inclusion. This occurs through daily living.

---

9. Ibid., 186.
10. Del Valle, "La interculturalidad como llamada y horizonte," 290.

Challenge to Experiment with Alternative Models

Raúl Fornet-Betancourt says:

> From a genuine intercultural viewpoint it must be emphasized that the discussion around cooperation between cultures and peoples is a sham, if not accompanied by a policy which seeks, in an efficient and unequivocal way, to redress the imbalance of power which characterizes the existing world "order," compounded as it is by ongoing globalization. Only by creating at a world level conditions of equality and social justice, can free interaction be guaranteed in which the cultures can, without fear of being colonized, accept and also promote from within mutual transformations in their way of life, work, community organizations, education etc.[11]

Keeping in mind their own history and contexts, different cultures have developed their own ways of making decisions, of seeking consensus, expressing disagreements, organizing time, prioritizing the use of resources, of exercising leadership, of relating to God, or placing limits on public and private space, etc. Therefore, every culture is specific and contextualized, and none can claim the right to establish what is particular to its own way of life as a "universal" norm for others. Nevertheless, this tension between the universal and the particular is to be found at the root of many challenges that confront the world today, and especially among the different ways of living out the Christian tradition. In terms of mission, this tension takes on a particular relevance in relation to concrete daily living, embracing as it does theological, ecclesiological, pastoral, and intercultural planning. The gospels give witness to Jesus' development toward a radical and egalitarian inclusive vision of the "other" in the project of the kingdom. We see this in his openness to dialogue and encounter with others.

Jesus, who was truly human, also shared his own cultural blind spots. Nevertheless, instead of denying or rejecting them, he allowed himself to be guided by the Spirit and overcame them through meeting, sharing, and encountering the "other." The story of the Syro-Phoenician woman is one of the paradigmatic examples:

> The woman was not Jewish, but of Syro-Phoenician origin. She went, and begged Jesus to expel the demon from her daughter. But Jesus said to her: Allow the children of the family to eat first, because it is not right that the children's bread be taken and given to the dogs. However she replied: But sir, even the dogs under the table eat the crumbs which

---

11. Fornet-Betancourt, "Interacción y asimetría entre las culturas," 13.

children allow to fall. Jesus replied: Because you have said this, go in peace. The demon has left your daughter. (Mark 7:27–29)

In this controversial and provocative story, we see how Jesus reacts initially from his own cultural prejudices but then opens himself up to encounter, dialogue, and change. This "encounter" challenges him to move beyond his own limits and discover that the project of the reign of God is a counter-cultural invitation to not allow religion to be enclosed by those parameters that are marked out by a limited cultural perspective. Jesus was changed by the encounter with this woman. Through his radical openness to meeting and dialogue, he—as a human being—was discerning how to be faithful to God by going beyond his own limitations and cultural contexts.

It is the same today. More and more women—and also men—are seeking dialogue, and question the church for its involvement in a patriarchal model, which on many occasions justifies the relegation and often oppression of women as though it were part of the "order" given by God.

> Roman Catholicism continues to give backing to cultural environments
> that accept the subordination of women and that give permission for
> men, as a social body, to function as a privileged human grouping that
> is allowed to degrade, humiliate and violate women. In most countries
> the Catholic Church has failed to offer alternative cultural models for
> transforming the apparent inertia of the cultural and social privileges
> enjoyed by men, and it has been negligent in abandoning the mentality
> of privileges that the present cultures reproduce.[12]

John Prior, SVD, suggests, from his missionary experience in Indonesia, that what is needed is not a revision of our theologies, biblical doctrines, or canon laws. What we are urged to do now, he suggests, is to revise the present interpretations and applications of the same. He says,

> We desperately need to re-educate pastoral workers (priests, bishops,
> catechists, pastoral councils) in order to read scripture, doctrine and
> Church law in healthy, holistic, contextual and non-discriminatory
> ways. . . . We need to learn how to read the scriptures with the eyes
> of "the other," with the eyes of women, the victim, the survivor. Many
> bible studies at the pastoral level ignore this issue and so unconsciously
> reinforce patriarchal values, and therefore abuse.[13]

---

12. María Pilar Aquino, "Feminist Intercultural Theology: Toward a Shared Future for a Just World," in María Pilar Aquino and María José Rosado-Nunes, eds., *Feminist Intercultural Theology: Latina Explorations for a Just World* (Maryknoll, NY: Orbis Books, 2007), 11.

13. John Mansford Prior, "Seeing with the Eyes of the Other," in Virginia Saldanha, ed., *Discipleship of Asian Women at the Service of Life* (Bangalore: Claretian Publications, 2011), 98.

Community life, which is in daily contact with diversity, urges one to cultivate a watchful and empathetic attitude toward any kind of exclusion, division, and boundaries. The very experience of being and accepting "difference," questions and develops new and creative forms of inclusion of those whom the political, economic, and religious systems force toward the margins and the frontiers of our societies, communities, and churches. The transition from *multi-* to *inter*-cultural living constitutes an urgent task for today.

Inserted Life as a Radicalization of an Incarnate Spirituality

The three challenges outlined here question the "*how*" of creating free spaces for intercultural relations in the world today. An incarnate spirituality urges us today to take on without fear cultural differences in order to open ourselves up to a process of radical conversion to God's project, which promotes alternative and counter-cultural forms of inclusion. This is done from a position of encounter and dialogue. These challenges are directed mainly at the centrifugal movement of the ministry of Jesus, which will bring the church to discover its universal mission. Nevertheless, Jesus lived out his openness to the "other" from what was at the same time a descending movement, bringing him to intentionally position himself at the margins of the world and of society. In this way missionary life today is challenged to review not only the *how* but also *from where* are intercultural relations embodied in keeping with this double displacement of Jesus.

Pope Francis urges today a profound renovation of the church from the paradigm of mission. In his apostolic exhortation *The Joy of the Gospel*, he reminds us, that from this paradigm, the option for the poor is an essential part of the faith of the church:

> For the Church the option for the poor is primarily a theological category rather than a cultural, sociological, political or philosophical one. . . . This option—as Benedict XVI taught—"is implicit in our Christian faith in a God who became poor for us, so as to enrich us with his poverty." This is why I want a Church which is poor and for the poor. They have much to teach us. . . . We need to let ourselves be evangelized by them. (EG 198)

The option for the poor that the pope speaks about does not refer to simply "helping" the poor or elaborating aid programs that attempt to alleviate "their" problems. His proposal is theological, and even though it has concrete social implications, it challenges us toward a movement that is much more radical than mere social assistance. The pope calls on Christians "to let themselves be evangelized" by them (the poor) and to appreciate the "poor in their goodness, in their experience of life, in their culture, and in their ways of living the faith" (EG 199). In a word, he asks us to animate ourselves for the "encounter." I will now present some elements of this encounter, which are taken from the experience of the inserted life among the poor in Latin America.

In the religious context of Latin America, the experience of the inserted life is born as a radicalization of the incarnate spirituality in the following of Jesus who divested himself and became poor *for love* (2 Cor 8:9). It is the practical and existential consequence of the option for the poor and the search for liberation. "It is clear that the type of poverty on which the theology of liberation is based," explains Gerhard Müller to European theologians, "does not refer to a humble and simple lifestyle, or the results of misfortune or disability . . . but (it is) the consequence of insurmountable existing structural conditions which destroy the lives of millions of human beings."[14]

In this context, insertion in Latin America refers in a concrete way to a geographical and social relocation of a religious community in order to implant itself, physically and in solidarity, among the poor and the oppressed of society. Inserted communities live, as distinct from those who are in institutions (schools, hospitals, monasteries, parishes, etc.) in an ordinary house in the barrio, and in this way share with the rest of the poor the same conditions, insecurities, shortages, and way of life.

Through insertion, the poor no longer are perceived as "objects" of welfare but rather are found to be "subjects" in a relationship of neighborliness and friendship. This new plane is what opens one up to a transformative experience where interrelationships and reciprocity are made possible. More than a "help" for the poor, the inserted life makes for an experience of God and space for renewal and personal and communitarian conversion.

Reading once again the story of the journey of religious life in Latin America, Victor Codina says: "It's not that inserted religious life is the only way of living out the preferential option for the poor, but . . . it is the option that reflects most clearly the love of God for the poor and his presence in them. For this reason it increases the radical position . . . as much in the people as in the institution."[15]

The geographical and social location from which one lives out mission is not neutral. Inserted living among the poor, as a chosen option, opens one up to a more radical process. Codina explains it in the following way: "The

---

14. Gerhard Ludwig Müller, "La teología de la liberación en debate," in Gerhard Ludwig Müller and Gustavo Gutiérrez, *Del lado de los pobres: Teología de la liberación* (Lima: Instituto Bartolomé de Las Casas, 2005), 91; English edition, Gustavo Gutiérrez and Gerhard Ludwig Müller, *On the Side of the Poor: The Theology of Liberation* (Maryknoll, NY: Orbis Books, 2015).

15. Víctor Codina, SJ, and José María Guerrero, SJ, "Hacer Memoria de la Vida Religiosa," *Revista CLAR* 38, no. 4 (2000): 10.

change of geographical location has followed from a social change from the center to the periphery, a theological change from a theology of poverty to a theology of the poor, and a spiritual change from a spirituality of trust in God to a prophetic spirituality of solidarity with the poor."[16] The following testimony of Benjamín González Buelta, a Spanish Jesuit missionary in the Dominican Republic, indicates to us some of the implications of this change:

> The fact of opting for the oppressed puts us in a new hermeneutic situation from which to analyze the social structures, theological reflection, the reading of the Word of God, and the very institutions of the congregation itself. It also judges us at the deepest level of our being. We do not live out this process merely as an intellectual adventure, but also as an existential adventure in the community of the oppressed which calls into play and risks our very personhood and our identity.[17]

And finally, the *kenosis* of Jesus does not romantically glorify poverty, suffering, and death but rather prophetically summons one to a project where the first place involves a radical inclusion of all. In the same way, the inserted life does not seek for itself suffering and the life of deprivation of the poor but is rather a deliberate and counter-cultural relinquishment of the inequality created by the so-called privileges of exclusion and the perpetuation of oppressive interpersonal relationships.

Missionary life is characterized by the centrifugal movement that leads one to cross geographic and linguistic frontiers. Today the model of the inserted life is a challenge for missionary and intercultural communities to cross over the most intangible frontiers of all that mark out various types of exclusion in the church and in society.

The dynamics of conversion implied in intercultural living challenge us, today more than ever, to cross over the frontiers leading us to insert ourselves at the margins of society. Jesus himself placed the call to universal inclusion at the margins of society. In today's terms, mission and commitment to justice, peace, and integrity of creation cannot be separated. Nevertheless, the social, geographical, and existential *from where* respond to this commitment and bring into play the radical nature by which we live the double movement that Jesus left us.

Conclusion

Multicultural living is nothing new for international congregations. We have an experiential treasure out of which we are called to contribute to the inter-

---

16. Ibid.

17. Benjamín González Buelta, *El Dios oprimido: Hacia una espiritualidad de la inserción* (Santander: Sal Terrae, 1989), 73.

cultural searches of the world and the church today. Nevertheless this same world awakens us to new challenges that question the forms and models by and from where cultural diversity is lived.

One of the most pressing challenges that arises on looking at these forms is to be found at the level of interpersonal relations, and the challenge to go beyond the *multi-* to *inter*-culturality. The ways for working on this transition are without doubt many; my work is approached from the perspective of the spirituality that sustains the missionary vocation and outlines steps that respond to the *how* and *from where* this challenge is embodied.

In relation to the *how*, I have outlined in this article three challenges that need to be addressed beyond the confines of this work, independently and in greater depth. From my own background and experience, intercultural living today requires more intentional work on differences, to be raised as a specific path of conversion, and to promote the creation of different forms of intercultural relations that reverse the injustice and oppression suffered by millions of people in the present world.

These challenges question the "*from where*" when we stop to look, interact, and transform reality. From the inserted life among the poor of Latin America I have presented some elements of the experience of being displaced geographically and socially to the margins and periphery of society. Insertion, shaped by the double movement—descending and centrifugal—of Jesus by which he lived out his incarnation to the end offers a way of conversion and radicalization.

From the viewpoint of the poor and the excluded today, intercultural living acquires a new relevance and urgency. The missionary dimension of the Christian faith by its nature challenges us to reach out to encounter the "other." In today's world this "other" challenges us not only beyond the geographic frontiers but also beyond the frontiers created by ever increasing modes of exclusion and oppression. From a multidimensional path of conversion and critical reflection, it is urgent that intercultural communities develop new forms of relating that promote the radical inclusive model, which is both fair and plural, and which Jesus himself has shown us.

Translated from Spanish by Brian O'Reilly, SVD

6

Programs for New Missionaries in Cross-Cultural Mission

Martin Ueffing, SVD

"Years ago, when young missionaries arrived in their mission country, one of the first things they were told was to look carefully around, especially at how the 'elders' worked and were still continuing their job. That advice was often accompanied by a warning to keep silent for the time since the young missionary was still too inexperienced to make judgments."[1] Times have changed, and also in the field of missionary activity the specific contribution of the young is increasingly exerting a reinvigorating influence on the older ones—not only because of their new theological insights but also because they undergo professionally conceptualized programs of formation and for the introduction of new missionaries in cross-cultural mission.

The XVI SVD General Chapter of 2006 stated that the introduction of new missionaries should be a priority for the receiving provinces worldwide: "All receiving provinces should seriously elaborate and implement this particular program. Failure to do so can be taken into consideration in making first assignments. Sending provinces should also organize such programs to aid in the preparation of new missionaries. Inter-zonal collaboration is strongly recommended."[2]

Martin Ueffing, SVD, finished his doctorate in missiology at the Pontifical Gregorian University in Rome. He was a professor of missiology and fundamental theology at the Divine Word School of Theology in Tagaytay City, Philippines, and of missiology at the Institute of Consecrated Life in Asia (ICLA) in Quezon City, Philippines. At present he is professor at the Philosophisch-Theologische Hochschule SVD, Sankt Augustin, Germany, and he is the provincial superior of the Divine Word Missionaries in Germany. He has been a formator for many years.

1. These are the opening lines of the booklet "Our Cultural Shadows," by Peter Koh Joo-Kheng and Jan Swyngedouw (Quezon City: Claretian Publications, 1998).
2. *Documents of the XVI General Chapter SVD, In Dialogue with the Word* (IDW), no. 6 (Rome: SVD Publications, September 2006), no. 103.

Without presenting such a program, this article will offer some general reflections on programs for new missionaries. The role and origin of missionaries in God's mission have changed, and there is an urgent need for a thorough preparation. The preparation of these missionaries and the introduction to work in another country/culture have increased.

Missionaries Today

In 1910, two-thirds of all Christian missionaries were Europeans. By 2010 this had dropped to approximately one-third. In 1910 half of all European missionaries were at work in Asia, but this dropped precipitously as colonial powers faded, and also for other reasons. Today, the principal destination for European missionaries is within Europe itself. The number of European missionaries sent out has been declining since 1970, while at the same time Europe receives more missionaries from the other five continents, especially from Asia. While the majority of missionaries from Africa and Asia today are working in their own continents, their number is increasing, nonetheless, also in Europe.[3]

The growth of Christianity in the Global South has also brought with it the reversal of the Christian missionary enterprise: while missionary projects continue "from the West to the rest," there are also an increasing number of missionary movements reaching back "from the rest to the West."[4] The great missionary movement is not over, but it has become omnidirectional, mission in and to six continents, and the leadership in mission is increasingly shaped by the Global South. This is true for all Christian denominations. The Second International Congress on World Evangelization concluded: "'Mission' is no longer, and can no longer be, a one-way movement from the 'older churches.' . . . Every local church is and cannot but be missionary. . . . [It] is responsible for its mission, and co-responsible for the mission of all its sister churches. Every local church, according to its possibilities, must share whatever its gifts are, for the needs of other churches, for mission throughout mankind, for the life of the world. . . . The Spirit of the Lord calls each people and each culture to its own fresh and creative response to the Gospel."[5]

Peter Vethanayagamony writes:

Missionaries from the Global South are faced with several challenges. They do not have the economic and political clout that those from

3. Todd M. Johnson and Kenneth R. Ross, eds., *Atlas of Global Christianity 1910–2010* (Edinburgh: Edinburgh University Press, 2009), 274–75.

4. P. Vethanayagamony, "Mission from the Rest to the West," in O. U. Kalu et al., eds., *Mission after Christendom* (Louisville, KY: Westminster John Knox Press, 2010), 59–70.

5. G. Rosales and C. G. Arévalo, eds., *For All the Peoples of Asia*, vol. 1 (Manila: Claretian Publications, 1997), 130.

the West had in the past. Christianity was once the religion of the confident, technologically advanced, and rising affluent, and sometimes those things were seen as a mark of God's favor. Christianity, now increasingly, is associated mostly with rather poor people and with some of the poorest countries on earth. Just like the Pauline mission, their mission is powerless in worldly terms and therefore dependent on the Holy Spirit. It not only lacks economic and political might; it also lacks the big organizational structure of the modern missionary movement.[6]

While the latter affirmation may not be true for many congregations and it may be true for some, the other observations are true. Missionaries from the Global South work from a position of weakness and powerlessness in worldly terms, but this may again be their strength in a missionary perspective. "More and more the agents of Christian mission come from among the weak, the broken, and the vulnerable. . . . More and more it is the poor who are taking the gospel to the rich. . . . Many migrants come from the new heartlands of Christianity and bring the flame of faith to the old centers in the north where the fire is burning low."[7]

In his reflection about mission in a time of testing, David Bosch[8] states that the position of Western mission agencies and missionaries has undergone some fundamental revision. No longer do missionaries go as ambassadors or representatives of the powerful West to territories subject to white, "Christian" nations. They now go to countries frequently hostile to Christian missions. And within the framework of the current mood of dialogue with people of other faiths, more and more missionaries are wondering whether there is still any point in going to the ends of the earth for the sake of the Christian gospel. Why, indeed, should one "suffer the pangs of exile and the stings of mosquitoes" if people will be saved anyway? It is, after all, "bad enough to have a difficult job to do, but much worse when one is left wondering if the difficult job is worth doing."

Missionaries, perhaps more than others, have tended to regard themselves as immune to the weaknesses and sins of "ordinary" Christians; it has taken them a long time to discover that they were no different than the churches from which they had come, and that, in the words of Stephen Neill, they "have on the whole been a feeble folk, not very wise, not very holy, not very patient. They have broken most of the commandments and fallen into every

---

6. See Vethanayagamony, "Mission from the Rest to the West," 65.

7. K. Ross, "Non-Western Christians in Scotland: Mission in Reverse," *Theology in Scotland* 12 (2005): 81.

8. D. Bosch, *Transforming Mission* (Maryknoll, NY: Orbis Books, 1991), 363–67.

conceivable mistake."[9] Indeed, in many parts of the world, including its traditional home base, the Christian mission appears to be the object not of God's grace and blessing, but of God's judgment. Repentance has to begin with a bold recognition of the fact that the church-in-mission is today facing a world fundamentally different from anything it faced before. This in itself calls for a new understanding of mission. We live in a period of transition, on the borderline between a paradigm that no longer satisfies and one that is, to a large extent, still amorphous and obscure. A time of paradigm change is, by its nature, a time of crisis—and crisis, we remind ourselves, is the point where danger and opportunity meet. It is a time when several "answers" are pressing themselves upon us, when many voices clamor for our attention. At this point, it may be helpful to remember some developments. The "success" of missionaries has a lot to do with their capacity to enter understandingly and sympathetically into the lives of others.

> This involves acquiring such an intimate knowledge of [persons] and of their environment that there results a deep understanding of their systems of thought and reaction. There will be mutual sharing of enjoyments, interests, and privileges resulting in such mutual sympathy that "we," "us," and "ours" are the spontaneous expressions for a sense of real community. One is no longer an outsider; one becomes an insider. The imagery of [others] is acquired; [their] point of view is appreciated so that the mutual insight and the sharing of mental states becomes possible. Fellowship and a sense of belonging is developed. . . .[10]

God's Mission

Mission has its deepest source in God, who,

> in His goodness and wisdom . . . chose to reveal Himself and to make known to us the hidden purpose of His will (see Eph 1:9) by which through Christ, the Word made flesh, man might in the Holy Spirit have access to the Father and come to share in the divine nature (see Eph 2:18; 2 Pet 1:4). Through this revelation, therefore, the invisible God (see Col 1:15, 1 Tim 1:17) out of the abundance of His love speaks to men [and women] as friends (see Ex 33:11; John 15:14–15) and lives among them (see Bar 3:38), so that He may invite and take them into fellowship with Himself. (DV 2)

---

9. S. Neill, *The Unfinished Task* (London: Lutterworth Press, 1960), 222.

10. D. Fleming, *Living as Comrades* (New York: Pub. for the Foreign Missions Conf. of North America by Agricultural Missions, 1950), 6–7.

God reveals himself to all men and women to invite all to friendship with God and to live in fellowship and communion with him. The initiative comes from God, and he wants that all come to share in the divine nature, i.e., have life. This thought is confirmed by *Ad Gentes* of Vatican II: "The pilgrim Church is missionary by her very nature, since it is from the mission of the Son and the mission of the Holy Spirit that she draws her origin, in accordance with the decree of God the Father" (AG 2). The church is called to participate in God's mission in the world and to follow God's own ways in this mission to invite people to relate with God, to have part in the divine nature, to be God's friends, and to live in communion with God and with one another.

On this foundation the missionary community of Christ's disciples began to grow and became church (see Acts 11:26: "In Antioch the disciples were called Christians for the first time"). Although there have been no programs for cross-cultural missionaries from the very beginning, there has been cross-cultural mission, starting at least with St. Paul.

The "Program" of St. Paul

The program of Paul may be summarized by 1 Cor 9:19–23. There we read,

> Though I am free and belong to no one, I have made myself a slave to everyone, to win as many as possible. To the Jews I became like a Jew, to win the Jews. To those under the law I became like one under the law (though I myself am not under the law), so as to win those under the law. To those not having the law I became like one not having the law (though I am not free from God's law but am under Christ's law), so as to win those not having the law. To the weak I became weak, to win the weak. I have become all things to all people so that by all possible means I might save some. I do all this for the sake of the gospel that I may share in its blessings.

Paul, the missionary *ad gentes* par excellence, became all to all—for the sake of Jesus Christ and his gospel. For Paul, everything starts with his own conversion. Senior and Stuhlmueller call this conversion the concrete starting point for Paul's Christian vision, with which Paul himself identifies his own missionary vocation.[11] This inaugural experience of Paul was such that it caused a radical revision in his way of life and his worldview. He calls it a "revelation" (Gal 1:12, 16), but he also refers to a visionary experience (1 Cor

---

11. Cf. D. Senior and C. Stuhlmueller, *The Biblical Foundations for Mission* (Maryknoll, NY: Orbis Books, 1983), 165.

9:1; 15:8). This revelation has shown him (1) that Jesus of Nazareth, who had been condemned to crucifixion, was, in fact, the Christ and had been raised from the dead and exalted as Son of God; (2) that through this Jesus, crucified and risen, God was offering salvation to all, both Jew and Gentile; (3) that, if Jesus was the Christ and salvation is offered to the Gentile world, for the understanding of a Jew the final age had begun; and (4) that he himself was called, in the manner of the prophets of old, to be the herald of God's word of salvation to the Gentiles.[12] His way may serve as a model until today—knowing Paul is an essential part of all programs for missionaries in cross-cultural mission.

Respecting Culture(s)

The young expatriate missionaries' encounters encompass the total cultural environment that they have become part of. In this respect, the young missionaries' experience is not so different from that of their seniors when they first arrived in their mission country. A similar enthusiasm fills their hearts. Although some subtle differences might arise when it comes to interpreting the aforementioned ideal of becoming "Jew with the Jews, and Greek with the Greeks," as St. Paul put it, their basic attitude toward the people around them is quite similar. They want to be of service, they want to respect culture(s), and for this they have to learn culture(s).

Therefore, another basis for mission is respect for cultures or contexts. This has already been stressed by the SCPF (Sacred Congregation de Propaganda Fide) in its very early years. In May 1658, the Sacred Congregation de Propaganda Fide presented Pope Alexander VII the first two candidates for the episcopate in Indochina. Before their departure for their mission, the new vicars apostolic received specific instructions from the congregation. Conditions were not favorable to Catholic missionaries in those countries at that particular time, and Propaganda Fide wished to ensure in missionaries the necessary qualities. More important, however, was the need to promote a local clergy. It was recognized as imperative to establish the local church with its own clergy and, eventually, its own hierarchy. The Propaganda Fide was also anxious to respect the traditions and customs of those countries, thus carrying on the early tradition of the church to assume into Christianity whatever was good in the ways of the people and gradually to eradicate what was not compatible with it.[13] The instruction was on Western customs that must not be introduced but local ones adopted:

---

12. Cf. Ibid., pp. 165–71.
13. Josef Neuner and Jacques Dupuis, *The Christian Faith* [ND] (New York: Alba House, 1996), nos. 1106–1110.

Do not in any way attempt, and do not on any pretext persuade these people to change their rites, habits, and customs, unless they are openly opposed to religion and good morals. For what could be more absurd than to bring France, Spain, Italy or any other European country over to China? It is not your country but the faith you must bring, that faith which does not reject or belittle the rites or customs of any nation as long as these rites are not evil, but rather desires that they be preserved in their integrity and fostered. It is, as it were, written in the nature of all men that the customs of their country and especially their country itself should be esteemed, loved and respected above anything else in the world. There is no greater cause of alienation and hatred than to change the customs of a nation, especially when they go back as far as the memory of ancestors can reach. . . .[14]

The point of departure for mission is the concrete people, the human community in a concrete context or cultural setting. Pope Paul VI insisted in *Evangelii Nuntiandi* (building on the advanced thinking of Vatican II and the 4th Synod of Bishops on Evangelization, in 1974) that the only correct attitude toward local ways of life would be nothing less than a "radical and profound understanding" of the local ways and values, an adjustment that would mean more than a "thin veneer" or that would be "purely decorative" in nature. On the contrary, the only proper attitude toward the ways and values of a local Christian community would have to touch the particular society "in a vital way," "in depth," and "right to the very roots"—in a word, "in the wide and rich sense of the Pastoral Constitution on the Church in the Modern World" (EN 18–20). Programs for cross-cultural missionaries are to be programs for culture learning, starting with language(s). It may be helpful to recall the following words from *Gaudium et Spes*:

It is one of the properties of the human person that he can achieve true and full humanity only by means of culture that is through the cultivation of the goods and values of nature. Whenever, therefore, there is a question of human life, nature and culture are intimately linked together.

The word "culture" in the general sense refers to all those things which go to the refining and developing of man's diverse mental and physical endowments. He strives to subdue the earth by his knowledge and his labor; he humanizes social life both in the family and in the whole civic community through the improvement of customs and institutions; he expresses through his works the great spiritual experi-

---

14. Alexander VII, "S. Congregation De Propaganda Fide—Instruction to the Vicars Apostolic of Tonkin and Cochinchina" (1659), in Neuner and Dupuis, no. 1109.

ences and aspirations of men throughout the ages; he communicates and preserves them to be an inspiration for the progress of many, even of all mankind.

Hence it follows that culture necessarily has historical and social overtones, and the word "culture" often carries with it sociological and anthropological connotations; in this sense one can speak about a plurality of cultures. For different styles of living and different scales of values originate in different ways of using things, of working and self-expression, of practicing religion and of behavior, of establishing laws and juridical institutions, of developing science and the arts and of cultivating beauty. Thus, the heritage of its institutions forms the patrimony proper to each human community; thus, too, is created a well-defined, historical milieu which envelopes the men of every nation and age, and from which they draw the values needed to foster humanity and civilization. (GS 53)

From "Accommodation" to "Inculturation"

Contextualization (inculturation) goes to the very roots of culture and views local cultures as already containing the germ of Jesus' message. The active presence of God in each context (or culture) began on the day of creation. This active presence continues today over the whole world, within and without the church. The church is therefore missioned not so much to introduce Christ to "others" (the people of other religions), as if he were a total stranger, but rather to help the "others" find him already present and active in the heart of all people. Comparing different approaches to mission, we notice major differences between a contextual and an accommodation approach:

- the primary agents involved in incarnating the gospel are the local Christian community and the Holy Spirit—not the sending church or the universal church;
- as important as church planting and the institutional church may be, the direct concern of mission is to proclaim the kingdom of God and salvation;
- the ultimate goal of incarnating the gospel is mutual enrichment, one that benefits not only the local Christian community but the universal church and the sending church as well;
- the depth of cultural penetration and identification with the gospel is incomparably greater in contextualization than in traditional accommodation;
- as important as the primary processes may be, the chief processes in inculturation are those connected with integration.

These points underline once more the challenge of knowing and understanding the "context(s)" of mission. Thus, it is not just accommodation but understanding the context and being part of the process of inculturation.

The attitude of Vatican II toward other religions underlines the richness of these religions. The Spirit acts in the depths of every person and offers to all the possibility to be made partners, in a way known to God, in the paschal mystery, whether they are within or without the visible borders of the church (GS 22; LG 16; AG 15; DH 6). All grace is of Christ. Without him there is no salvation (GS 22).

Long before the evangelizer appears, God is already active laying out the foundation on which the evangelizer must build. The presence of Christ experienced in this germinal form must, as much as possible, be allowed to grow and blossom in the congenial climate of the particular culture and tradition. With this understanding, mission today has this concept of the incarnation: Christ is incarnated once again, not, however, as a Jew of two thousand years ago or as a Westerner of the twentieth century but as someone born here, in the native soil. Cross-cultural missionaries need to be listeners—listeners to the word of God—but also listeners to the people to whom they are sent. Programs need to include the improvement of listening skills—getting in touch with realities different from the missionary's own—to be able to participate in God's mission in a given context. This kind of approach ("inculturation") poses the important and difficult question: How would Christ behave and what would he teach if he were born, for instance, in Japan in our times, or as a tribal Filipino born in Kalinga. Mission must make it possible for Christ to be reborn again and again in every time and place. It is especially to cultural anthropology that one must go to understand what culture (the "context" in contextualization) is and how it operates. It should be remembered that the ones who understand the culture most profoundly are the people who live the culture. Cross-cultural missionaries are persons of dialogue—able to enter into dialogue with people and their cultures, because the source of their life is dialogue with God. Dialogue is a central theme of all programs for cross-cultural missionaries.

Cross-Cultural Missionaries

In the early church, Christians knew that baptism made them full members of the church and, likewise, collaborators in continuing Jesus' mission. The catechumenate process laid the foundation; house churches, Christian networks, community prayer, and ritual provided building blocks; on this basis Christians witnessed to their faith and the community of disciples continued to grow. Up to the sixteenth century, mission became more and more associated with a select group of specialists, the missionaries. Since Vatican II the missionary calling of all is stressed again. *Ad Gentes* 35 says that "the whole Church is missionary and the work of evangelization is the basic duty of the People of God." Paul VI stresses, "Thus, it is that the whole Church receives the mission to evangelize, and the work of each individual member is important for the whole" (EN 15).[15] According to *Redemptoris Missio* "there is a new awareness that missionary activity is a matter for all Christians, for all dioceses and parishes, Church institutions and associations" (RM 2). Mission is no longer an activity of a selected few specialists but an essential part of being church and Christian, and all are called to participate in it. Both Paul VI and John Paul II also stress the role the laity has to play (see EN 71; RM 74). But there are also those who participate in God's mission by crossing religious, cultural, and economic borders in more deliberate and explicit ways. "Such ordained, religious, and an increasing number of lay Christians are identified as missionaries."[16]

Here, we are talking about cross-cultural or foreign missionaries, who are sent from one country/culture to another. This surely does not exclude other missionary vocations and other ways of participating in God's mission. In fact, mission today is more and more about collaborating with different groups and individuals who in one way or another respond to the calling to be missionaries in more explicit ways. The importance of laity and collaborating with them is also underlined in the document "SVD—Laity: Mission Partnership."[17] There we read, "Thus, the Church of today finds herself at a privileged era. In no other century has she been gifted with such a widely and highly educated laity—many among whom are now generously taking part in pastoral leadership and mission service. One unforeseen consequence is the mounting tension between ordained ministers and lay leaders. Some see in it a serious problem of potential rivalry to resolve. But it may be better to welcome it as a creative process whose faithful pursuit bears the promise of ecclesial rebirth."[18]

And later: "Thus, as priestly vocations and regular churchgoing decline in their midst, Catholics in Europe live more and more with the sad closure or merging of their once-flourishing parishes. Yet, a counter-trend seems to foretell another Europe that is not the graveyard of Christendom but a greenhouse for a new Christianity. It shows itself through the rise and spread of various and numerous ecclesial movements—ranging from 'conservative' to 'progressive' in social or cultural orientation, and mainly led by the laity."[19]

---

15. R. Schroeder, *What Is the Mission of the Church: A Guide for Catholics*, revised and expanded (Maryknoll, NY: Orbis Books, 2018), 101.

16. Ibid., 105.

17. IDW, no. 8 (December 2008).

18. Ibid., 17.

19. Ibid., 21.

There are many ways for "lay people" to engage as cross-cultural missionaries. In some parts of Europe, e.g., in Germany, the "MaZ-programs"
(MaZ = Missionare auf Zeit; missionaries for a certain time) are flourishing.
The programs for preparation and accompaniment are well developed, and
are used for these lay missionaries. They include a period of preparation in
the home country of the future missionaries, as well as regular meetings
during their mission exposure. For SVD religious missionaries, the Constitutions [c.] stress: "Whoever joins our Society must be ready to go wherever
the superior sends him in order to fulfill our missionary mandate even if this
entails leaving his own country, mother tongue and cultural milieu. Such
readiness is an essential characteristic of our missionary vocation. Confreres
always have the right to volunteer for missionary service in another country
or culture" (c. 102).

While a readiness for cross-cultural mission is a basic SVD requirement,
all members of the Society always have the right to opt for mission outside
their home country and culture. While a basic availability for the needs of
the congregation is important, the liberty to choose a certain mission area
may be helpful for the mission motivation of the members. In his latest letter
about new mission assignments,[20] Fr. Superior General writes that, before
taking their perpetual vows, candidates are requested "to make known to
the Superiors both the country or Province/Region and the kind of work for
which they feel themselves best suited (c. 116.1)." For this, "the following
considerations need to be given emphasis:

- *Lifelong Commitment*: The goal of every missionary should be the commitment to become one with the people to whom he is sent. This entails seeking to adopt a new people and culture and to allow oneself to be adopted
  by a new people. Saint Joseph Freinademetz is our model in this regard.
  He once wrote: "China has become not only my homeland but also the
  battlefield on which I will one day fall. . . ." The First Assignment, then, is
  a lifelong commitment.
- *Missionary Motives*: Choices should be made on the basis of genuine missionary motives ("Where am I needed?") rather than of personal desires
  ("What do I want?"). They should be made in the spirit of the prophet
  Isaiah: "Then I heard the voice of the Lord saying, Whom shall I send, and
  who will go for us? And I said, Here am I; send me!" (Isa 6:8).
- *Difficult Missions*: The General Council and I wish to challenge our young
  confreres to be ready to choose our more difficult missions and not just
  those where they think they might be comfortable.
- *Prophetic Dialogue*: The young confreres should also keep in mind the perspective of our "fourfold prophetic dialogue" when expressing their desire

---

20. Taken from the letter of December 20, 2010, to all provincial and regional superiors.

for a particular type of missionary work. In today's world, we are facing the new challenges of urban ministry, work with migrants, refugees, and displaced people, ministry among indigenous peoples, with those suffering from HIV/AIDS, etc.[21]

An important element in missionary preparation is the application process for the future assignment. This process is a period of discernment and clarification of understandings of mission, and of mission purposes and goals. Mission will not work if missionaries are only sent by superiors and comply because of "obedience." This is also true for those who come to another country during their formation years, to complete their initial formation there. The needs of the Society are to be considered, but also personal interest and motivation to work in the place where one plans to be a missionary are important. The third of the above-mentioned points needs attention: there are different experiences and reasons to call a mission "difficult." These may be of an economic or social nature: poverty, injustice, violence, etc., in a given place surely make mission there difficult (whatever the understanding of mission). But even a continent like Europe may be a difficult mission. Secularization, religious indifference, individualism, materialism, etc., may be reasons for difficulties as well the situation of church and religious life on the continent. Europe is of many different realities, contexts, and cultures at the same time. In addition, history—the role of Europe in the history of Africa and Asia, as well as European history itself—may make mission difficult. Feelings or even experiences of superiority and inferiority are to be taken seriously on all sides.

Programs for New Missionaries

After all that has been said about programs for cross-cultural missionaries, there are other considerations to be taken into account. It is strange that, whatever has been said, until not too long ago relatively little attention had been given in missionary circles to preparing people in a systematic way for encounters with other/new cultures. Whereas in the present age of globalization in society at large, an increasing need is felt, and responded to, for formal training in what is called "intercultural competence," missionaries have been slow in joining the example. Sure, there have been exceptions. A few missionaries have indeed been pioneers in cultural anthropology, and some among them have tried to widen the knowledge they gained from studying one particular foreign culture to establish more general principles for intercultural living.[22] But to this day it is hard to find satisfactory and helpful sources on intercultural living or about the role of missionaries in cross-cultural mission.

---

21. Ibid.
22. The Anthropos tradition in the SVD is only to be mentioned at this point.

In preparation for the Edinburgh 2010 conference, commissions were created to reflect on nine themes identified as being the key to mission in the twenty-first century. Commission V dealt with the preparation of missionaries.[23] The rapidly changing world situation was seen to challenge churches to produce a higher standard of missionary. Missionaries need to be men and women who combine genuine vocation with the highest possible professional and theological training. According to experiences recorded by missionaries, there is a marked disparity between their ideals and their actual or working standard. This is true for both the standards of personal preparation (physical, social, intellectual, spiritual) and for the professional training of missionaries. In his article "The Philosophy of Intercultural Formation" Ivan Illich writes:

> For what else is spiritual poverty but indifference, willingness to be without what we like? Just as spiritual poverty implies not the absence of likes, but freedom from them; so the attitude of the missioner carries him not to the denial of his background but to communication with that of another, and this is a difficult goal to achieve. It is difficult to become indifferent—detached from all exterior comforts. It is even more difficult to become indifferent to intimate gifts such as physical conditions supporting a healthy life, or the presence of those we love, or our reputation or our success. It is much more difficult again to become detached from convictions deeply rooted in us since childhood about what is and is not done. Yet it is this last detachment which the missioner will have to achieve if he wants to be truly an instrument of the Incarnation rather than an agent of his own culture. No missioner has the right to insist, in the name of the Gospel, on acceptance of his own human background, and thus to make Baptism or full Church membership dependent on a degree of spiritual poverty in the convert which he himself is not willing to practice.[24]

Missionaries should be excellent communicators who can bring people together. Team ministry seems to be the only appropriate pastoral method that corresponds to the idea of collegiality, communion, and partnership as a way of being church and "doing" mission.[25] Franz-Josef Eilers stresses: "One must see very clearly, however, that one of the basic needs along these lines is also to be aware that without a sufficient insight into one's own culture, into

---

23. D. A. Kerr and K. Ross, eds., *Edinburgh 2010: Mission Then and Now* (Eugene, OR: Wipf & Stock, 2010), 155–77.

24. I. Illich, "The Philosophy of Intercultural Formation," *SEDOS Bulletin* (1981): 268.

25. Cf. A. Bellagamba, *Mission and Ministry in the Global Church* (Maryknoll, NY: Orbis Books, 1992), 70–92.

one's personality and religion, one cannot really communicate interculturally: how did and does my culture shape and influence my own knowledge, behavior, understanding and communication and where is the limit to be kept, or where do I have to transgress the boundary of my own heritage?"[26]

Missionaries who are sent to a foreign country are strangers to the place to which they are destined. They are "strangers" whose personalities have been formed by a culture entirely different from that of the place where they are supposed to work—they are called to transcend the frontiers of their own culture. A. Bellagamba draws the following profile of today's missionaries:

> Missionaries must be persons who live in, or have lived in, more than one culture, who have made contact with more than one nation, who have prayed with disciples of more than one religion. They have learned more than one language. They are at home everywhere, but not quite at home anywhere. They are persons who can move easily from one place to another, from one culture to another, and not become confused, or lost, or incapable of action.

As humanity moves closer to a world community, only those individuals who have developed these qualities and skills that the missionary ought to possess and become an example of will be able to live in that global village, grow, operate, and be happy. "People who cannot accept multiculturalism, multiracism, people who are afraid of moving from one place to another, people who cannot master more than one language will find it hard to live the next stage of human existence. Today's missionary is the type of what all people must become in the next era of the development of humanity."[27] In former times, missionaries left their home countries, usually never to return. We cannot but admire their spirit of heroism and abnegation in the face of the many adversities they had to confront. Nowadays, missionaries share the same life expectancy as their contemporaries; they frequently travel by air, and communicate via E-mail. The former adventurer–conqueror–martyr model has given way to that of a bridge-builder, a communicator, a partner.

Missionaries today cannot rely any more on the same ideological foundation as their predecessors. These could sacrifice their lives for the sake of "saving souls" from eternal perdition and of establishing the church. Their identity was clearly defined by a sense of divine mission to preach, convert and baptize (see Matt 28:16–20). Missionaries today need that conviction of being sent, but their sense of identity may be more obscure and blurred. To work and serve with conviction, and yet without ideological baggage, to offer oneself and yet feel empty-handed, are part of a new way of mission. In

---

26. Franz-Josef Eilers, *Communicating between Cultures* (Manila: Logos, 1992), 164–65.
27. Bellagamba, *Mission and Ministry in the Global Church*, 10.

perhaps new ways, sacrifice and self-emptying continue to be part and parcel of the life of a missionary who takes his task seriously. Louis Luzbetak writes:

> The most common, most painful, and most important but generally unrecognized form of self-immolation is the call to small but real and continuous daily sacrifices. . . . We refer, for instance, to the enormous sacrifices that will be required of all engaged in cross-cultural ministries in learning and appreciating the ways and values of the community ministered to; there are also the drudgery and the countless humiliations and frustrations associated with any real effort to master an apparently "insignificant" local dialect; there is the violence to self that is required when adapting to local standards of human interactions; and there is the humiliation of having to serve as junior partner in the Third World only because one is a foreigner, even if the expatriate has had a far better education and far more experience in the particular ministry than his or her indigenous counterpart. Not the sacrifice of the luxuries of one's home nor the consolations of relatives and friends of long standing but the sacrifice of one's ways and values will be the missionary's greatest sacrifice, a sacrifice that, in fact, may even become a slow martyrdom. The missionary who claims that he or she has never felt the weight of this sacrifice has most likely never made it.[28]

Experience shows the importance of the preparation of cross-cultural missionaries as well as the preparation of those who will stay in their own culture to work with those coming from outside. SVD missionaries want to live in international, multicultural communities (teams) in the diverse contexts to which they are assigned. The preparation of missionaries has—besides many other aspects—to include both learning international/intercultural living and learning the new context/culture. There may even be conflicts resulting from the attempts to be missionaries both in intercultural communities and enculturated at the same time.

> It is common to distinguish two dimensions in our religious missionary vocation: the personal dimension and the ministry dimension. The process of growth as a person and the need to cope with the accompanying changes in one's personal life are factors to be reckoned with. Moreover, as far as our missionary action and service are concerned, the context of the rapidly changing world opens up new possibilities, but also poses unaccustomed challenges. By its very nature, then, our vocation necessitates ongoing formation in both dimensions.[29]

---

28. L. Luzbetak, *The Church and Cultures: New Perspectives in Missiological Anthropology* (Maryknoll, NY: Orbis Books, 1988), 5–6.

29. IDW, no. 4 (December 2004), *SVD Ongoing Formation*, 12.

The initial years in mission are for learning from the people and the actual context of the mission. The temptation to enter too soon into active ministry on one's own initiative and on one's own responsibility should be avoided. It is crucial at this period to have a suitable support structure. . . . There should be a well laid out plan for the introduction and the language learning of new missionaries. This would include personal accompaniment by a confrere with experience and understanding. Regular meetings of the young newly assigned confreres have also been found to be very valuable. Special attention should be given to introducing them to live and work in international and intercultural teams.[30]

The SVD *Handbook for Superiors* deals in one section with "new missionaries."[31] After underlining that "missionary work is the end and the aim of our Society" (Prologue of SVD Constitutions), the purpose of the given directives is explained: "The directives given below are intended to facilitate the transition of those confreres who have to leave their homeland to assume a new life and activity in another country and/or another culture. Since the first period spent by a confrere in a new culture, as well as the beginning of his work after basic formation, is critically important, the Society places special emphasis on the first three years after completing basic formation."[32]

About the introduction of new missionaries we read:[33]

- The introduction of a new missionary into his field of work is an important and critical period that has a decisive influence on his future. Both he and the superior are responsible for its success (c. 518). This introduction entails both a well-organized program of introduction and the cooperation of experienced confreres.
- The new missionary has the right to a thorough introduction into the language and culture, the ecclesial and pastoral situation, as an important prerequisite for fruitful missionary labor. The provincial superior of the province to which the confrere is appointed is responsible for planning and carrying through this program (c. 518.1).
- The most important dimension of the care of the newly arrived missionaries involves the personal guidance needed to help them deal with the problems of culture shock, difficulties in adapting to a new situation, transition to a greater independence, and contact with local SVD communities. The

---

30. Ibid., 42–43.
31. Society of the Divine Word, *Handbook for Superiors* (only for internal circulation), Rome, 2002, A 5 New Missionaries, 23–25.
32. Ibid., 23–24.
33. Ibid., 24–25.

new missionary should be accompanied by a confrere appointed for this purpose. The confrere in charge of accompaniment should organize periodic evaluations that will include the different dimensions of the study experience as well as of the religious life of prayer and integration of the new missionary into his new province.

- The introduction of new missionaries and their ongoing formation should lay special stress on:
  - ◊ language learning;
  - ◊ knowledge of the religions of the country so as to enable them to engage in dialogue with those of other beliefs;
  - ◊ study of the culture and history of the country from the local viewpoint so as to become sensitive to the values, symbols, and behavior patterns of the culture(s) within which they are to work.
- The method and duration of this introduction will be determined by the provincial council and must correspond to the norms established by the bishop and the bishops' conference.
- Where it is possible and appropriate, the Society should develop a detailed program in cooperation with other institutes and make it obligatory for the new missionary (c. 518.2).
- No new missionary destined for pastoral ministry is to be appointed at once to an isolated post but rather is to be introduced to his work by a competent confrere for a period of about three years (c. 518.3).

It is interesting to note that for language learning there is still a section in the *Handbook* that quotes from the SVD tradition:

> In a letter written in 1895 Arnold Janssen [the founder of the SVD] wrote: "There is one very important point I would like you to take to heart, namely the mastery of the language of the country in which you are. If you fail to do this, you will ever remain an outsider in this land and you will not be able to accomplish for God's kingdom what you should accomplish." Constitution 518.1 puts great emphasis on language learning as "an important prerequisite for fruitful missionary labor" and on the right every new missionary has to a thorough study of the local language.[34]

Missionary training should integrate spiritual, moral, and intellectual elements. Since the spiritual element is purely a gift from God, it has to be nurtured throughout a missionary's life, in which training both before and

---

34. Society of the Divine Word, *Handbook for Superiors*, 2002, A 6 Language Learning for New Missionaries, 25–27.

during missionary service is essential. Missionaries must be people of faith.[35] Moral training should cultivate four qualities: *docility* in the sense of always being open and willing to learn; *gentleness* or *the spirit of courtesy*, which enables missionaries to understand the customs of the people among whom they are called to live; and *sympathy*, which empowers missionaries to love the people they serve. These qualities combine to produce a fourth that all missionaries should seek to attain: namely, *leadership* with respect to "the special duties and responsibilities of a missionary's position."[36] In addition to such qualities, intellectual training is of great importance. The missionary must have the best education that his own country and the church can give him, whatever is to be his kind of work. Professional competence is an important requirement of religious missionary formation and should remain a criterion in all programs of ongoing formation and specialization.

Ideally, formation should take place in close proximity to real missionary situations and in constant interaction with missionary personnel active in the field. Through a guided process, the *formandi* should be encouraged to make a realistic assessment of the missionary response taking place in their vicinity so that they can analyze its lights and shadows. Realities that one encounters in the mission should become impulses for learning new lessons. Such learning becomes possible through opportunities for a hands-on experience of actual missionary activity. It should become a regular ingredient of our formation programs. Direct experience of mission helps the *formandi* to gather a realistic idea of what to expect as they enter the field at the end of their initial formation. We have certain established processes to provide such hands-on experience of mission: Regency, Cross-cultural Training Program (CTP), Overseas Training Program (OTP), Exposure and Immersion Program (EIP), Clinical Pastoral Education (CPE), and supervised pastoral ministry. To ensure that these programs become more effective in contributing to our missionary formation, we should make use of the action–reflection–action model.[37]

Today, the priests and religious and lay missionaries can assert, "there are three special moments when we must imitate the Lord's 'Passover.' We are called to pass over when we enter another culture, when we become one with the poor, and when we engage in dialogue."[38] The experience of missionaries of diverse cultures, religions, and ways of life qualifies them as persons who can bring together different peoples and ways of life, reconcile them, make

---

35. Bellagamba, *Mission and Ministry in the Global Church*, 93–114; Luzbetak, *The Church and Cultures*, 2–8.

36. Kerr and Ross, eds., *Edinburgh 2010*, 156.

37. *Re-imagining the Pathways of Our Common Vocational Journey* (Rome: SVD Publications, 2010), 26–27.

38. *Following the Word* 1, in *Nuntius SVD*, 12, no. 5(1988 [1990]): 693.

them intelligible to one another, and instill respect for one another. Missionaries live in a continuous process of "passing over" and "coming back," passing over from one culture to another, from one religion to another, and coming back to their own way of life, their own religion.[39] For example, many Christian missionaries from Africa or Asia sent to Europe encounter people and societies whose cultures have been deeply influenced by Christianity. But they also have to face present-day realities of European Christianity and religiosity—new challenges and questions, secularization, critical stances toward the church, etc.

An attitude of openness to the unknown and a desire to "go beyond" one's own world, culture, and religion are important. The present global context demands of missionaries a sensitivity to emergent needs. It may be useful to integrate the study of culture and cultures into different programs for the preparation of missionaries. Such programs surely start already before departing for the place of assignment in another country or culture. The point of departure of all programs is the motivation of the cross-cultural missionary to really enter a new culture and to participate in an intercultural team in God's mission in the given place and among the people present. Programs for new missionaries in cross-cultural mission must rely on foundations laid in the home countries of the missionaries, and have to be drawn up in concrete contexts based on the Good News of Jesus Christ of God's reign of life offered to all.

---

39. Cf. John Dunne, *The Way of All the Earth: Experiments in Truth and Religion* (Notre Dame, IN: University of Notre Dame Press, 1978), 1.

7

Interculturality and Conflict

Barbara Hüfner-Kemper
and Thomas Kemper

"Be patient toward all that is unsolved in your heart and try to love the questions themselves. Do not now seek the answers, which cannot be given you because you would not be able to live them. And the point is to live everything. Live the questions now."[1]

Cultural Awareness Not Competence

Our experience in working with people in intercultural settings, as missionaries, organizational leaders, and as trainers or counselors over the last thirty years, has been an enriching experience of cultural awareness. It has deepened our understanding and knowledge about people from other cultures and circumstances of life. However, it has also been an experience of *not* understanding—of misinterpreting, misjudging, and being misjudged. Situations of tense irritation and real embarrassment forced us to get in touch with our own limitations and vulnerability in cross-cultural settings.

Barbara Hüfner-Kemper holds a master's degree in social science and is trained in concentrative movement therapy and brainspotting. She has experience in Brazil and Germany as a therapist. Currently she works as a life coach with Brazilian immigrants at *TACC Training and Counseling Center St Luke's*, Atlanta, GA, and teaches as adjunct professor at Candler School of Theology, Emory University, Atlanta, GA. Focus areas of her work are stress, trauma, and cross-cultural conflict transformation.

Thomas Kemper holds master's degrees in development sociology and adult education. He taught at the Methodist Theological School in Rudge Ramos, Sao Paulo. Later, in his native Germany, he worked for the Reformed Church in Lippe, and also led the international mission work for the German United Methodist Church. Since 2010 he heads Global Ministries, the mission and development agency of the United Methodist Church with its headquarters in New York. It works in more than 130 countries with missionaries, projects, and partners. He is married to Barbara Hüfner-Kemper, and they have three adult children.

1. Rainer M. Rilke, *Letters to a Young Poet* (New York: W. W. Norton, 1934).

In exploring our topic, interculturality and conflict, we are working with a definition of culture as a system of beliefs, habits, behavior, values, attitudes, and symbols. People rarely stop to think about culture in form or content. Culture is passed along by communication and imitation. It is a field of possibilities and limitations and boundaries. Culture is never static; it is always dynamic, in change and transition. While we can enhance awareness, our own experiences and our definition of culture make it very clear that we will never be fully culturally competent.

Objective and a Reminder

This chapter tries to articulate and make suggestions as to how we can deal with misunderstandings and conflicts that arise for mission work within intercultural settings. From our Western perspective, one of the major challenges in such settings comes from our conditioning in an achievement-oriented society of quick responses. We explain, we solve, and we fix problems and misunderstandings. And that success-oriented society has us in its thrall. It seduces us with the false image of cultural superiority. We are well advised in mission content to recall that Christianity teaches us surrender, acceptance of limitations, and suffering, and the art of being present with people in unresolved situations. Our faith teaches us that we never get closer to God than when we accept our own vulnerability and surrender to God.

Culture and the Iceberg Model

An iceberg model helps to explain many of the common challenges in intercultural relations and communication. Only a small part of culture, like an iceberg, is visible at the surface. Cultures have their hidden parts—an unconscious component—even as we humans do. The visible and conscience part of culture is what we see and know. For example, clothes, languages, architecture, food, and art.[2] The invisible is the unconscious part of culture and the reason for uncountable misunderstandings and conflicts in cross-cultural mission settings. "The important part of culture exists safely hidden below the level of conscious awareness."[3]

Interestingly enough, Joseph Shaules, in "Two Minds Abroad: What Neuroscience Can Teach Us about Global Living," explains "culture shock" as a cognitive overload in the brain linked to the unconscious mind. The conscious mind searches for intercultural experience, and on the surface conscious learning and knowing take place; however, the deeper learning accrues

---

2. J. R. Von Wogau, H. Eimmermacher, and A. Lanfranchi, *Therapie und Beratung von Migranten—systemisch-interkulturell denken und handeln* (Weinheim/Basel: Beltz Verlag, 2004), 34.

3. E. T. Hall, *Beyond Culture* (Garden City, NY: Anchor Books, 1976).

not when we are taking vacation in a different culture but when we live in a place. Intercultural living is a deeper learning. It affects the unconscious mind and can be seen as a reconfiguration of cultural patterns. This overload can lead to culture shock,[4] which is the cause of many inner and interrelation conflicts abroad.

Culture shock can be productive. Gisela Führing[5] says that the key situation for intercultural learning is exactly this moment of culture shock. The overload and the judging unconscious mind raise irritation, misunderstanding, and embarrassment. The moment when we are aware that we do not understand, when we misinterpret and put ourselves and others in embarrassing situations, that is the very moment when our intercultural learning starts.

The partial overload is part of that learning process, and it assures us that we never will be totally competent when it comes to cross-cultural learning. We need to take into account the unconscious elements of a culture, or a mind, and that means the cognizance of failure, an awareness that we can get lost, that we may not know—the recognition that we must try again.

Attitude of Vulnerability

The cultural overload that Shaules and Führing talk about is not only contemporary. Consider the biblical account of the wandering Hebrews, not always sure where they were geographically and encountering a range of cultural customs and taboos. The apostle Paul seems a bit lost in Acts 16:6–8— so many cities, so far away from each other, more than hundreds of miles in opposite directions, a zigzagging from place to place. Interculturality in mission includes getting lost sometimes. Mission is "unfortunately" not the straight path. Missionaries are sometimes not sure of what to do or where to go. And it is okay to get lost when in mission, to know there is no GPS help. Here offered is one experience that stands for several other similar stories told, heard or experienced by us over the years:

> When I came to the "mission field" I was so excited and happy. After all that time of preparation, finally I arrived! Now it was really going to start. I felt surrounded by such nice people, so welcoming and open-hearted. The wonderful weather and the variety of fruits at the market, just beautiful. I jumped into the work. So much appreciation for my person and my efforts. I did things that I had never done before. So sure and so convinced of myself. I felt so gifted and equipped.

4. J. Shaules, *Webinar: Two Minds Abroad—What Neuroscience Can Teach Us about Global Living*, Families in Global Transition, 2014.

5. G. Führing, *Begegnung als Irritation* (Münster: Waxmann, 1996), 115.

But after some time I felt completely lost. Surrounded by all these wonderful people, I felt really alone. At the beginning my knowledge about the host culture made me feel secure and undeterred. Now I realized that deep down I didn't understand anything.

Crises like this are the important teaching/learning moments in intercultural mission work. We have the choice between hiding or accepting. To hide our vulnerability means to play the role of the superior, possibly Western missionaries with our own ways of dominating or manipulating in uncertain new circumstances. To accept our vulnerability and ask for help is the way to become a real part of the community; then mutual learning can start. We can pass from knowing something about the culture to becoming part of, being in that culture. This way vulnerability becomes a gift and a strength.

This attitude is especially important for missionaries from countries with dominant cultures such as Germany or the United States. If we are not in touch with our own vulnerability we run the risk of continuing to be or becoming arrogant. To have this kind of experience saves us from feeling superior, it makes us humble. It makes us sit down, look eye to eye and to be on the same level. It makes our nonjudgmental mission possible. And that's how Paul's mission started. Not helping others, but being helped. That's how nonjudgmental mission works. We are helped and we are helping. It goes both ways.

Very close to this line of thought is the concept of "Konvivenz" (convivencia) which was developed by the missiologist Theo Sundermeier to describe mission for the twenty-first century. Mission in this perspective means living together, "convivence," co-serving, co-learning, and co-celebrating. Sundermeier came upon "Konvivenz" in his work with Brazilian liberation theology and base communities. He sees its *Sitz im Leben* (place in life) in communities or neighborhoods where people help one another and live in solidarity. The people share advice and knowledge, very often traditional wisdom and rituals, about nutrition, health, birth, and death. They learn in community. They also celebrate as a community, the celebration often being protest against resignation and death. When we enter into co-serving, co-learning and co-celebrating, intercultural understanding can take place.[6]

Circumstances of Life and Culture

Human reality is diverse and never explained by reference to culture alone. Graphic 1 explains and illustrates how through a "Triangle of Differences"

---

6. T. Sundermeier, *Den Fremden Verstehen: eine Praktische Hermeneutik* (Göttingen: Vandenhoeck & Ruprecht, 1996).

we can start to learn to delineate between types of differences, and not simply see everything through the lens of culture.

Graphic 1: Triangle of differences

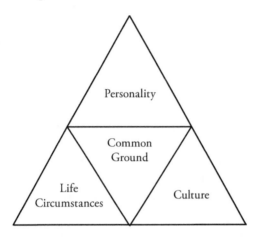

When it comes to culture, we have observed over the years two recurring attitudes. One is that we use our knowledge about cultural differences in order to dominate, that is, as knowledge that helps us to keep or gain power over people. A second attitude is to blame culture for everything we do not understand. Here two examples:

- A missionary in Kenya tells us about his new work and how happy he is with his co-workers. Everything seems to go very well. But his secretary was arriving late at least three times a week. The missionary assumes with a smile on his face "I guess that's her culture."

The missionary drives his own car to the church office every day. The secretary, who lives in a faraway neighborhood, must depend on the very unreliable public transport system. The circumstances of her life, not her culture, make her late.

Another example comes from a Filipina church leader who told us:

- In September 1972, when Martial Law (ML) was declared in the Philippines, the people, including church folks, were numbed by fear, as it wasn't clear what ML would mean for our lives, for our freedom of movement and expression. I was a 22-year-old director of Christian education for a large local church.

    One of my tasks then was to produce every week a summary of the adult Sunday school lesson. On that first Sunday after ML, I added in the Sunday school material a question about possible implications of

ML on our civil liberties. It did not take long for some of our church leaders to inform me that Sunday school was not the place to raise such questions.

After five or six years of Martial Law, exercising caution and being constantly on guard became second nature for me. One day we were going to launch an event related to human rights—in other words, it was politically sensitive. I suggested that we scrutinize our guest list. I invited a U.S. missionary to the event, but I informed him that we weren't sure everyone should be invited. With his classic liberal concept of inclusiveness, he scoffed at the idea. He rather suggested that he would not feel comfortable going to an event where not everyone was welcomed, and misunderstood it as being part of our noninclusive culture.

I don't believe this missionary knew that my home had been ransacked by military intelligence agents or that my two sisters were taken blindfolded to some remote location before they were returned home, physically unharmed, but psychologically traumatized. He did not know in those difficult times how important it was to be always alert about with whom you communicated.

The U.S. missionary insisted on his value of inclusiveness against the apparent value of selectivity, while the storyteller's behavior was based on very concrete circumstances of life in a dictatorial regime rather than a culture of exclusion. You could call it the limits of hospitality in times of repression, not cultural difference. These are two examples that demonstrate the evidence and importance of having the triangle of differences in mind when we deal with cross-cultural misunderstandings or conflicts.

The mission story in Acts 16:11–13 describes on the other hand the *encounter* of differences. It is astonishing that, despite all the differences, Paul and Lydia are not just getting along. No—it is the story of a really successful mission endeavor. Paul is meeting Lydia and a group of women who are gathered by the river. This encounter of so many different people cannot only be explained by culture. On the one side, we have women who are settled down, doing a hard job, sustaining the children, gathering and praying outside the gates, being part of an excluded people. And on the other side, we have men who are traveling and preaching.

This encounter of differences encompasses different cultures, different languages, different genders, different religions, different circumstances of life, and most likely different personalities. Interculturality is the encounter and the recognition of these differences, and going beyond them to ask the question: what do we have in common?

And to ask this question in an attitude of sitting down, coming down, trying to understand, listening and responding. That means not judging, not interpreting and not dominating. Therefore, we find Marshal Rosenberg's "Non-Violent Communication" (NVC) very helpful.[7] This method is very appropriate when it comes to cross-cultural communication, especially in conflict situations.

Using Culture Research as an Orientation, and Not as a Tool for Labeling Other Cultures

This section presents three sets of research findings about personal and cultural differences that can be used to improve communication in intercultural settings. Very often such findings are used in an almost fundamentalist way as proven fact about how the others are. We highly recommend avoiding that perspective; rather, use these findings for orientation, tools to help us ask more questions and reach more reflective observation followed by the respective action. The knowledge should be used to build hypotheses rather than serve as assumptions.

The first research comes from Geert Hofstede whose theory of cultural dimensions describes the effect of culture on the values of its members and how these values relate to behavior. His work is widely cited in cross-cultural learning and psychology. Hofstede is a Dutch psychologist and his research on cultural differences is a framework for all cross-cultural communication. Hofstede's research covers fifty-two countries worldwide, and describes the effects of different cultural values on its members and how these values relate to human behavior. We want to mention three of his cultural dimensions that we find the most helpful.[8]

Power distance	
High	**Low**
It is accepted and expected that power is distributed unequally. The power of others is based on where they are situated in certain formal and hierarchical positions.	People relate to one another more as equals regardless of formal positions.

An example: A good friend of ours rose in the ranks of a Catholic order but continued to be his humble self. Whenever he went on visitations to other provinces, especially in Asia, he was not allowed to participate with

7. M. Rosenberg, *Living Nonviolent Communication* (Boulder, CO: Sounds True, 2012).
8. G. J. Hofstede, P. B. Pedersen, and G. Hofstede, *Exploring Culture* (Yarmouth, ME: Intercultural Press, 2002).

his brothers in the cleaning of the dishes after a meal. His attempts to do so were blocked because this was not seen as his role as a superior coming from Rome. The brothers themselves were experiencing a terrible conflict as to whether to stop him, since he was a superior who should not do these manual chores, or to let him go ahead, as he was their superior and could do what he thought best to do.

Uncertainty "avoidance"	
High	**Low**
Members of a society attempt to cope with anxiety by minimizing uncertainty. They try to minimize the occurrence of unknown and unusual circumstances and to proceed with careful changes step by step by planning and by implementing rules, laws, and regulations.	Cultures accept and feel comfortable in unstructured situations or changeable environments and try to have as few rules as possible. People in these cultures tend to be more pragmatic and are more tolerant of change.

An example: A Korean missionary couple shared with us their experience in doing mission work in Kenya. One of the greatest challenges for them was to realize that they felt insecure and very uncomfortable in not being able to plan and organize things in the way in which they were accustomed. Many things seemed to be chaotic to them. They needed a great deal of patience with themselves and others to refrain from getting angry. Their need for planning and control was very often not met. It took them a long time to realize that people can feel good in unstructured situations and that "unstructured" does not mean "ineffective."

Collectivism or Individualism?	
Collectivism	**Individualism**
Individuals act predominantly as members of a lifelong and cohesive group or organization	Self-realization and standing up for yourself is a very important value. Stress is put on personal achievements and individual rights.

An example: When we started working in Brazil as a young couple many years ago, we were invited almost every Sunday following Sunday school in the morning to stay with one of the church families for the whole day: having lunch together, watching TV, talking and, very important in Brazil, taking a shower and then going at night together to the worship service. Even after worship they asked us again to come to their houses. They wanted us to feel at home and be part of their families. We were very happy about the kindness and friendship, but we, however, as Germans coming from a very individualistic culture, felt the need of having some time for ourselves—for privacy. We came to understand that the Brazilians felt sorry for us because in their understanding, coming from a collective culture, we must have felt very alone so far away from our German families.

Other research data we find important comes from Lothar Käser and his work on "Fremde Kulturen" (foreign cultures) as an introduction to ethnology. His work has important implications for mission work from a Christian-oriented worldview. He argues that members of a collective-oriented society react mostly with shame when it comes to failures or fault in their behavior. In an individualistic-oriented society, the members react mostly with guilt.[9]

Building of consciousness	
Mostly shame orientation	**Mostly guilt orientation**
Collective-oriented worldview with fear of losing face in the group.	Individual-oriented worldview with fear of feeling guilty.
In case of a failure in one's behavior	
When the wrongdoer assumes his/her fault directly, it is socially considered as a huge impertinence.	When the wrongdoer assumes his/her fault directly, it is socially considered as honorable.

An example: A young American teaching intern in Tanzania was enthusiastic about her work until she encountered a crisis: someone stole money from a classmate. She confronted the class directly, asking the child who had taken the money to come during lunch break, bring the money back, and talk privately with her about the issue. She felt confident that one of the kids had done this, and was happy about having found such an indirect approach for resolving the conflict. However, there was no follow up. Nobody came to see her. She was very upset. In her understanding, coming from a guilt-oriented culture, she expected the wrongdoer to assume the fault. She didn't know that in a shame-oriented culture the most shameful thing you can do is to say: "It was me!" Once she gained this awareness, she continued to have a good relationship with all of the children in her class. Differences in expectations in situations like this can result in uncountable conflicts in the mission experience.

A third area of research that we find helpful for intercultural communi-

9. L. Käser, *Fremde Kulturen: eine Einführung in die Ethnologie* (Erlangen: Verlag der Ev.-Luth. Mission, 1998).

cation is the Linguistic Awareness of Culture (LAC)[10] model. This looks at the differences in language. It assumes that language is a complex entity of conventions. Some of the main findings are summarized below.

The Meaning of the Word

The translation of a word into another language never corresponds 100 percent to the original. What do the terms "rain," "compromise" or "siblings" mean? Does "rain" mean good or bad weather? Is a "compromise" a sign of weakness or a good solution? Are "siblings" just children from my parents or the kids from my aunt and uncle as well?

Conversation Has Structure

In a conversation, several phases follow one another, whereby every phase has its duration regulated by convention. When such rules are ignored, the hearer may feel you are being treated impolitely.

Person from culture A has this structure	Person from culture B has this structure
Greeting	Greeting
Signs of goodwill	Signs of goodwill
Connections to Family and Groups	Wish or concern
Search for commonality	Exchange of ideas
Wish or concern	Appreciation
Exchange of ideas	Saying Good-bye
Appreciation	
Saying Good-bye	

In a conversation, Person A will probably think that Person B is impolite and rude. Person B will probably think that A is not getting to the point. Conflicts can arise as a result of different structures and roles in conversation.

Paraverbal Signs

The tone of voice and the sound of what is said provide information about the speaker to the receiver. People pay attention to both what is said and to how it is said. Such things as loudness, modulation, speaking breaks, and speaking speed are weighed in different cultures differently. Is speaking low a sign of authority or shyness? Is speaking loudly is a sign of authority or disrespect?

---

10. B. Mueller-Jacquier, "Linguistic Awareness of Cultures," in *Principles of a Training* (Leipzig Studien zur internationalen Unternehmenskommunikation, 2000), 20–49.

Nonverbal Signs

Nonverbal signs are those one sees when a person is speaking: gestures, mimicry, body posture, eye contact and the spatial distance between conversation partners. These are interpreted as well as seen. Is looking into one's eyes a sign of respect or disrespect? Is laughing after someone does something wrong a sign of arrogance or shame?

The LAC approach illustrates the many ways we can misunderstand one another. Therefore, we believe it is most helpful to ask a mentor or bridge builder what to do in the following example situations, even if one thinks that one already knows:

How do you —

> say "How are you,"
> say "Good bye,"
> ask for something,
> accept an invitation,
> decline an invitation,
> invite somebody,
> praise someone,
> criticize someone,
> agree on something,
> give a "heads up,"
> accuse someone,
> apologize,
> give compliments,
> make a promise?

And don't forget to ask about the non- and paraverbal signs!

How Different Cultures Deal with Conflicts Differently

As shown in the triangle of differences (see Graphic 1), it is very important to be aware of differences and the various types of differences that may be interacting. This awareness is the departure point for the search of commonality. When we are aware of differences we can search for the common ground and find one another.

Differences in Communication Styles

Since different styles are a constant source of misunderstanding, being aware of differences in communication styles can prevent conflicts. The columns below present one of the most common style differences, which is the difference between direct and indirect communication.

Indirect	Direct
Relationship oriented	Information and fact oriented
The information comes in the middle or at the end of the conversation	The information comes at the beginning of the conversation
Avoid saying "no"	Acceptable to say "no"
Expressions of appreciation are highly valued	Criticism is acceptable
In a conflict people search for a third person as a mediator or agent who can speak for you or the other person involved	In a conflict you can speak directly with the other person involved

Differences in Conflict Styles

Hammer's research[11] about intercultural conflict styles also differentiates between the direct and indirect style. The direct style is more often used in individualistically orientated cultures with a need for self-realization—the objective being the achievement of personal goals. The indirect style, however, places greater importance on the need and goals of the group to which people belong. A second aspect of cultural differences is manifest in the way in which people express or restrain their feelings. As a result, Hammer defines four communication styles in conflict. See Graphic 2.

Discussion style is used by people who want to keep emotions out of the conflict. They try to control their feelings and speak directly about the concern or disagreement with the other person or group involved. They want to stay objective and use facts rather than opinions or feelings to overcome a conflict.

Accommodation style is practiced by people who prefer to keep their emotions under control. They speak indirectly and their major concern is the possible damage that the conflict can do to the relationship. Therefore they use metaphors or other techniques to prevent a conflict from escalating.

Engagement style is used by people who are more comfortable with expressing their feelings openly. They communicate directly their concerns and are passionate in their conversation style.

---

11. M. R. Hammer, "The Inter-cultural Conflict Style Inventory: A Conceptual Framework and Measure of Intercultural Conflict Resolution Approaches," *International Journal of Intercultural Relations* 29 (2005): 675–95.

Dynamic style is used by people who are expressive regarding their own emotions, but don't feel comfortable talking directly about the content. It's a more associative argument structure and relies on a third neutral person from outside, for example, a mediator, to deal with the conflict.

Graphic 2:

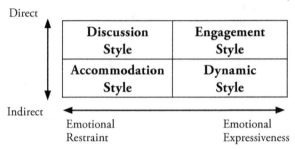

A Model of Intercultural Conflict Style

	Discussion Style	Engagement Style
	Accommodation Style	Dynamic Style

Direct ↑ Indirect ↓

← Emotional Restraint ——————— Emotional Expressiveness →

Differences in Attitudes toward Conflict

Another difference between cultures in dealing with conflict is described by Glasl. He sees three different attitudes toward conflict.[12] The three are rarely found in a pure form, and the biggest challenge seen in this model comes when a vicious circle develops between conflict avoiders and conflict seekers.

Provoking	Managing	Avoiding
Would rather hurt someone than appear to be a coward.	Realizes that conflict helps overcome situations or circumstances or dynamics that need to be changed and don't work anymore.	Is afraid to hurt others.
Has emotional outbreaks (explodes, can't control his/her emotions).		Avoids speaking about conflict.
		Suppresses and hides his or her feelings.
Underestimates potential damage.	Considers differences as valuable and enriching.	Overestimates the potential damage.
Directs aggression and anger toward others.	Aggression is seen as energy that can be used positively.	Directs anger against him- or herself.
	Energy is used in favor of her/himself and others.	Is afraid to be hurt by others

---

12. F. Glasl, *Selbsthilfe in Konflikten* (Stuttgart: Verlag Freies Geistesleben, 2000), 13.

Here are two important questions to ask in order to understand and analyze a conflict with the lens of differences in attitudes. (1) What is the attitude toward conflict you use, and (2) which attitude is your conflict partner practicing?

Different Types of Conflict

Conflicts are part of interpersonal relationships, just as joy and happiness are. Life experiences and skills usually allow us to resolve these conflicts without them ever becoming an issue.

However, it is necessary to deal actively and intentionally with conflict when it occurs, or spreads, or when group members begin to withdraw because of it. When the conflict starts to dominate people's energies in such a way that they can no longer function properly, then the urgency for a solution is obvious. Berkel differentiates three general types of conflict.[13]

Conflicts about Content: The group shares a common goal, however, does not agree on how to achieve it and which resources to use.

Conflict about Relationships: People feel hurt by others. This conflict can be resolved in a healing process. The conflict needs the spirit of generosity. Our own experience, and what we have heard from others living in cross-cultural settings, is an astonishment about the generosity and willingness of our counterparts for unconditional forgiveness and a good sense of humor that can overcome difficult and tense situations.

Conflicts about Values: Different people, especially those coming from different cultural backgrounds, have different values. Arguing about different values can lead to endless discussions without any outcome. We want to emphasize value conflicts here, because they are, at least to our knowledge, the most common in cross-cultural living.

A Small, Simplified Example: For Brazilian Methodists, a good Christian does not drink alcohol. For German Methodists alcohol is not a problem at all, but a good Christian does not use tobacco, a behavior that is not a problem for a British Methodist.

Many such conflicts are resolved without becoming huge issues. In this example, I can simply respect the mores where I am, not drinking in Brazil and not smoking in Germany when around Methodists. This requires respect for the expectations of a dominant culture, and possibly the recognition that neither drinking nor smoking is good for health, and both Brazilian and German Methodists have valid points.

But when it comes to sexual orientation, marriage, celibacy, or women's rights, the conflicts become much more heated and difficult to address. We

---

13. K. Berkel, *Konflikttraining. Konflikte verstehen, analysieren, bewältigen* (Heidelberg: Sauer-Verlag, 2002).

encounter those every day in all kinds of Christian and non-Christian environments, and experience huge differences—differences that tear us apart and separate us from one another. These types of value conflicts lead to endless and, very often, paralyzing discussions. In some situations, if a group wants to stay together, value discussions may be impossible.

How do we deal with value conflicts and how can we end them? In the following we describe in phrases or very short sentences possible approaches and solutions that can be used. One possible resolution is to find a consensus, or some part of the group that is willing to give up its position. In a democratically organized group, a vote can be taken to make a decision, while in a more autocratic group, the leader makes a decision that group will accept. There is also the possibility of agreeing to disagree, perhaps to the extent of separation.

Differences in Values

Schulz von Thun's "Quadra of Values"[14] provides an additional helpful tool to deal with value discussions. He says that every value or each guiding principle needs a positive counterpart to avoid exaggeration. People committed to the value of steadfastness can get in conflict with people who are eager for change. Or the value of attachment can conflict with the value of distance.

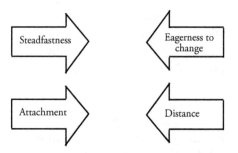

Instead of fighting, competing, or arguing, it is important to search for the virtue in the opposite value and to try to integrate that part as an enriching view of the world in one's own value system. And it especially helps to avoid exaggeration and fundamentalist thinking and behavior.

Coming from a Western culture with an individualistic approach, typical exaggerations are egocentrism and selfishness. The healing process in collective organized cultures is the feeling of being part of a community—to feel safe and welcome. To make personal and cultural values clear and visible allows for them to be recognized and possibly reconciled, rather than for them to remain hidden and unconsciously compete with each other.

---

14. D. Kumbier and F. Schulz von Thun, *Interkulturelle Kommunikation: Methoden, Modelle, Beispiele* (Reinbek bei Hamburg: Rowohlt Taschenbuch Verlag, 2001), 14–15.

Having Doubts about Your Own Assumptions and Sharing Them with Your Bridge Builder

As mentioned before, it is important to find in mission contexts a bridge builder in order to gain more knowledge and to immerse deeper into the host country's culture. A bridge builder is someone from your host country with whom you can develop a trusting relationship. The bridge builder can be a mentor or friend, and can prevent many misunderstandings and conflicts.

However, not everything can be resolved by asking questions.

- A wonderful youth exchange program between young adults from Zimbabwe and Germany was taking place in Zimbabwe. The young people had a lot of fun together, a great experience for everyone. There were also misunderstandings, but fortunately the group had mentors, or bridge builders—people who had a deeper understanding and knowledge of both cultures. The two groups had initially spent a great time together in repairing a youth center. Now it was time to get to know the beautiful country and to grow even closer together on a bus trip. After two or three days on the bus, the Zimbabwean youth realized that the Germans sometimes became very upset. It seemed they, the Zimbabweans, were doing something wrong, but they could not quite figure out what it was. After some time they realized it happened each time they threw trash in plastic bags out of the bus windows. The Zimbabweans did not understand why this should be a problem, and they asked their German bridge builder for advice. He said that he would love to explain the reasons, but because of the importance of their joint intercultural learning he wanted the Zimbabweans first to figure out for themselves why in these moments the Germans were so upset. So the Zimbabweans reflected together about the situation, and after a time they came up with an explanation. It was not throwing the trash out of the window that angered the Germans, the Zimbabwean assumed, because this was the most common thing to do and should not bother anybody. No, it was because in Germany vehicles drive on the right side of the road and not on the left as in Zimbabwe. So the Zimbabweans concluded that the Germans were upset because the trash was being thrown out of the wrong side of the bus.

  Very happy and relieved the Zimbabweans collected the trash again in plastic bags and threw it out on the right side of the bus. A great frustration and astonishment appeared when they realized that the Germans were still upset.

This is one of our favorite examples of cross-cultural misunderstanding and learning. The youth groups were really trying hard to understand their peers from another culture. With the triangle of differences in mind, we realize that the Zimbabweans were emphasizing circumstances of life, which in this case means to be aware of differences in traffic rules between the two countries. The German concern arose from a set of rules about trash disposal.

A tool to understand intercultural misunderstandings is the ladder of abstraction. As human beings we are all very quick to interpret or draw conclusions about events and things beyond our knowledge and experience.

Steps of the Ladder of Abstraction

Read from bottom to top (read as though you climb the ladder):
   7. I act based on my belief.
   6. I develop beliefs in relation to the world.
   5. I draw conclusions.
   4. I make assumptions based on the meaning I added.
      I interpret. I confuse my interpretation with facts.
   3. I add meaning to it (personal, cultural).
   2. I select one piece of information from my critical observation.
   1. I observe data and experiences.
      (as if you push play back on a video recorder).
So let's connect this model to our example:

Step 1: The Zimbabweans and Germans are traveling together in a bus.

Step 2: The Zimbabweans pick one piece of information: the upset German faces after trash is thrown out of the window.

Step 3: The Zimbabweans add meaning to it, and think there is a connection between throwing out the trash and the Germans getting upset.

Step 4: They make the assumption Germans don't like to throw trash out of the window, but can't understand why because there is no way somebody could get upset just because trash is being thrown out of a bus window, which is the most common thing to do.

Step 5: The Zimbabweans continue to reflect in order to fully understand why the Germans are upset, and conclude that the Germans don't like it because they are throwing the trash out of the wrong side of the bus.

Step 6: The Zimbabweans believe this is due to the traffic regulations in Germany, where they drive on the other side of the road.

Step 7: The Zimbabweans act on their belief, and throw the trash out of the other side of the bus.

This happens with all of us every day and the really tricky thing is that we often unconsciously confuse our interpretations with fact, which stops further searching for new facts to confirm our assumptions. To avoid misunderstandings it is important to build in a break when we climb the ladder of abstraction, right about Step 4, at which we have gained some critical information or observation in our daily life abroad. At this point, we need to reach out for the bridge builder and communicate our cultural or personal assumptions in the form of questions, seeking further clarification.[15]

Rosenberg's Non-Violent Communication (NVC) has a helpful methodological suggestion for the moment described above. He offers five steps that start with observation. His method starts a conversation about a critical incident with a *concrete observation,* but without interpretation or assumption. The model of the ladder of abstraction helps us to understand that we need to keep referring to the first step; a clear and simple observation. When we stay focused on the real observation, we are protected from misunderstanding and misjudging or blaming others. At the start of a critical conversation, this way allows for the people involved to open up without becoming offended at the beginning.

The second step in the NVC concerns *feelings.* It is important to connect the observation with the feelings of the observer: To be honestly in touch with feelings, to assume full responsibility for those feelings, and not use those feelings to blame the other person. Often in conflicts people misuse the expression of feelings in a manipulative way, or they may even express so-called pseudo feelings. For example, someone says, "When you talk with me like this I am very sad." This expression of sadness can be a manipulative way of assigning blame, and blaming never opens up a respectful conversation. Blaming only leads to offensiveness and new attacks. However, the challenge is to keep blame out of an honest conversation. I shouldn't blame anyone for whatever I am feeling. My feeling is my responsibility, my choice. In this understanding, NVC offers a direct and clear but nonconfrontational approach.

The third step connects feelings with *needs.* For Rosenberg, so-called negative feelings such as anger, sadness, and frustration are not considered negative. They are important because they indicate unmet needs. So the challenge is to go deeper into the uncomfortable feelings to figure out those needs. Rosenberg has a very helpful list of feelings and needs.[16] This kind of list is helpful because, often in conflict situations, it is hard to figure out what exactly my feelings or needs are. This method tries to connect and not to separate. While recognizing the differences, it searches for the communality. Human beings are different because of their culture, circumstances of life, or personality, but all human beings have feelings and needs. The ways in which we express these feelings differ; however the common ground and starting point for reconciliation and forgiveness are in our commonalities.

---

15. Kumbier and Schulz von Thun, *Interkulturelle Kommunikation,* 345.

16. M. Rosenberg, www.cnvc.org, Center for Nonviolent Communication: An International Organization.

The fourth step is to *make a request* to the other person in order to satisfy an unmet need. Here again, such a request has to avoid a manipulative attitude in which the request is not an honest asking but a hidden manipulative way of demanding. A request is only a request when the person to whom the request is made has the honest freedom to agree or disagree. It is only in this spirit of acceptance, and not wanting to change others, that a conflict can be resolved.

A fifth step is that of *thankfulness*, the expression of gratitude, to the collaborating person. The spirit of an open heart and the importance of creating a good atmosphere are familiar tenets of an indirect communication style, and a great value in many cultures worldwide.

Intercultural living requires for all of us a process of patience toward everything that is unsolved in our hearts. It requires our moving back from assumptions to questions. It asks us not to look for quick answers, which cannot be given to us because we would not be able to embrace or to live them. And the point in intercultural living is to "live" everything, to connect to the asking and live our questions now!

Be patient toward all that is unsolved in your heart and try to love the questions themselves. Do not now seek the answers, which cannot be given you because you would not be able to live them. And the point is to live everything. Live the questions now.[17]

Other References

Cashman, K., *Leadership from the Inside Out: Becoming a Leader for Life* (San Francisco: Berret-Koehler Publishers, 2008).

Elmer, D., *Cross-cultural Conflict: Building Relationships for Effective Ministry* (Downer's Grove, IL: IVP Academic, 1993).

General Board of Global Ministries, *A Mission Journey: A Handbook for Volunteers* (Nashville: Discipleship Resources, 2013).

Hauenstein P., and M. Rosenberg, *Living Nonviolent Communication* (Boulder, CO: Sounds True, 2012).

Hauenstein, P., *Mittendrin — und doch am Rand,* (Neuendettelsau: Erlanger Verlag für Mission und Ökumene, 2002).

Hixon, S., and T. Porter, *The Journey* (New York: United Methodist Women, 2011).

Leu, L., *Nonviolent Communication: A Practical Guide for Individual, Group, or Classroom Study* (Encinitas, CA: Puddle Dancer Press, 2003).

17. Rilke, *Letters to a Young Poet.*

Mayer, C. H., and K. M. Boness, *Interkulturelle Mediation und Konflikt-bearbeitung* (Münster: Waxmann, 2004).

Montada, L., and E. Kals, *Mediation: Lehrbuch für Psychologen und Juristen* (Weinheim: Beltz Verlag, 2001).

Porter, T., *The Spirit and Art of Conflict Transformation: Creating a Culture of Just Peace* (Nashville, TN: Upper Room Books, 2010).

Ting-Toomey, S., and J. G. Oetzel, *Managing Intercultural Conflict Effectively* (Thousand Oaks, CA: Sage Publications, 2001).

8

Conversion from Ethnocentrism

Philip Gibbs, SVD

Ethnocentrism

There are many dimensions of cultural difference influencing the way we interact with others. Philip Harris and colleagues have listed ten such general dimensions of culture: sense of self and space, communication and language, dress and appearance, food and feeding habits, time and time consciousness, relationships, values and norms, beliefs and attitudes, learning, and work habits and practices.[1] There are aspects of all these dimensions that any particular person will most likely consider "normal." I may speak four languages, but there will be a way of communicating that I will feel more comfortable within any given situation. I might enjoy "eating out" at a restaurant with food from one ethnic group, but that is why I go, because it is different from what I would "normally" eat. I will have ideas as to what constitutes being early or late.

Ethnocentrism considers this "normal" response in a negative way. It involves cultural or ethnic bias—whether conscious or unconscious—in which a person views the world from the perspective of his or her own group. This may result in an inability to adequately understand cultures that are different from one's own and in value judgments that show preferential coopera-

Philip Gibbs, SVD, was born in New Zealand and has been serving in Papua New Guinea since 1973. He has an MBA, a postgraduate diploma in anthropology, and a doctorate in theology. Philip Gibbs has served as a parish priest, director of a pastoral center, seminary lecturer, and researcher. Currently he is professor of social research and vice president of research and higher degrees at Divine Word University, Madang, Papua New Guinea. He is also a visiting fellow at the School of Culture, History and Language at Australian National University.

1. Philip Harris, Robert Moran and Sarah Moran, *Managing Cultural Differences: Global Leadership Strategies and the 21ʳ Century,* 6th ed. (New York: Elsevier, 2004), 5–8.

tion with a defined in-group. Thus, one's own group is the center, and others are scaled and rated in reference to it.

Below is an account of the experience of a Papua New Guinean SVD priest discovering variations in what is considered "normal."

> I know what is normal for us on my island. I went to work in the Highlands and I used to talk and behave in a low-key way, because in my home we are taught to respect others and not express ourselves too strongly. But in the Highlands my "normal" way of speaking didn't work. It seemed like people were shouting at me and I had negative feelings about it. I realized that they were thinking that my low-key approach made me appear as a child in their eyes. So I had to learn to talk and I changed my way of relating. I learned how to be more assertive. One time I was on the phone with my cousin at home speaking in a way that had become normal for me, and he accused me of shouting! I said, "I'm not shouting, I am talking to you." Another time when I visited home I was carrying a baby and the baby started crying, and they accused me of shouting at the baby.

The priest who went to work in another part of Papua New Guinea adapted to a more assertive way of speaking to others. This became normal for him, and he realized the ethnocentric views of his family when they reproached him for being culturally eccentric.

Intercultural Development Continuum

Social researcher Milton Bennett has developed an Intercultural Development Continuum with six levels in two main stages.[2] The ethnocentric stage includes three levels: denial, defense, and minimization. The second stage, which he calls ethnorelativistic (equivalent to what I call intercultural), includes three levels: acceptance, adaptation, and integration. One moves along the continuum as one grows in intercultural competence and the ability to accept cultural diversity. I will consider the first four of these levels in turn using examples from my experience of multicultural living in Papua New Guinea, both in international missionary communities and as an expatriate living with people of Papua New Guinea.[3] Cultural competence

---

2. Milton Bennett, "Towards Ethnorelativism: A Developmental Model of Intercultural Sensitivity," in R. M. Paige, ed., *Education for the Intercultural Experience*, 2nd ed. (Yarmouth, ME: Intercultural Press, 1993), 21–71.

3. I consider here only four levels to simplify the discussion, since I consider the positive dimension of minimization as a form of interculturality. So I am discussing levels of ethnocentrism (monoculturality) and two of interculturality and consider it unnecessary for

is achieved by people moving beyond the ethnocentric stage to levels at the intercultural stage of relating.

Denial

Denial represents a low level of capability for understanding cultural differences. At that level, cultural difference has no meaning, or through selective perception people do not notice differences. Sometimes when overseas I have been asked questions such as, "How many witches have you met in PNG? Are most people there cannibals?" Such questions come from a broad, poorly differentiated understanding of Papua New Guinea as a place noted for witches and cannibals. There seems little knowledge other than such stereotypes. People asking such questions do not intend to be derogatory but demonstrate stereotypes in which genuine cultural difference is ignored.

At this level one can also experience separation. This can be intentional, with the erection of physical or social barriers, or strong nationalism, which keeps one at a distance from others. How many times have I experienced "community" gatherings where once the formal part ends and people go into informal groups, they end up in national linguistic groups, where because they are speaking their own language, I feel hesitant to intrude.

Here is the experience of another Papua New Guinean SVD student with a group of expatriate missionaries.

> I was working in a parish with two priests and a sister from a certain country. One time we had a visitor—a doctor from their place. I was cooking and they were speaking their own language. Usually we could eat around 7 pm. They went out speaking their language and they didn't come back, so at 7 pm I ate my share and went to sleep. Later they came back. I was upset. At least they should have told me what they were doing. Later they came and looked for me. It happened another time, and it seemed to me that they didn't acknowledge my presence. So I went and spoke to our district superior, who is from the same country as them. He told me, "You have thousands of people in the village speaking a language you don't understand, so why are you complaining about those four?" Later after two months I asked for a change. I still feel a tension when I see people from that country.

The student relating the story felt that cultural difference was ignored by those he was living with and his district superior. He could not see a way to change what he considered unacceptably ethnocentric attitudes, so he opted to move elsewhere.

---

my argument to discuss the levels of adaptation and integration.

Defense

At the second level, that of defense (sometimes called polarization), people will counter specific cultural differences or promote strongly what they perceive as "normal." Sometimes it is accompanied by a judgmental orientation grounded in a sense of "us" and "them." I have noticed how frequently the word "they" is used in expatriate missionary circles. Often this is a form of negative cultural stereotyping or denigration that classes everyone else in the "they" category, usually seen in a negative light. It does not help to respond to inaccurate assumptions because the problem is not misinformation but, rather, ethnocentrism.

Everyone wants to be respected, and when people do not experience the respect they feel is their due, they can respond defensively with passive or overt aggression, as illustrated in the following example.

> I was watching an English program on TV and improving my English, and another member of the community came in and took the remote and changed the channel to BBC. I didn't like it, but I said nothing and remained quiet. Then another time he did it again, and another time, again. The fourth time I got so angry that I threw the remote at him, saying, "I am a priest too." He went to his room. Later he came to apologize. I said, "I am doing this to improve my English, please ask if you want to change the channel." Maybe he grew up under a cultural situation. People like him come across as "boss" or "I'm longer here." If someone from his country were there he probably wouldn't have done it like he did to me.

The younger SVD priest in the example above reacted angrily to the denial of mutual respect by the older confrere. The situation could be one of sheer insensitivity, but the younger priest interpreted the affront in cultural terms, thinking that the older man would not have acted that way with someone from his own country. He added, "Now he shows respect and it is ok."

Minimization

Minimization is the level between the more monocultural mindset of denial and defense, and the intercultural orientations such as acceptance. At this level, one tends to bury difference under the cover of cultural similarities based on our shared humanity. When a group of Divine Word Missionaries from various countries were tested using Hammer's Intercultural Development Inventory (IDI), the majority (including the writer) was classed as being at the stage of "minimization."[4] How might one experience this level

---

4. Mitchell Hammer, "The Intercultural Development Inventory," in M. A. Moodian,

in community life? An SVD brother offers a relevant comment on language and minimization below.

> We have the policy that in all public events we should use the language of the country, which here means either English or Tok Pisin. I agree with the rule. But when it comes to liturgy and the prayer of the church I find it really quite dry and boring. Some of us in our home country are used to singing and chanting the psalms. Recently I noticed that none of us in the group had English as our first language, and there we were reciting the prayer of the church, including the hymn, in rather poor English.

The brother commenting realizes the importance of having a common language in the community, but that can also lead to a form of "lowest common denominator" in the case he refers to, where spiritual exercises appear dull when stripped of cultural distinctiveness.

What might this mean for a missionary congregation? In religious circles there is a trend toward a form of what Bennet calls "transcendent universalism," which considers us all created by God and sharing the equal dignity of being made "in God's image."[5] From this perspective, difference is not trivialized but is seen relative to what we share in our common humanity. The downside of this view may be seen in some missionary strategies that look for common cultural traits simply to facilitate communicating one's own worldview. In such cases, interest in cultural difference is less about appreciating the other, but rather that knowledge of difference will better allow one to implement conversion. For example, identifying indigenous community structures can then be used analogously to explain what it means to be "church."

Behind the limitation of minimization is the assumption that deep down everyone is the same, and that this commonality can be tapped for communication. This assumes that one's ideas and behavior are easily understandable by others with a different worldview, and allows one to maintain a fairly comfortable state of ethnocentrism. There can be a sense of "let's go along to get along." In this way, minimization through the use of commonality strategies is a way to focus attention away from deeper cultural differences and to maintain cordial relations in the community.

The positive side of identifying universalizing elements may be found in its potential for genuine inculturation. Here missiology tends to diverge from anthropology. The latter favors the relative uniqueness of various cultures,

---

ed., *Contemporary Leadership and Intercultural Competence* (Thousand Oaks, CA: Sage, 2009), 203–18.

5. Bennett, "Towards Ethnorelativism," p. 43.

while missiology focuses more on integrating cultural diversity with the uniqueness of the gospel message. In the "Statement of the SVD Fifteenth General Chapter," inculturation is described as a two-way process whereby the "Good News becomes an integral part of a people's way of life," and "the impulses emerging from the different cultures influence the interpretation of the Gospel."[6] So long as a dynamic view of culture is adopted, the two-way process can be a genuine appreciation of cultural difference, and in my view may be seen not as ethnocentrism but as a level of interculturality.[7] The "One heart, many faces" image used by the Divine Word Missionaries during their centenary celebrations illustrates this point. Focusing on the one heart could be viewed negatively as an assumed universal characteristic, but if viewed in terms of unity in diversity it can be seen as appreciating cultural difference.

Beyond Ethnocentrism

Moving beyond ethnocentrism in Bennett's continuum requires the facility to move from one's own worldview to that of another. It involves the capability to at least partially take the perspective of one or more cultures, bridge between different cultural systems, and change behavior in culturally appropriate and authentic ways. One recognizes cultural patterns understood from the perspective of the other in a way that cultural difference is appreciated. Compare, for example, the following two accounts of the same event.

1. The bus circled endlessly around the market area picking up passengers, and it was ages before we left town. I was feeling impatient, and it seems to me what they call "PNG time" is an excuse for just wasting time. I won't do that again.
2. The bus went around picking up various passengers and bringing with them food and a variety of valuables. After an hour or so, with the bus full, we departed for Mount Hagen. The whole journey was amazingly PNG!

In the first case, cultural difference is seen as problematic, and the person decides to avoid that sort of interaction with life in the future. In the other case, the experience is seen as interesting and culturally fascinating. Here are two ways of experiencing difference. One sees it as avoidable and the other enjoyable. It is enjoyable largely because the person giving the account values difference.

Bennett calls this positive view an ethnorelative orientation. I prefer the

---

6. Divine Word Missionaries, "Listening to the Spirit: Our Missionary Response Today," in *In Dialogue with the Word* (IDW), no. 1 (Rome: SVD Publications, 2000), 64–67.

7. By a "dynamic" view of culture I mean culture as an interpretation of reality rather than a collection of cultural traits. One does not "have" culture; one engages in it.

term intercultural orientation because I am not entirely convinced that Bennett avoids the limitations of both cultural and ethical relativism. With total relativism there is no good or bad, only difference. Yet I consider that one must be able to appreciate and value cultural difference without giving up one's own cultural values and principles. Acceptance involves increased self-reflexiveness in which one is able to experience others as both different from oneself yet meriting equal respect. For example, funerals are an important feature of life with varying cultural values. From an individualistic perspective, funerals in which the body is brought "home" by air and where hundreds of people will stop work and travel long distances to attend might appear a waste of money. Yet from the communitarian perspective of some cultures, such costly arrangements are very important to fulfill obligations to the extended family, even if it means a costly plane trip home. From an intercultural viewpoint, one can appreciate the value of both perspectives on funerals.

The move to an acceptance viewpoint may be seen in the commonly cited difference between sympathy and empathy. Sympathy is ethnocentric in that it demands only a shift in assumed circumstance and not a shift in frame of reference that one brings to that circumstance. Empathy is like the intercultural approach that requires a shift in one's frame of reference—apprehending from the other's perspective. It is based on the assumption of difference and implies a respect for that difference and a readiness to temporarily give up one's own worldview in order to participate in that of the other.[8] Consider the following experience in which an SVD brother comes to acknowledge and respect cultural difference.

> Recently a seminarian accompanied me on a fairly long drive to another province. We got talking about politics, and I started being very critical about the political situation, patronage, corruption, and related social evils. He just listened and didn't say much. At one stage we stopped and met his aunt, who invited us for something to eat. In fact she provided a delicious meal. After we continued on our way I was very appreciative of his aunt's generosity, and I began to feel ashamed of all the negative things I had said before. I realized that the seminarian with me was much closer to the situation and understood it much better. Who am I to judge? I felt embarrassed, and since then I make a point of not being overly critical of the social situation. In fact, I realize now that what I labeled as corruption and favoritism was often informal reciprocity, providing security that would normally be provided by the formalized social security system where I come from.

---

8. Bennett, "Towards Ethnorelativism," 53, gives the example comparing "What I'd do in his position" (sympathy) with "I feel different about this when I imagine him viewing it" (empathy).

The driver was applying labels to behavior based on his home experience. By changing his frame of reference (prompted by the experience of kindness), the empathy coming from viewing the situation in terms of security in a very different setting caused him to feel embarrassed about the way he had been so judgmental before. This does not mean that he can never criticize corruption, but by considering the situation from a different viewpoint he could come to an opinion that valued an intercultural perspective.

Double Vision

Cornelius was a Gentile centurion residing in Caesarea, who, after the vision of an angel, sent his servants to call for Simon Peter. In the meantime, on Simon the Tanner's housetop in Joppa, Peter was experiencing the vision of a sheet coming from heaven with all kinds of animals, reptiles and birds of the air that he was asked to kill and eat (Acts 10:13). He was surprised at this command. Because some were nonkosher (unclean), it went against his belief as a Jew. When Cornelius's friends arrived to fetch him, Peter did not know that his visitors were Gentiles. Normally, a faithful Jew like Peter would not associate in this manner with Gentiles. Despite Peter's previous resistance at being asked to eat unclean food ("Not so, Lord!" Acts 10:14), he invited the Gentile visitors in and entertained them as guests. This runs contrary to Jewish custom with Gentiles and is the first indication of a change in Peter.

Centuries previously, another Jew had come to Joppa with a solemn message from God, in which he was commissioned to bear a message to the Gentiles. Jonah, the prophet, did not share God's heart for the lost. He took a ship from Joppa and ran from God's call. Peter, however, was willing to reexamine his traditions and prejudices. He went with his visitors to the house of Cornelius in Caesarea. By entering a Gentile's home, Peter showed a change of heart, surely learning a lesson from the vision of the great sheet. Thus, as John Stott points out, "The principal subject of this chapter is not so much the conversion of Cornelius as the conversion of Peter."[9]

When asked to speak, Peter began with the words, "I perceive that God shows no partiality, but in every nation anyone who fears him and does what is right is acceptable to him" (Acts 10:34). This statement goes completely against the prevailing Jewish thought at that time, that God certainly did show partiality toward the Jews and against the Gentiles. Even Jesus is recorded as saying that he was sent first to the lost children of Israel (Matt 15:24). What is really novel is the idea that God loved and blessed the Gentiles just as God loved and blessed the Jews, and God did this while they were still Gentiles. It challenged the Jewish assumption that a holy and pure

---

9. John Stott, *The Message of Acts* (Lancaster: Intervarsity Press, 1990), 189.

God would not pour out the Holy Spirit on profane, common, and unclean Gentiles, unless they became holy and ritually pure through becoming Jews.

While Peter was still speaking, the Holy Spirit came upon those Gentiles in Cornelius's household in a Gentile Pentecost, and they began to speak in tongues and to praise God (Acts 10:46). At that, Peter declared, "Can anyone forbid water for baptizing these people who have received the Holy Spirit just as we have?" The "converted" Peter, realizing that they all belonged to the same messianic community ("having received the Spirit just as we have," Acts 10:47), accepted Cornelius and the others and ordered "them to be baptized in the name of Jesus Christ" (Acts 10:48) without submission to the prior rite of circumcision. This introduced an innovation that would bring about the opposition of the circumcised Jewish Christians and others. Leading members of the Jewish church were worried that table fellowship with "unclean" Gentiles would defile them as well (Acts 11:3).

One could trivialize the concerns of the church leaders, labeling them "legalists," but their concern for purity was really a concern for the solidarity of the whole Christian community. They were being asked not only to share earthly goods but also spiritual food. They might have expressed their opposition to table fellowship with non-Jews, but really the issue was sharing the Holy Spirit with "unholy" Gentiles, which went against the whole trend of privileging Jews in the social practices of the faith community. Peter had the advantage of the "double vision" of Cornelius with the angel and himself with the sheet. The Jewish Christian leaders had to struggle to appreciate that, though they were chosen, there could be others (symbolized in the uncircumcised Cornelius) with different beliefs and customs who were equally chosen. This incident was an important moment in a massive shift in the trajectory of the church's mission in its earliest days.

Spirituality of Nonpartiality

We see in the account of Peter with Cornelius several features that provide guidance for a spirituality of nonpartiality—or what I will refer to as interculturality. In Acts 10:34, where Peter declares that God shows no partiality, he uses the concept *lambano prosopon* (literally, to receive the face).[10] To greet a social superior, one lowered the face, and if the one greeted raised the face of the greeter, it was a sign of recognition and esteem. Peter applies this quality to God's dealing with persons from every nation (*ethnos*) and announces that persons in every *ethnos* who fear God and do good are acceptable to him. This relates to the vision of the sheet with a mixture of clean and unclean

---

10. "Peter's Witness to Cornelius," IVP New Testament commentaries, https://www.biblegateway.com.

creatures. God was challenging Peter to relate the distinction between clean and unclean foods to clean and unclean people. Peter came to understand and spoke out: "God has shown me that I should not call any man common or unclean" (Acts 10:28).

Peter exhibits several qualities that can assist us in developing a spirituality of nonpartiality. I note here six qualities: faithfulness, trust, respect, listening, openness, and acceptance.

Peter is horrified or, as the RSVB puts it, "inwardly perplexed" at the prospect of killing and eating creatures considered by his faith as unclean. He replies, "I have never eaten anything that is common or unclean" (Acts 10:14). He was well aware of Jewish food laws and had every intention of faithfully following them. However, his faith was challenged when he discerned that, through the vision, God was asking him not only to be open to a prohibited custom but also to actually put it into practice. Peter was perplexed precisely because he was faithful to his Jewish tradition.

Peter also shows the quality of trust, not only in what he discerns as coming from God in a vision but also in trusting strangers. The men sent by Cornelius came to the gate of the house where Peter was lodging and called out for him. He discerned that the Spirit was calling him to go down and accompany them "without hesitation." Here were Gentiles who were complete strangers, and Peter invites them to come in. He trusts them and his host Simon the Tanner enough to provide hospitality, and invites them to stay the night as guests in the house of his host.

Another quality is respect. When Peter comes to the house of Cornelius, his host "fell down at his feet and worshiped him." Peter immediately responds, "Stand up, I too am a man" (Acts 10:26). Peter did not wish to receive special treatment, and reminds Cornelius that they are both human beings with the same human dignity and worthy of the same respect. It does not matter if one is a Gentile or marginalized, there is spiritual equality that leads to acceptance across racial, class, and ethnic lines. Peter then respectfully listens to Cornelius's story before he responds.

All through this episode, Peter shows great openness and acceptance, whether it be openness to the promptings of the Spirit, openness to what Cornelius has to say, or being open to God's offer of salvation to Gentiles. This is confirmed in the Spirit "falling" on Cornelius's household, and in them speaking in tongues and praising God in a new Gentile Pentecost. The alienation of Jews and Gentiles was symbolized in different languages, but here they speak the same language praising God.

Peter experienced conversion from faithful Jewish belief to an attitude that accepted people who according to Jewish law were considered unclean. His conversion provides an example for us in our day for moving from ethnocentrism to interculturality.

When Is Conversion?

Two common English definitions of conversion originate from the Greek terms *epistrophe*, which can mean "conversion" or "turning around," and *metanoia*, which can mean "repentance" or "to turn around," with an emphasis on the inner transformation of the convert.[11] The term conversion within Judeo-Christian circles is most often used to describe a believer's faith in God or commitment to new beliefs, rituals, and a religious community.

How much change is necessary for the change to be considered conversion? Some people consider that conversion entails an abrupt and radical religious reorientation, while others hold that conversion processes are gradual, with the converts progressively entering a new religious tradition or deepening their commitment to their present tradition. The example of Peter at the beginning of this chapter provides an example of an abrupt reorientation, from one of faithful Jewish belief to an attitude that accepted people who according to Jewish law were considered unclean.

For others it might be gradual process. I associate the most important development in my appreciation of interculturality to a period in my life when, living with a family in an isolated village setting and with no contact at all with outsiders, I spent six months learning a local language in Papua New Guinea. Sometime afterward, I wrote in my diary,

> The time there was a learning experience in many ways as people's lives and feelings were revealed. I started to understand so many things which had been just questions and things I didn't even know enough to even question before. A child died in the family I was with and another close family member died in an accident. I got to see or participate in many aspects of people's traditional religious life, and at the end of it I felt as if I was just standing at the door of a house ready to step out into a whole new world where previously I had simply been looking out through the window. The whole experience helped open me up to religious experience outside of the traditional Christian belief and practice—a sort of cosmocentric view which I think has greatly influenced me since then.

Unlike Peter, I experienced the change gradually over six months. However the same qualities identified in Peter, faithfulness, trust, respect, listening, openness, and acceptance, were equally important for me in moving from an ethnocentric attitude to one of interculturality. I should add that subsequently I have faced situations where I reach a sort of plateau, where I considered my level of intercul-

---

11. Lewis R. Rambo and Charles E. Farhadian, "Conversion," in Lindsay Jones, with Mircea Eliade and Charles J. Adams, eds., *Encyclopedia of Religion* (Detroit: Macmillan Reference, 2005), 1969–74.

tural competence as "good enough," and thereby risked regression since in new situations the challenge to conversion is on-going.

Important Considerations for Intercultural Living

Seen in terms of conversion, intercultural competence may be seen as a constant challenge to appreciate cultural difference. Here I suggest some positive strategies associated with the qualities found in Simon Peter's spirituality of nonpartiality.

To develop in intercultural competence one should be faithful to one's tradition and not abandon or reject it even if "inwardly perplexed" when challenged by other viewpoints. A person with only a shallow understanding and acceptance of his or her home culture will find it difficult to appreciate another, since in true dialogue one needs to be culturally grounded and have a position to start with. A mature appreciation of Christian faith should open a person to the "other" in a genuine exercise of catholicity.

Intercultural competence requires moving out of what is familiar and trusting in the good will of others. The familiar might be associated with time, space, language, feeding habits, or work practices, and it is a matter of trusting others and oneself to go out of the comfort zone to encounter new cultural differences. It concerns me to see some younger missionaries today spending long hours on the Internet communicating with "home" when there are immense possibilities for them to enter into quality relationships in their new environment.

I associate listening and respect with the terms "we" and "us." When the table conversation includes many references to "they" and "them" I wonder if the speakers are appreciating cultural difference or rather perceiving that difference in terms of a dualistic "us" and "them." I echo the words of Peter, "I too am a man," in pressing for the basic recognition of every person as having human dignity that merits equality and respect in the way we refer to them and relate to them.

Openness and acceptance require spending time with people. It may mean having to deal with values and behavior that I might initially define as inappropriate, insensitive, or incorrect (spitting?). There is always much to learn. For example, who do people understand are the "victims" in witchcraft accusations? From a modern scientific viewpoint, the victim is the person accused of being a witch, whereas from the local perspective the victim might very well be the person thought to have been killed or maligned by the witch. I do not have to agree with them, but it is important to appreciate the cultural difference in such situations. Interculturally competent moral or ethical judgments are made by considering the meaning and value a cultural practice represents in a different cultural community.

Such considerations as those above will surely contribute to the ongoing conversion required to move from ethnocentrism to a more intercultural orientation that recognizes and appreciates cultural differences.

Conversion from Ethnocentrism

Advancement in intercultural competence may be seen as a conversion from ethnocentrism when one can take the perspective of another without losing one's own perspective. This requires moving beyond monocultural orientations such as denial and defense in which one's own culture is perceived as central to reality toward an intercultural orientation in which cultural differences are understood relative to one another. The change can rightly be considered conversion because it requires a radical reorientation toward cultural difference. Whether the change happens instantly or over time, it is accompanied by qualities such as faithfulness, trust, respect, listening, openness, and acceptance. Simon Peter's conversion was confirmed by the manifestation of the Holy Spirit among the Gentile believers. Conversion toward interculturality in any context will surely be blessed by the Spirit of God, who "shows no partiality" (Acts 10:34).

9

Building Intercultural Competence

Jon P. Kirby, SVD

Communication and Culture

Building intercultural competence starts with the question How does someone in culture A communicate with someone in culture B? There are two ways to answer this. One focuses on personality characteristics that are sensitive to cultural difference. This approach is exemplified in Muriel Elmer's "Intercultural Competence Scale" (ICS).[1] Here the task of building competence focuses on how to improve weak characteristics. Although the characteristics approach is attractive because it is easy to understand, testing is straightforward, and it offers a well-designed developmental regimen[2] to improve a learner's weaker characteristics, it does not sufficiently address the complex dynamics of culture.

The second and far-better answer focuses on both culture and communication. In the 1960s, the popularizing anthropologist Edward Hall helped business people communicate better overseas by treating culture as a kind of "silent language."[3] Besides understanding the other culture, they needed to become, through sensitivity to difference, less bound by the constraints of their own culture. Cultures differentiate differently because they have fundamentally different worldviews. Benjamin Lee Whorf[4] and Hall pointed out

---

Jon P. Kirby, SVD, obtained his MPhil and PhD degrees in social anthropology at Cambridge UK, in 1983. He was founder-director of Tamale Institute of Cross-Cultural Studies (TICCS) in Ghana for twenty-five years. He held the chair of mission and cross-cultural studies at Washington Theological Union, in Washington, DC. He has written and edited twenty-five books and more than sixty articles. His latest book is *The Power and the Glory: Popular Christianity in Northern Ghana* (2013).

1. An online test to assess intercultural competence based on twelve sensitivity characteristics to cultural differences (see http://icsprofile.org/).

2. ICS "Skill Builders" (see http://icsprofile.org/).

3. Edward Hall, *The Silent Language* (New York: Doubleday, 1973).

4. Benjamin L. Whorf, *Language, Thought and Reality: Selected Writings of B. L. Whorf,* ed. J. B. Carroll (New York: John Wiley, 1956).

that we each experience the world through our own cultural lenses and that cultural differentiation is crucial for attempts to understand and communicate cross-culturally. Milton Bennett[5] and Mitchell Hammer[6] follow in their footsteps when they insist that intercultural competence is about both communication and culture. Accepting this is the beginning of development. This needs to be the primary grounding for an SVD approach to intercultural development. The ICS is useful but only as an additional supplement. In this chapter we will, therefore, focus on Bennett's "Developmental Model of Intercultural Sensitivity" (DMIS) in the slightly modified form of Hammer's "Intercultural Development Inventory" (IDI).[7]

Assessment

If learners are to improve they must know their starting point, their level of intercultural competence, or their present experience of cultural difference. Hammer's IDI provides this. It is based on the fact that sensitivity is affected more by difference than by sameness, *which tends to be ethnocentrically biased and illusory*. Developing intercultural competence is always prevented when we negate difference. Thus, the IDI measures a person's levels of impedance—the degree to which learners are not recognizing difference.

We account for differences by comparing and contrasting cultures. We do this in ways that are culture-specific (emic) and culture-general (etic, e.g., individualism vs. collectivism). Competence requires skills in both. Geert Hofstede has detected six culture-general categories[8] for contrasting differ-

---

5. M. Bennett, "Towards Ethnorelativism: A Development Model of Intercultural Sensitivity," in R. Michael Paige, ed., *Education for Intercultural Experience* (Yarmouth, ME: Intercultural Press, 1993).

6. M. R. Hammer, "The Intercultural Development Inventory," in M. A. Moodian, ed., *Contemporary Leadership and Intercultural Competence* (Thousand Oaks, CA: Sage, 2009), 203–18.

7. See Hammer, "Intercultural Development Inventory." And M. R. Hammer, "Solving Problems and Resolving Conflict Using the Intercultural Conflict Style Model and Inventory," in M.A. Moodian, ed., *Contemporary Leadership and Intercultural Competence* (Thousand Oaks, CA: Sage, 2009), 219–32.

8. 1. Handling inequality: extent that underprivileged accept unequal power structure
PDI Power distance: from high to low
   2. Dealing with the unknown: extent threatened by ambiguity/unknown and try to control this
UAI Uncertainty avoidance: from strong (control future) to weak (just let it happen)
   3. Dependence on others: the degree of interdependence in a society among members
IDV Individualism to Collectivism
   4. Gender roles: focusing on emotion/drives
MAS from Masculinity (competition) to Femininity (caring, nurturing, having fun)

ence, and more are being discovered. These basic ways to structure cultural difference are often revealed in proverbs (e.g., "Blessed be the child that makes it on its own"—individualism vs. "The rafter that sticks out is the first to rot"—collectivism). We can readily see that "Africans are collective" and "Americans are individualistic," but there are people, code shifters, who are both, who can shift back and forth. The IDI helps us to be like them—to shift to another cultural reality.

Intercultural Competence

An advanced level of intercultural sensitivity should be a missioner's goal. But such competence is not an inborn talent, nor does it come automatically with novitiate, theological studies, or by taking vows. It must be learned; but more than that—it is an ongoing transformative experience that involves the construction of a new self, a new cultural identity.

Intercultural competence is not simply about mastering another culture or developing a set of skills that helps us communicate better in the context of other cultures. It is about the ongoing construction of one's reality as increasingly able to accommodate cultural difference. Further, it is about both the process of constructing and taking on the new realities. Bennett[9] says that we build culture by embodiment—we create our context, and then our context creates us. It is a process involving the establishment of worldviews that support separate, and very different, experiences of cultural difference. It is about the mastery of a process involving cross-cultural learning, communication, and human relations. The process involves experience *and* understanding, as well as the cumulative readjustment of that understanding through further experience and more understanding.

Culture affects your identity. Your cultural identity, or who you are as a participant in a cultural context, is at the heart of intercultural communication. Today we see multilevel or hybrid cultural identities. These are people with an expanded-worldviews repertoire. In the past this was rare but, due to globalization, it is becoming widespread. They can operate in any number of other cultures, at least a little bit. The more you operate in these different worldviews, the more this starts to affect you and become who you are. I have been socialized to operate within a West Coast American middle-class world and several West African worlds. This combination is now part of who I am.

---

5. Time perspective: from long-term (future orientation) to short-term (immediate gain)
6. Dealing with natural drives: from indulgence to restraint
   Also see https://www.youtube.com/watch?v=U-XdlbgFxZo "Map of the World"
9. See Bennett, "Towards Ethnorelativism."

I can live either way. I am not an African as such, but I can operate in those contexts. More and more people are starting to define themselves in this way.

Not everyone sees it this way. Cultures limit our understanding of difference by their absolute categories. Those with a monocultural worldview see such biculturalism as a threat to their identity or interpret it as paranoid or schizophrenic. The interculturally sensitive are not restricted by these assumptions. They perceive behavior, values, and identity not as reality itself but as a *process* of constructing reality. They go beyond the boundaries of their culture and make choices based *not upon* the "universal principles" of their own culture but on a repertoire of possibilities derived from different cultures. These are the basic assumptions underlying the possibility of acquiring intercultural competence. Such competence must be learned as a process that involves constructing new identities and expanded repertoires by experiencing and taking on difference. Simply being present to other cultures does not insure an intercultural experience. As the saying goes, "You can have thirty years' experience or one year's experience repeated thirty times." "It is the successive construing and reconstruing of what happens that enriches experience."[10]

The Development Process

Development progresses from less sensitive "monocultural" to more sensitive "intercultural" orientations.[11] The process involves three movements: (1) the experience of difference; (2) the appreciation of cultural patterns; and (3) the construction of identity. At first, difference is barely noticed; there are no categories for it. Development occurs when differences are finally perceived and understood as factors of culture rather than as physical or moral defects. Then you begin to create increasingly differentiated cultural categories. Appreciation of cultural difference increases, and your way of interpreting the world is viewed as only one of seven thousand. You become conscious of yourself as no longer just a product of a culture but also a producer, a "meaning maker." You develop intercultural sensitivity as you begin to experience yourself as a member of more than one culture (e.g., as a Vietnamese American or even a biculturally American and Chinese person). Then the "meaning maker" takes charge. As you combine aspects of many different cultures you begin to construct an intercultural identity. You experience yourself as both the product and producer of meaning. You develop greater sensitivity as you consciously select and integrate culturally different aspects of your identities, and cultural difference becomes an opportunity for identity expansion.

---

10. George Kelly, *A Theory of Personality* (New York: Norton, 1963), 73.
11. Hammer refers to them as "monocultural" vs. "intercultural."

This process is the basis for Bennett's theory of intercultural development.[12] These three movements are accompanied by shifts from cognition, to affect, to behavior. Development starts with cognitive structure—generating relevant situations and categories for cultural difference. This leads to affective reactions. Difference becomes a threat to the stability of your worldview. This elicits actions as the developmental response to the affect. The response to this is cognitive, consolidating differences into universal categories. Then, the increased knowledge of difference sparks insecurities, leading to another affective response. This results in new behaviors, applications, and intercultural skills. The process continues in a spiral leading to increased awareness and expanded understanding. There are other processes between and within each movement, and it is not a one-way progression—it can regress—nor is it permanent. Finally, all three are integrated in what Bennett calls "constructive marginality."[13]

We take as our model for the intercultural development process the DMIS as refined by Mitchell Hammer in his intercultural development continuum.[14] It delineates five stages from the monocultural orientations of Denial and Polarization (defense/reversal), through the transitional mindset of Minimization, to the intercultural mindsets of Acceptance and Adaptation.[15] In monocultural orientations one's own culture is the only reality. In more sensitive intercultural orientations, reality is not limited to any one culture, and cultural differences are understood in relation to each other. Here, you are most able to shift your perspective and adapt your behavior to a given cultural context.[16] Progressing through these various levels of sensitivity can take years, but with direction and intentionality it is possible to achieve a higher level of orientation in six to eight weeks. We will now take up these stages and the process of development at each orientation.[17]

---

12. See Bennett, "Towards Ethnorelativism," 22.

13. An advanced state of persons who operate outside normal cultural boundaries on the margins of their cultures. For them all is relative. There is no absolute right or wrong behavior in every circumstance. When a person has arrived at marginality after going through the development stages, they are in charge of the process (Bennett, "Towards Ethnorelativism," 64).

14. Hammer's IDI and continuum are highly respected for their thoroughness, validity, accuracy, and cross-cultural applicability.

15. At first, the DMIS included Integration as the endpoint. It is no longer viewed as a distinct stage in this sequence but as a factor influencing progress at each stage.

16. Bennett, "Towards Ethnorelativism," 46.

17. These steps are taken from Bennett, "Towards Ethnorelativism," and M. Bennett and Janet M. Bennett, "Cultural Marginality: Identity Issues in Intercultural Training," in R. Michael Paige, ed., *Education for the Intercultural Experience* (Yarmouth, ME: Intercultural Press, 2000).

Denial

People at Denial are isolated from other cultures and are not able to experience cultural difference. They demonstrate benign, nonaggressive stereotyping (well meant but ignorant or based on naïve observations) and superficial statements of tolerance. But stereotypes make others less than human, which is dangerous because people who are objectified must be controlled and dealt with (e.g., immigrants and the homeless). One eliminates the problem by eliminating the people. Only the dominant group denies others' reality. Nondominant groups must recognize the differences that are being denied. Typically, they try to stay out of trouble by filling the dominant group's expectations through reversal—exchanging one reality for another.

Denial is sustained by isolation and separation. Persons may be isolated naturally, living in very parochial rural towns, or they can purposely construct and maintain it by exclusion strategies like, "keeping the neighborhood clean." Outsiders are expected to fit in and be just like them. The differences others bring to social interaction are typically ignored or not recognized. Others are simply "foreigners," or "Asian," etc. Separation is overcome by getting into contact with other cultures and difference. But they purposely build barriers against this, like ethnic neighborhoods and nationalistic organizations, etc. Isolation makes them more inclined to separation. Then, through exclusion, they create the conditions for more tension and isolation, which inhibits progress.

At this stage there is no cognitive structuring because difference is not recognized. The affective quality is a benign "live and let live" approach, but it harbors deep racism, which is potentially genocidal, and the enormous possibility of exploitation by the dominant group.

The Development Task at Denial

People develop from Denial to Polarization when they overcome separation and are forced to deal with difference—as when more people from different culture groups move into your neighborhood or organization. Development occurs by noticing cultural differences and setting up categories for understanding them. Greater openness to difference increases sensitivity.

Learners need support in helping them to recognize difference. Facilitators should encourage them with nonthreatening activities in an inclusive no-blame atmosphere, always building on what learners already know. They should try to arouse their curiosity and help them move beyond separation through cultural-awareness activities like international nights and cultural-awareness weekends, with ethnic music, foods, costumes, and activities, and dos and don'ts for traveling. Slide shows, films, history lessons, courses, visits to museums, and discussions aimed at increasing understanding and experience of different cultures are important here. But at later stages they are not effective. Efforts must also be made to avoid introducing deeper, more significant cultural differences which will be ignored or used as reasons for going deeper into Denial.

The development plan must always be matched to the trainee's orientation level. Based on those who have already taken the IDI, we are anticipating that the average orientation of SVDs is Minimization, so it is reasonably safe to focus introductory workshops at this level. But if there is any doubt, a rough assessment can be done by trained facilitators using the descriptions and "typical comments" presented here.

Learners at this level should aim to develop the ability to recognize differences and gather appropriate information about culture, the initiative to explore aspects of their own culture, and attitudes of trust, friendliness, and cooperation.

Typical comments at this stage:
"Live and let live, that's what I say."
"All big cities are the same—lots of buildings, too many cars, McDonalds."
"What I really need to know about is art and music."
"As long as we all speak the same language, there's no problem."
"The main concerns I have involve knowing how to get around and ordering in restaurants."
"With my experience, I can be successful in any culture without any special effort."
"I never experience culture shock."
"All I need to know about is politics and history—I can figure out the rest of it as I go along."

Polarization

Polarization, either by defense or reversal, is a reaction to a threat against one's culture-bound sense of reality—one's very identity. The greater the difference is, the more the threat. It is characterized by "us vs. them," with negative stereotyping. It embodies an evolutionary view of the world with modern at the top and "underdeveloped peoples" at the bottom (e.g., the perspective of USAID). Differences are recognized and polarized. Those at the bottom are proselytized.

There are two defensive postures: denigration and superiority. Denigration uses negative stereotypes to reduce the threat of race, age, gender, ethnicity, or any status characteristic. It is often combined with a rationale that makes it dangerous for others to object (e.g., Nazis stereotyping Jews). Superiority exaggerates the positive aspects of one's own culture, and to see others positively is viewed as an attack against them. Reverse polarization is the tendency to embrace the other and malign one's own. The poles are reversed but polarization persists.

Cognitively, the categories for cultural difference are more defined but the original worldview stays the same; no integration. The affective quality is one of defending privilege and identity. The behavioral emphasis is on exclusion and segregation, with backlash through supremacists and hate groups if the other group asserts itself. Power is exercised by exclusion and denial of equal opportunity.

The Developmental Task at Polarization

The way to development is *not* through more information. The problem is ethnocentrism, not ignorance. Development is fostered for those in Defense by mixing them with those who are the threat. At first, help them see in-group/out-group distinctions, different learning styles, and personality types within their group, and the way they deal with emotions differently. The process at this point avoids cultural contrasts but rather focuses on similarities. Opportunities should be structured, as a way to build cooperation, for learners to share about their own group.

Missionary groups, like the SVD, need to move beyond a Defense/Superior orientation or we will take a particular cultural form of the gospel to be the perfect expression of the Word itself. As missioners, we need to see other cultures as having valid ways of viewing the world. We need to evangelize cultures. However, until missioner learners reach Minimization, where the emphasis shifts to recognizing cultural difference, they are not yet ready for deeper experiences focusing on cultural relativity.

Facilitators should try to help learners be more firmly rooted in their own culture. Before departure to an assignment, facilitators could help them focus on the good qualities and history of their own culture, and on the commonalities of shared needs and goals between in-groups and out groups. The process should stress conflict mediation, team building, and promote cooperation. The transferable skills in dealing with difference should be identified. Skills to be developed at this stage include self-control, patience, tolerance, and the ability to manage anxiety.

Typical comments at this stage:

"I wish these people would just talk the way we do."

"Even though I'm speaking their language, they're still rude to me."

"When you go to other cultures, it makes you realize how much better the United States is."

"These people don't value life the way we do."

"Boy, could we teach these people a lot of stuff."

"What a sexist society!"

"These people are so urbane and sophisticated, not like the superficial people back home."

"I am embarrassed by my compatriots, so I spend all my time with the host country nationals."

"I wish I could give up my own cultural background and really be one of these people."

Minimization

Minimization is recognition and acceptance of superficial cultural differences (e.g., eating and customs, etc.), while maintaining that human beings are essentially the same. Learners at this stage emphasize similarity of peoples and values, but they silently define the basis for commonality as their own culture. There are two types: physical universalism and transcendent. Physical emphasizes our common physical qualities ("we are all human!"). Transcendent emphasizes our commonality as being under a particular God, religion or social philosophy (e.g., "We are all children of God, whether we know it or not."). It is not morality or belief per se that is questioned here but the narrow framing of beliefs by one's culture (e.g., Ghanaians call God "Grandfather," not Father).

The cognitive structure here is that one's own worldview is protected by saying "we are all the same." The affective quality is the tendency to be superficially "nice." The behavioral emphasis is to actively support our own special "universals"—our religious, moral and political philosophies. Power is exercised by accepting for granted the institutionalized privilege of the dominant group. Interreligious dialogue attempted at this stage will yield no results.

The Development Task at Minimization

The task at Minimization is to develop greater self-awareness. In support of their learners, facilitators need to help them clarify the definitions of culture, race, ethnicity, stereotypes, and other generalizations about culture. Learners need to understand the dynamics of culture, what is meant by perception and worldview. Minor subjective differences between cultures such as nonverbal behavior, or communication styles need to be explored. But the cultural contrasts (e.g., between communication styles) should not go into much depth—just enough to startle and increase their curiosity about their own culture in relation to others.

At this stage learners are excited about culture. Facilitators should make use of this to encourage them further and challenge them to develop new categories and frameworks for their discoveries. In this way, they will also come to understand their own culture more fully, both the externals and the deeper values and beliefs. Power relations need to be better understood, especially how the dominant group is privileged in comparison with oppressed groups. Facilitators should use examples and materials that are authentic and current (e.g., advertising and the media, etc.) from their own culture.

Trained resource persons at a high level of intercultural competence should be brought in to give demonstrations and coach structured activities (e.g., using culture-drama)[18] that will enable learners to experience difference. Also opportunities with other culture groups, such as visits and exchanges, can be arranged. The discussions afterward should always focus on self-awareness.

Intercultural skills that learners need to develop include greater knowledge about culture in general, more open-mindedness, greater knowledge of their own culture, intensification of their listening skills, an increase in their ability to perceive others accurately, and the ability to be nonjudgmental in their interactions with others.

Typical comments at this stage:
"The key to getting along in any culture is to just be yourself—authentic and honest!"
"Customs differ, of course, but when you really get to know them they're pretty much like us."
"I have this intuitive sense of other people, no matter what their culture."
"Technology is bringing cultural uniformity to the developed world."
"While the context may be different, the basic need to communicate remains the same around the world."
"No matter what their culture, people are pretty much motivated by the same things."
"If people are really honest, they'll recognize that some values are universal."
"It's a small world, after all!"

The Transition to Intercultural Mindsets
When learners move past the midpoint of Minimization, they are making a major shift in their understanding of things. The major task in moving into the intercultural mindset is recognizing and appreciating cultural differences in behavior and values. It begins with acceptance of cultural difference as good, enjoyable, and inevitable. It is not evaluated. Here, learners begin to

---

18. Culture-drama is an important development tool at the level of Acceptance/Adaptation because it develops empathy by putting you inside the other's world through action. It provides a safe environment to learn and test out new, more adequate intercultural behavior. Learners engage in cross-cultural encounter, learning to shift their cultural frames of reference. The fact that learners have experienced deep empathy is shown by their comments during the sharing at the end of a culture-drama session: "Now I really know how you felt. It is so real, yet so different from the way I think about it." For more on culture-drama see https://spiritualityandculture. com.

perceive cultures as relative and to accept cultural differences as viable alternatives to the way they organize their life. They begin to interpret phenomena as always being within a context, and they consciously and deliberately develop specific categories of difference.

As learners move more toward Acceptance they develop the ability to analyze complex interactions in culture-contrast terms. At first, respect for difference is placed on concrete behavioral differences (language, customs, foods, and clothing, etc.) because these are easy to manage. But they soon realize that behavioral differences embody more than just different codes to express the same ideas. They come to sense that there are actually quite different ideas here. This challenges the universalist perspectives held earlier. Then they begin to see outward differences as indicators of much deeper differences in worldview. Style differences start to become apparent in language and actions, e.g., the length and importance of greeting rituals, action chains, inductive vs. deductive speech, linear vs. circular discourse, emotionally expressive vs. restrained interaction, etc. Differences in nonverbal behavior, as in proxemics and kinesics, become apparent.[19] At earlier orientations it was just assumed that all nonverbal behavior was universal. Now you see it is not, and you are looking for new categories for incorporating this unfamiliar behavior.

Learners also become more aware of the relative nature of values and beliefs. They begin to see different worldviews (including their own) and the values or beliefs attached to them as culturally constructed systems. It is here that a sense of process emerges. Values are no longer "things" but something we make. It all depends on the cultural context. Hall calls this way of thinking about values as things "extension-transference"[20]—when the extension takes the place of the process extended. We value our worldview and extend this process of valuing into things that we then call values. We don't "have values," but their existence is assumed in response to the way we organize and value our world. By participating in the culture, we give it worth and perpetuate it as part of an ongoing process.

In the latter part of Minimization, at the cusp of Acceptance, the cognitive structure works on the differentiation and elaboration of cultural categories and the development of a stance outside of one's culture for interpreting all cultural difference, including one's own culture. The affective quality is curiosity and interest in other cultures. The behavioral emphasis is on ever-greater acquisition of knowledge about cultures, one's own included. Power is no longer exercised in defense or destruction, but it is simply inactive in a kind of liberal stasis.

---

19. Edward Hall, *Beyond Culture* (New York: Doubleday, 1976).
20. Ibid., 25.

Typical comments at this stage:

"The more difference the better! More difference equals more creative ideas!"

"You certainly wouldn't want to have all the same kind of people around—the ideas get stale, and besides, it's boring."

"I always try to study about a new culture before I go there."

"The more cultures you know about, the better comparisons you can make."

"Sometimes it's confusing, knowing that values are different in various cultures and wanting to be respectful, but still wanting to maintain my own core values."

"When studying abroad, every student needs to be aware of relevant cultural differences."

"I know my homestay family and I have had very different life experiences, but we're learning to work together."

"Where can I learn more about Mexican culture to be effective in my communication?"

Acceptance

People in Acceptance are able to perceive and respect the valuing that others do in their cultures but without necessarily valuing as they do. Valuing is a process. Reification, or seeing value as a thing, impedes Acceptance. The task for learners at Acceptance is to further develop, refine, and deepen their analysis of cultural contrasts.

Facilitators need to challenge and support learners to increase their experience of difference with more profound contrasts. They do this by offering increasingly complex experiences of subjective cultural differences along with value analysis, and by helping them to develop and refine more categories for cultural contrast and comparison. This will help them better appreciate the relationship between different cognitive and communication styles.

Learners need to connect instances of communication with practical applications, and to begin to fit them into a broader cultural context, e.g., Ghanaians measure a child's height with palm up and an animal's with palm down. This yields clues to what is considered "good" or "bad" behavior. Analysis tells us that children (humans) are different from animals and "you shouldn't hold them down." They are meant to grow and advance until they become ancestors. Animals don't become ancestors; they are food to be eaten. Treating animals like humans, by petting them or feeding them, therefore is bad. Broadening the cultural frame, we see that the words for "animal" and "meat" are the same. They distinguish only between "house meat" (domestic) and "bush meat" (wild).

While focusing on cultural differences, facilitators should also help learners deepen their cultural self-awareness—how they speak, act, and think differently from others. At this stage facilitators start preparing their learners to make concrete shifts in cultural frames of reference—from their world to others'. They do this (1) by helping them appropriately apply (when, where, how, and under what circumstances) culture-general (etic) categories (e.g., individualistic vs. collective) and the culture-specific (emic) categories that are particular to each culture, and (2) by helping them to understand and deal with issues of cultural and ethical relativity.

As an example of ethical relativity, there is a tendency to think of some values of other cultures as offensive (e.g., human sacrifice, cannibalism, and patriarchy). If American women understand patriarchy as a reified, immovable, offensive African value, they are reacting from a Polarization orientation through superiority or denigration ("When will they get it?"), or from Minimization ("They don't really feel that way do they?"). But when they see this as part of the way they organize their world as a whole, its value becomes apparent, and this new information broadens their categories and increases their sensitivity. Although the women may still feel strongly that men and women are equal, they are not being ethnocentric in this view.

At this stage facilitators build on learners' new enthusiasm for seeing differences by providing opportunities in face-to-face action. Bennett says, "These activities might include dyads with other-culture partners, facilitated by multicultural group discussions, or outside assignments involving interviewing people from other cultures. Training in the practice of empathy is also appropriate. As much as possible, activities should be related to real life communication situations."[21] Now the learners are self-movers. But facilitators must guide and provide hands-on experience. They can arrange homestays, or set up situations for them to interact with people of other cultures on specific issues such as how to make friends, build relationships, or intervene in conflicts. Interaction, requiring intercultural empathy, can be done through simulations, role-playing, and culture-drama.

Skills to be acquired by the learner at this stage include culture-specific (emic) knowledge of different cultures in specific situations; cognitive flexibility or the ability to withhold one's own interpretation of a cultural scene or action chain in order to search for a different set of meanings; a deeper knowledge of other cultures; knowledge of how we communicate through context (high-context vs. low-context cultures) and how interpretation is affected by context; greater respect for others' values and beliefs; and a heightened tolerance of ambiguity as one works toward broader levels of integration.

The Development Task at Acceptance

Moving toward Adaptation, or full intercultural communication, requires a further development of communication skills through empathy. This is the

---

21. Bennett, "Towards Ethnorelativism," 58.

ability to consciously shift one's perspective into elements of an alternative cultural worldview and act in ways that are culturally appropriate in those worlds. This is much more than "sympathy," which is an ethnocentric projection of your own worldview onto the situation. It implies that others will feel the same in similar circumstances (e.g., "What I'd do in his position is . . ."). Empathy requires a shift beyond this, "an intentional attempt to understand by imagining or comprehending the other's perspective."[22]

At this stage the cognitive structure is concerned with intentionality—linking up knowledge and behavior by conscious efforts. Here learners seek new cultural categories, and, as they do so, they begin to experience their category boundaries becoming more flexible and permeable. The affective response is striving for greater competence, and the behavioral emphasis is on intentionality—purposely taking the perspective of the other in empathy. Learners are able to recognize and respond to power in specific cultural contexts and have some ability to exercise power appropriately in other cultural contexts.

Typical comments at this stage:
"To solve this dispute, I'm going to have to change my approach."
"I know they're really trying hard to adapt to my style, so it's fair that I try to meet them halfway."
"I greet people from my culture and people from the host culture somewhat differently to account for cultural differences in the way respect is communicated."
"I can maintain my values and also behave in culturally appropriate ways."
"In a study abroad program, every student should be able to adapt to at least some cultural differences."
"To solve this dispute, I need to change my behavior to account for the difference in status between me and my counterpart from the other culture."
"I'm beginning to feel like a member of this culture."
"The more I understand this culture, the better I get at the language."

Adaptation[23]

At Adaptation, learners define their cultural identity in pluralistic terms that are the internalization of more than one complete worldview where behavior shifts into different frames without much conscious effort. They see themselves "existing within a collection of various cultural and personal frames

---

22. Ibid., 53.
23. Adaptation is not to be confused with "assimilation" or absorption by another culture, which is a Polarization-reversal response.

of reference,"[24] and developing skills for shifting their frame of reference. Facilitators support learners by helping them to understand different models of culture shock and adaptation. They provide learners with opportunities to practice behavior in other cultural contexts, especially on topics that require intercultural empathy (e.g., humor and distinguishing deviance in other cultures). Facilitators and informants should be well trained and interculturally competent. They should conduct interaction sessions (e.g., culture-drama) using various techniques so that learners will be able to continue learning on their own.

In order to communicate across cultures, learners need to make shifts in their cultural frames of reference. Doing this demands a high level of intercultural development. This involves increased knowledge of other cultures, facility in other languages, communication styles, and nonverbal communication styles. But, most important, it involves experiences of code shifting, of how situations just "feel different" when different cultural values are applied. Learners make progress by constantly joining this knowledge with practical applications.

The Development Task at Adaptation

The task for learners at Adaptation is to develop a broader cultural identity. They need to internalize bicultural or multicultural frames of reference and maintain a definition of their cultural identity that is marginal to any particular culture. They do this through a constant process of integration: "the integrated person understands that his or her identity emerges from the act of defining identity itself. This self-reflective loop shows identity to be one act of constructing reality, similar to other acts that together yield concepts and cultures. By being conscious of this dynamic process, people can function in relationship to cultures while staying outside the constraints of any particular one."[25]

The intercultural skills that are to be developed at this stage include empathy, risk taking, problem solving, interaction management, and flexibility. Facilitators should provide opportunities for learners to interact in new cultural contexts and help them to address deeper anxieties, like internal culture shock and identity conflicts. As one becomes more interculturally sensitive, one's first culture is usually kept and new skills are added to it from other cultures. But some lose their first culture, which leads to a kind of internal culture shock.

Integration occurs at every stage but especially at Adaptation. Here the integration process moves from "Contextual Evaluation" to "Constructive Marginality." Contextual Evaluation is the ability to use multiple cultural

---

24. Bennett, "Towards Ethnorelativism," 59.
25. Ibid., 60.

frames of reference in evaluating phenomena (e.g., being *indirect* when correcting Asians and *direct* when correcting Americans). Constructive Marginality is the acceptance of an identity that is not primarily based in any one culture. It includes the ability to facilitate constructive contact between one's own culture and another culture. In Bennett's words, it is where "one is a constant creator of one's own reality."[26] To some extent this means being marginalized, not belonging to any one culture. Your "group" now becomes that of other "marginals."

At this stage the cognitive structure sees worldview categories as "constructs" that people make to provide meaning. The affective quality is both confusion at being marginal and authenticity in the sense of being true to a greater and truer reality. The behavior emphasis is now on forming and maintaining "constructed affiliation groups" that offer support, and on mediation between cultures. The exercise of power now hinges on whatever is most culturally appropriate for the situation. This tends toward the consensual, or a balance.

Adaptation is not the end. Becoming more interculturally sensitive is an open-ended process. We are always in the process of becoming a part of, and apart from, a given cultural context. The greatest limitation at Adaptation is the inability to generalize one's cultural adaptivity to other cultures and nationalities (e.g., "I know Ghana but don't ask me about Asia"). This ability can be enhanced by experiencing culture-general frameworks through action, as in culture-drama.

Typical comments at this stage:
"Everywhere is home, if you know enough about how things work there."
"I feel most comfortable when I'm bridging differences between the cultures I know."
"Whatever the situation, I can usually look at it from a variety of cultural points of view."
"In an intercultural world, everyone needs to have a transcultural mindset."
"I truly enjoy participating fully in both of my cultures."
"My decision-making skills are enhanced by having multiple frames of reference."

Summary

Adaptation is not the end. Rather, it is an orientation toward the world and the other that is both the basis and prerequisite for any true incarnational ministry. In today's diversity, a missioner's first task is to be more intercultur-

---

26. Ibid., 64.

ally sensitive. The five developmental orientations described in this chapter provide a guide and a set of directives to accomplish this. But they are not something that, once achieved, can be put aside for the next task. They are at the very heart of our missionary endeavor—inculturating the gospel leaven into an ever-changing human condition. We are always in the process of becoming a part of and apart from any given cultural context. Continually adapting with increased sensitivity is, therefore, a life-long and open-ended process.

If I could simplify this process in one word, it would be "empathy." Empathy both presumes and fosters an intercultural mindset because it is based on an assumption of difference and it demands a shift in one's frame of reference. Besides respecting difference, it implies a readiness to give up temporarily one's own worldview in order to imaginatively participate in the other's. Empathy makes code shifting possible—experiencing an aspect of reality differently from that which is offered by one's own culture—and thus makes common meaning possible through relationships.

I have mentioned culture-drama as a key tool for honing this sensitivity because, more than any other exercise I know of, it helps us to learn empathy and build relationships. It dramatizes empathy and makes it experiential. It develops empathy by putting you palpably inside the other's world, and through this dramatized encounter you learn to shift to their cultural frames of reference; you move from sympathy (your world) to empathy (their world). Having had this experience you can say, "Now I really know how you feel. . . . It is so real, yet so different from the way I think about it." As missioners we need to be able to say this in our every encounter.

10

A Sign for All Peoples
Internationalization, Communication Styles, and Behavior Patterns

Frans Dokman

This article is about the effects of internationalization on communication styles and the behavior patterns between members of religious institutions. In their concern about working for a better world and communicating about the Christian faith, international religious institutions do meet a diversity of cultures. This diversity is reflected inside and outside their organization. Missionary orders and congregations are especially used to an international composition. But nowadays, as an effect of globalization and the center of gravity of Christianity moving to the South and East, communities are much more composed of brothers and sisters of diverse nationalities. Here, orders and congregations are going through a complicated process that requires much from leadership and, in many cases, also from the individual brother or sister. Internationalization influences not only the composition of communities and management, but also communication and collaboration, behavior patterns, management style, leadership, spirituality, and education. In short, internationalization affects religious institutions to the core, and because of diversity in cultural orientations, miscommunication and misunderstandings easily occur in their relationships and ministries.

The Process of Internationalization within International Orders and Congregations

During a Congress at the Nijmegen Institute for Mission Studies in 2003, the internationalization of religious institutions was a central theme. One of

Frans Dokman is a senior researcher for International Management and Religion, and director of the Nijmegen Institute for Mission Studies, Radboud University, The Netherlands. His research and training focus on internationalization of orders and congregations.

136

the speakers was Michael Amaladoss, SJ. He spoke about important points to consider in the internationalization process. Amaladoss warned religious institutions of the notion that cultural differences can be overcome by bringing people together in an international setting. Instead, he emphasized that within international institutions there is always the chance that a dominant culture will emerge. A characteristic of this dominant culture is the functional and financial position of power it occupies within the institution. According to Amaladoss, European culture still remains a dominant culture within religious institutions, and this is partly due to the big financial contribution of the European provinces. He does not reject the idea of pluralism, certainly not, but cultures do not treat one another with equality. About this Amaladoss says: "Multiculturalism is always a problem. Cultural pluralism is welcome and can be enriching. The problem is that in most situations the cultures do not encounter each other as equals. One culture always tends to dominate over the others. The reasons can be cultural, financial or political."[1]

Amaladoss agrees with the idea that Asian and African religious who come to Europe for administrative and leadership functions could lend a multicultural meaning to these religious institutions. But herein, says Amaladoss, financial motivations also play a role: "Many Asian and African religious institutions may see their presence and involvement in Europe as fundraising ventures."[2]

In a response to Amaladoss, Elsy Varghese, SSpS, sketched a picture of her missionary work within the multicultural context of The Hague in the Netherlands. According to her, she experienced much respect for her culture and identity. Inside her community, this Asian perspective is also valued. The community offers space for religious sisters with different cultures so that they can meet one another on an equal footing. Varghese puts it this way: "When speaking of international institutes, we should not speak of a culture; they can be and are often a structure in which cultures can meet on equal terms. As a member of a different cultural group, I am also a foreigner. Yet, it is often my cultural difference that allows me to offer something new to the community which welcomes me and with which I live and work."[3]

Varghese emphasized that an international community needs well-balanced members. She is inspired by the effort of her international community to be a mirror for society, a sign for all peoples.

---

1. M. Amaladoss, "Mission Institutes in the Millennium," in F. Dokman, ed., *The West and the Rest of the World in Theology, Mission and Co-funding* (Nijmegen: NIM, 2005), 74.

2. Ibid., 76.

3. E. Varghese, "Mission Institutes in the New Millennium," in F. Dokman, ed., *The West and the Rest of the World in Theology, Mission and Co-funding* (Nijmegen: NIM, 2005), 92.

Cultural Dimensions within International Organizations

Amaladoss and Varghese experience and consider the encounter of cultures differently. The former thinks about the unequal relationships among the diverse cultures, focusing on the superior and inferior culture. The latter sees and experiences equality. Both Amaladoss and Varghese basically speak about power and equality. Analysis of the relation between power and equality receives much attention from various disciplines, including theology and philosophy. However, to obtain a more empirical view of the process of intercultural interaction, including the relation between power and equality, we will turn to studies of intercultural communication. Another reason to benefit from this field is that this article's focus is on internationalization, communication styles, and behavior patterns.

Intercultural communication teaches how to go about with diversity within an international community and is aimed at preventing conflicts from escalating. It has been Geert Hofstede who has made a remarkable start in this field. The theme of Hofstede's work[4] deals with diversity in thinking, feeling, and action of peoples all over the world. Even though the varieties in human thinking are great, he recognized a structure in this diversity. Recognizing this structure can serve as the basis for mutual understanding.

Geert Hofstede is among the most widely cited scientists in the field of intercultural communication. Hofstede's great contribution is that he raises awareness of the importance of cultural dimensions. His research is aimed at deep-rooted and, therefore, oftentimes unconscious values. Hofstede differentiates national cultures in which people learn and acquire positive as well as negative values. These values are internalized and influence acting, thinking, and feeling. Hofstede treats five cultural dimensions to point to the characteristics of national cultures:[5]

- power gap
- individualism vs. collectivism
- masculinity vs. femininity
- avoidance of uncertainties
- Confucian dynamism

According to Hofstede, these cultural dimensions can be expressed in numbers and indexes. With the help of questionnaires, he was able to compute the score of every land or region in each of these dimensions. The cul-

---

4. G. Hofstede, *Culture's Consequences: Comparing Values, Behaviors, Institutions and Organizations across Nations* (Thousand Oaks, CA: Sage Publications, 2001); G. Hofstede, G. J. Hofstede, and M. Minkov, *Cultures and Organizations: Software of the Mind, Intercultural Cooperation and Its Importance for Survival* (New York: McGraw-Hill, 2010).

5. Hofstede, Hofstede, and Minkov, *Cultures and Organizations*, 29–32.

tural dimensions mention collective facts, but the manner of thinking and acting of a group is not, per se, identical to the thinking and acting of an individual. The culture of an individual is the result of his /her upbringing in the family, in school, and at work, and also determined by individual experiences and personality type. Every person has his/her own cultural orientations, but Hofstede believes that the individual differences do not undermine the validity of the research. He claims that the individual differences within a national culture are always much less than the diversity among national cultures.

In my opinion Hofstede's cultural dimensions clarify the differences in behavior and communication among cultures. Dealing with power, time, communal thinking, etc. is experienced differently by every culture, and it is good to have awareness of this. At the same time, Hofstede's categories are indications, suited for discussions, but not applicable to any individual at any place or time. Individual behaviors may well show a difference from the analyzed behaviors of a national culture.

As mentioned, Hofstede has computed indices for national cultures and cultural dimensions. Index 0 is the lowest score; 100 is the highest. Hofstede shows the facts or statistics for fifty national cultures and three groups of countries, which are West Africa, East Africa, and Arabian countries.

Cultural Dimensions and the Society of the Divine Word

As this article contributes to a publication of the Society of the Divine Word, countries with communities of SVD missionaries have been selected for a comparison, and this is based on Hofstede's research on communication styles and behavior patterns. Countries have been chosen from each continent where the SVD is active: India, Brazil, Germany, Australia, and the United States. Nigeria is taken as a representative of the African continent. The score of Nigeria is based on the results for West Africa.

Working in over seventy-seven countries and on every continent, the Society of the Divine Word is one of the largest religious institutes in the Roman Catholic Church, with approximately six thousand members (priests and brothers) worldwide. SVD's membership reflects the international nature of the congregation, and it is considered as representative for our study here. In any country where the SVD is present, members from diverse nations work together. In a world that is divided by cultural, social, and religious diversity, Divine Word Missionaries' mission is dedicated to encourage people to open their hearts and share God's love. "One heart, many faces" was the theme of the canonization of Arnold Janssen, their founder, and Joseph Freinademetz, their first missionary to China. It underlines that all people are included in God's plan and their diversity is valued.

Power gap

This dimension illustrates the way of dealing with the differences in power within an international community. It concerns this pair of concepts: equality and hierarchy. Whenever a hierarchical, unequal distribution of power is found to be "normal," then the power gap is bigger. In a more equal distribution of power, the power gap is smaller. This was the theme that caught the attention of Amaladoss and Varghese. In cultures that have a wide power gap, inequality between people is expected and also wanted; whereas in cultures with small power gap, this inequality among people is made as small as possible. In a culture with a big power gap, people expect to be told what they should do. On the contrary, in a culture with a small power gap, people expect to be consulted first.

The scores for the selected countries are as follows:[6]

India	77
Nigeria	77
Brazil	69
United States	40
Germany	35
Australia	35

India and Nigeria appear to have scored quite high, 77, as countries with a big power gap. Brazil presents a score of 69. This is closer to the outcomes for Nigeria and India than it is to the United States, Germany, and Australia, with low scores of 40, 35, and 35 respectively. From this we can conclude that within the cultures of India, Nigeria, and Brazil things are treated and handled through a big power-gap dimension, whereas the cultures of the United States, Germany, and Australia characterize themselves with the presence of equality. It is interesting to see if this connects with the observations within religious congregations.

The relationship among religious coming from different cultures may have a long history. The socio-anthropologist Nico Vink recognizes and accepts the role of memories herein. According to Vink,[7] in the interaction between peoples of various cultures the past or history can play a crucial role. For instance, when Dutch and Surinamers speak with one another, their shared colonial history has an effect on the way they speak and relate with one another. This can lead to lack or loss of trust. This must be neutralized first, if they want their communication to be conducted on an equal footing.

Conscious or unconscious memories of the past play a role. In the case

---

6. Ibid., 57–59.

7. N. Vink, *Grenzeloos Communiceren: Een Nieuwe Benadering van Interculturele Communicatie* (Amsterdam: KIT, 2001), 47.

of international religious institutes there existed a power gap between Western missionaries and the local clergy. These memories are interwoven in the interaction between members of an international community. Very actual and really visible is the strong financial position of missionaries from the North. This somehow affects the relationships between religious in international communities, whether they like it or not. On the other hand, the missionary institutions in Southern and Eastern areas feel they can be on their own, and they are strong because of the continuous growth in their numbers. This is contrary to what is happening in Europe, where the number called to our vocation is minimal. The idea crops up and the feeling prevails that the future of these religious communities depends on those called to the vocation outside Europe.

Another example of international diversity in the way of dealing with the power gap is the manner in which decision making within religious institutes is made. Religious institutions that originally began in Europe are strongly equal and democratic, and during a chapter the majority vote counts. But how does this work in cultures with a more authoritarian leadership? Or how do you deal with the principle that the majority counts, but one prefers government by consensus?

The World Council of Churches (WCC) has been confronted with this thinking pattern.[8] In 2003, the Kenian Methodist Dr. Samuel Kobia was appointed to be the first African secretary general. After his appointment, Kobia announced his plan to lead the organization according to an African way of management, Ubuntu, in which the consensus method of decision making plays a big role. The majority standpoint is not pushed anymore, but the opinion of the minority is nevertheless heard and used in decision making. Consideration is given to all participants' viewpoints. The leadership has, of course, the natural right to make fast decisions, but on important themes and strategies, consensus has to be reached. During the Assembly of the WCC in Porto Alegre in February 2006, decisions were made for the first time by consensus. This was inspired by Ubuntu but also supported in particular by the United Church of Australia.

Individualism versus Collectivism

A society is individualistic when the relationship among the people is not binding or is noncommittal, and everyone is expected to exclusively take care of himself or herself and his or her own family. There is collectivism wherever people, since birth, are taken into strongly close groups that offer them security, life-long protection in exchange for unconditional loyalty. Examples of

---

8. F. Dokman, *De Zevende Dimensie: De Rol van Religie Binnen International Management* (Leidschendam: Quist, 2013).

an individualistic attitude are "taking your identity from yourself," or "you say what you are thinking." Examples of a collectivistic attitude are "you take your identity from your social network" or "harmony always has to be maintained and direct confrontation avoided."

The scores[9] will probably not surprise you:

United States 91
Australia   90
Germany   67
India   48
Brazil   38
Nigeria   20

The United States and Australia have an almost identical high individuality index of 91 and 90. Germany follows with 67, over 20 points less. There are also differences between the more collectivistic countries India (48), Brazil (38), and Nigeria (20).

In the world of religious institutions, these scores indicate that within collective countries as India, Brazil, and Nigeria leading a community means leading groups, whereas in the individualistic societies leadership needs more emphasis on accompanying individuals. Another point of attention is the difference in contacts and the absence of the social context. Brothers and sisters from the South with a mission in Europe say how they miss the community life at home and feel lonely, especially when in their new community a language is spoken that is difficult for them.

Another concrete example of individualism versus collectivism is the joke (but one with a serious component) among European missionaries: when you ordain an African priest, you also gain the "extended family." It is also said that it is better not to ordain the eldest son of an African family because in our European opinion this means asking for problems; the parish house soon becomes the family home. Notice how in this case cultural notions about property differ between the individual and the community.

Masculinity versus Femininity

Masculinity stands for a society in which the gender roles are clearly divided. Men are expected to be assertive and tough, competitive and focused on material success. Femininity stands for a society in which gender roles overlap. Both men and women are supposed to be discreet and tender and focused on the quality of life with "feminine" values such as care, solidarity, and maintaining warm personal relationships.

---

9. Hofstede, Hofstede, and Minkov, *Cultures and Organizations*, 95–97.

Here according to Hofstede[10] the scores of the selected countries are:

Germany   66
Australia   60
United States 61
India   56
Brazil   49
Nigeria   46

Germany, Australia, and the United States have a reasonably high ranking with scores around 60 and 70 on the Masculinity index. India follows closely with 56. Brazil and Nigeria have almost the same scores, with 49 and 46.

The culture within the world of religious institutions is mostly "feminine," focused on solidarity and attention for interhuman relations. On the whole, conflicts are either being avoided or solved by compromises. The dimension of masculinity does not so much play a role in direct contact between members of the religious institution. However, according to Hofstede, societies with a more masculine orientation do have a strong preference for large and well-structured organizations. This orientation helps the worldwide expansion of both business organizations and religious institutes with roots in the West.

Avoiding Uncertainty

The dimension of "avoiding uncertainty" indicates how the members of a culture feel threatened by insecure or unknown situations. A culture has a high avoidance of uncertainty when there is a great need for rules and formal procedures. In such a culture, there is an inner urge to work hard. There is a low avoidance of uncertainty, when not everything has to be laid down in procedures.

Based on the research of Hofstede[11] the scores of this cultural dimension are:

Brazil   76
Germany   65
Nigeria   54
Australia   51
United States 46
India   40

Brazil has the highest preference for avoiding uncertainty, followed by Germany. The scores of Nigeria and Australia are almost the same, 54 and 51.

---

10. Ibid., 141–43.
11. Ibid., 192–94.

The United States and India follow with 46 and 40. On a scale of 100, the cultural dimensions of avoiding uncertainties are probably similar in these pairs of countries. Noteworthy is that the separation between Western and Southern countries, seen in the dimensions examined earlier, is not seen here. There is not such a clear West–South split, but a clear reason for this is not known.

What is clear however is that religious institutes for the most part excel in setting down rules and procedures that minimize uncertainties. There is a need for precision and formalization, not only written down in constitutions and life rules but also noticeable in a strong bureaucracy.

Confucian Dynamism

The dimension of Confucian dynamism reveals long-term versus short-term orientations. Long-term orientations stand for striving for virtues that will be honored in the future, such as perseverance and frugality. Short-term orientations stand for striving for virtues that are connected with the past and the now, especially respect for tradition and fulfilling social obligations. Geert Hofstede has examined this time-thinking in various countries. According to him, Asian cultures are directed toward long-term thinking. In European cultures, it is average. African cultures are especially more directed toward short-term thinking.

Hofstede's analysis[12] relates to countries below as follows:

Brazil	65
India	61
Germany	31
Australia	31
United States	29
Nigeria	16

Nigeria has a low score of 16, manifesting the short-term orientation. Germany, Australia, and the United States form a middle group, while Brazil and India exhibit a more long-term orientation.

The significance of this index is to be conscious of the differences in planning in communities. Many Western-style planning concepts do work with an annual planning, short-term planning of up to two years, and long-term planning of up to four years. Leadership should consider, in an international context, which cultural orientation it should adopt in the communities of various countries or cultures, the short term or the long term. General Chapters might provide input on policy development for six years, but this will

---

12. Ibid., 255–58.

be more challenging to find results for the short term, i.e., in the first two or three years and the long-term orientations, i.e., five or six years.

Communication

The communication dimensions of culture are difficult to observe. They can cause misunderstandings when people from different cultures communicate with one another. People are usually not aware of their own standards and values, let alone those of another culture. It is very important for members of religious communities to gain more knowledge of cultural differences in the field of communication, because orders and congregations are becoming more and more international.

Hofstede[13] makes a distinction between three phases of learning how to communicate interculturally: awareness, knowledge, and capabilities. Without awareness of one's own mental programming one can travel across the world with an attitude of superiority, deaf and blind to all signals of the relativity of one's own mental programming. When working together with other cultures it is necessary to understand which value patterns these cultures have. In intercultural communication people are called to be aware of their own cultural perspective, as well of that of the other. Varieties in ways of thinking and social interaction between people can be explained by the diversity in cultural dimensions. People act and react out of the dimensions that are provided and shaped by their culture.

Because of globalization, it seems that lifestyles homogenize in a worldwide way, but underneath this outer layer there is a lot of diversity. Intercultural communication is influenced by diverse cultural dimensions. In cultures close to a center of power, communication is most direct. The status of the persons concerned is not so relevant unless a formal meeting with a very big hierarchical difference is involved. Cultures with a larger distance from a center of power know relatively many indirect and nonverbal ways of communication. This is strongly aimed at the form of communication, and these depend on the mutual positions of the partners in conversation.

In most Asian cultures there is more distance between social classes or generations, and as a result the way of talking is more indirect. Communication is strongly focused on form and very dependent on the mutual position of conversation partners. There is sophistication in language use too. An interesting example could be Bahasa Indonesia, a language that has five words to say "yes." However, two of these words actually mean "no." Such a sensitive language expresses a very different cultural reality: out of respect

---

13. Ibid., 419.

for the other, you are positive; you don't like the other to lose face. This is in contrast to a culture with a small power distance. Conformity and harmony are appreciated but communication forms and language are more direct.

Intercultural Mediation

It is good to accentuate the positive dimensions of internationalization. Intercultural contacts are experienced as inspiring. Members of international orders and congregations appreciate the fact that they have a familiar home among their foreign sisters and brothers. But there is a human aspect that overrides the scores and that is harder to accommodate. People react very differently to cultural contrasts. Intercultural dimensions can easily lead to tensions that will have a great influence on the individuals or communities involved.

Some people within communities and organizations are unable to communicate in intercultural settings and also unable to appreciate misunderstandings. In these situations, one loses sight of that which binds people together. Tensions can run so high that an independent process counselor is needed to mediate. The goal of "intercultural mediation" is to make people aware of cultural dimensions, to get to the essence of this, and to stimulate dialogue with a positive effect on individuals and organizations, so that they are better equipped to deal with conflicts.

Within "intercultural mediation" a distinction is usually made[14] between two opposing attitudes with regard to conflicts. On the one hand, avoidance of conflict, and, on the other hand, an eagerness to engage in conflict. When conflict is avoided, people are reserved, there is a fear of disputes, and irritations, emotions are suppressed, and differences of opinion are not openly discussed. People are afraid that they will appear cold and inhuman if they show aggressiveness. They are afraid that they will provoke others or harm themselves. That is why they do not want to settle conflicts in an aggressive way. They suppress feelings and put on a reserved attitude. When, on the other hand, some people are eager for conflict and they take negative pleasure from conflicts, personal emotions are shown and differences of opinion are openly fought out. People with this mindset are afraid that they will not be assertive enough to others and that they may appear too friendly to others. They don't want to be considered a coward or insecure, and thus they prefer fighting to withdrawing.

Cultural dimensions also affect attitudes toward conflicts. Within some cultures, for example in Asia, it is considered rude to bring conflicts out in the open. Conflicts can of course also be between individuals or among con-

---

14. F. Glasl, *Help! Conflicten* (Zeist: Christofoor, 2001).

flicting characters. Typical for "intercultural mediation" is that both cultural dimensions and conflicting characters are recognized. From that basis a solution, acceptable to each and everyone involved, is sought.

Spirituality Transcending Tensions

Cultural dimensions, however, also offer international religious communities a path to spiritual learning in which brothers and sisters encounter understanding and misunderstanding, and connection and disconnection with themselves and their fellow brothers and sisters. These experiences do raise questions such as the following:

- Why does a brother or sister from another culture behave or believe so differently?
- Why is it sometimes difficult to get in contact with one another?
- How do I deal with my brother's or sister's cultural customs?
- Does my behavior express cultural dominance?
- Do I obey my cultural orientations or the spirituality of my community?

These are intriguing questions, and part of a process leading to insights, breakthroughs, recognitions, solidarity, and communication with brothers and sisters.

As such, internationalization presents a possibility to deepen the spirituality of brothers and sisters, both on an individual basis and in their communities. The shared spirituality of a congregation creates an opportunity to transcend cultural dimensions and to construct common ground. International literally means "between nationalities," just as intercultural means "between cultures." Spirituality presents the possibility to fill the space "between nationalities," to fill the space "between cultures," and to find together in that space common ground, where compassion with ourselves and with others sanctifies our contacts and connections with the world.

In fact, it might be seen as a task for international orders and congregations to find such common ground, not only for themselves but also for the societies in which they live and work. As a result of globalization and migration, the composition of a population in society has become more and more intercultural and also interreligious. In many societies there are strong tensions between people from different cultures and religions. There is a deep gap between diverse groups, and there is a context in which people do have an "us and them" orientation. Such an "us and them" orientation actually precludes intercultural communication. It leaves no common ground, which is by definition very problematic for intercultural and international societies.

Conclusion

Hofstede's analysis of behavioral patterns and communication styles by means of cultural dimensions, does give insights into the deep-rooted and often-unconscious values of people. His research clarifies cultural diversity in thinking, feeling, and acting of peoples all over the world. And even though the varieties are huge, a structure in this diversity can be recognized and explained with the help of cultural dimensions.

Consciousness of cultural dimensions is very important for international religious communities. Their boards and communities become more and more intercultural. Intercultural contacts and cooperation are often experienced as valuable. However, the diversity in orientations may also lead to misunderstandings, and these can lead to distance in, and avoidance of, contact between brothers and sisters. The concept of cultural dimensions provides a tool for understanding the misunderstandings. At the same time, it is necessary to realize that an individual is more than his or her cultural dimensions.

Especially in a context in which people use an "us and them" approach to construct barriers between intercultural and interreligious groups, international religious communities can be a mirror for and of diverse societies. The communities offer a platform to give witness to living and working interculturally. Thanks to the challenges of internationalization, religious communities even have an opportunity to show societies that, despite theological debates, spirituality is a universal way of transcending the dimensions of diversity. In their search for common ground, religious communities can be an example for all peoples of how to move from the international to transnational, from the intercultural to transcultural, from formation to transformation.

11

Ecological Concerns
A Mission Perspective

Mary Motte, FMM

Ecological Concerns at the Heart of Mission

Theological shifts of the Second Vatican Council have given a new motivation for mission. Roger Schroeder describes these shifts as recognition of the missionary nature of the entire church (AG 2); God's presence in the world as "signs of the times" (GS 4); the need for collaboration with members of other religions (NA 4); and the possibility of salvation without baptism (LG 16). He goes on to point out that these shifts "undercut the pre-Vatican motivation for mission as the salvation of souls and the establishment of the visible Church."[1] The resultant changes in mission have been continuously researched and studied over the last fifty years. Tools advancing the study of ecological concerns from a mission perspective have been discovered through the collaborative efforts among international mission congregations of men and women who are members of SEDOS.[2] The *SEDOS Bulletin* and the published results of major seminars held in 1968, 1981, and 1990 testify to the depth of these studies and to the intercultural approaches to the questions.[3]

Mary Motte, FMM, is presently director of the Mission Resource Center–Franciscan Missionaries of Mary, US Province. She is engaged in mission study, research, and formation in collaboration with both Catholic missionary congregations and ecumenical organizations. She has contributed articles to *International Bulletin of Missionary Research, International Review of Mission,* and *SEDOS Bulletin.*

1. Roger P. Schroeder, SVD, "Catholic Teaching on Mission after Vatican II: 1975–2007," in Stephen B. Bevans, ed., *A Century of Catholic Mission* (Oxford: Regnum Books, 2013), 112.

2. SEDOS is a membership organization of international missionary congregations in Rome, Italy, which was begun after the Second Vatican Council.

3. See *SEDOS Bulletin* and seminars at www.sedosmission.org. Also, SEDOS, ed., *The Foundations of Mission Theology* (Maryknoll, NY: Orbis Books, 1972); Mary Motte, FMM, and Joseph R. Lang, MM, eds., *Mission in Dialogue: The Sedos Seminar on the Future of Mission*

Progress in ecological understanding makes it possible to retrieve, many centuries or decades later, the concerns that Francis of Assisi and other prophets such as Hildegard of Bingen, John Woolman, and Pierre Teilhard de Chardin had for the care of the earth and the integrity of creation.[4] Unfortunately today, ecological concerns are frequently motivated by an acute realization of the profound loss resulting from planning and practices rooted in purposes harmful to creation. These realities question mission in its understanding of the human- and gospel-based commitment to the poor, the obligation to care for creation, and the vision of a new future in the kingdom of God. New issues emerging from scientific studies of the universe also question our missionary understanding of how we are to proclaim the gospel. Scientists now verify that the process of creation continues.[5] Some of this data indicates all life forms are characterized by relationships, which are apparent throughout the evolutionary process in even the most infinitesimal particles of life. Hence, there is a pattern of relationship running through the make-up of the universe. W. Stoeger calls these "constitutive relationships which give an entity its unity, consistency of action and identity."[6] Such factual information from the scientific community challenges theologians to reach for deeper insights into the mystery of the Trinity in its relationship with all creation. Missiologists and mission practitioners are likewise challenged to consider how this might relate to an ecologically conscious communication of the gospel proclamation of the incarnation and resurrection. Such ecological commitment, rooted in the missionaries' faith in the incarnation, death, and resurrection of Jesus, opens the way for them to explore new developments in missionary spirituality.[7] As Denis Edwards reminds us, "the incarnation and its culmination in the resurrection and ascension of the crucified Jesus mean that the Word of God is forever matter, forever flesh, forever a creature, forever part of the universe of creatures, but part of all this is now radically transfigured."[8] Sandra Schneiders notes, "One particular

---

(Maryknoll, NY: Orbis Books, 1982); William Jenkinson and Helene O'Sullivan, eds., *Trends in Mission: Towards the 3rd Millennium* (Maryknoll, NY: Orbis Books, 1991).

4. Stephen B. Bevans and Roger P. Schroeder, *Constants in Context: A Theology of Mission for Today* (Maryknoll, NY: Orbis Books, 2004), 376.

5. Denis Edwards, *How God Acts: Creation, Redemption and Special Divine Actions* (Minneapolis, MN: Fortress Press, 2010), 1–4.

6. Cf. W. Stoeger, "Reductionism and Emergence: Implications for the Interaction of Theology with the Natural Sciences," in Nancy C. Murphy and William R. Stoeger, eds., *Evolution and Emergence: Systems, Organisms, Persons* (Oxford: Oxford University Press, 2007), 229–47.

7. Sandra Schneiders, IHM, *Buying the Field: Catholic Religious Life in Mission to the World* (Mahwah, NJ: Paulist Press, 2013), 63.

8. Denis Edwards, *Partaking of God: Trinity, Evolution, and Ecology* (Collegeville, MN: Liturgical Press, 2014), 62.

contribution Religious can make is to help keep the ecological commitment of Christians truly Christian, by their deep knowledge of and explicit articulation of the rootedness of such commitment to the biblical soil of creation and Incarnation."[9]

In this chapter I will consider the overall rapid development of ecological concerns among missionaries and will cite a few instances that are illustrative of ways in which these concerns are expressed and of the interculturality that is basically assumed by the international missionary congregations. I will then consider briefly the challenge ahead for missionaries to develop their spirituality in relation to concrete ecological practices and the unfolding evolution in the universe. To do so they will need to recognize the relationships between these two realities of ecology and evolution and to deepen their contemplation of God–Trinity in relation to creation.

Ecological Mission Orientations

Energizing thoughts and conversations, orientations and actions, projects and research around the topic of ecology abound. Orientations and convictions rooted in and formed by the gospel are part of this conversation and research. The Holy See, several episcopal conferences at continental, national, and local levels, and the religious orders of women and men, apostolic associations of the laity, and, ecumenically, the World Council of Churches are all involved in ecological engagements.[10] Their reflections and studies show how these ecological engagements carry out the concerns of the gospel and its communication in present times. Francis's ecological concerns have been in evidence since the beginning of his pontificate. In May 2014 he spoke of the gift of knowledge of the Holy Spirit, and describing the relationship of this gift to all of Creation he said: "it is a special gift which allows us to grasp, through Creation, the greatness and love of God and His profound relationship with every creature." He continued: "When our eyes are enlightened by the Spirit, they open to the contemplation of God in the beauty of nature and the grandeur of the cosmos, and lead us to discover how everything speaks to us of Him and everything speaks to us of His love. All this arouses astonishment and a deep sense of gratitude in us! . . . Before all this, the Spirit leads us to praise the Lord from the depths of our hearts and recognize, in all that we have and are, a priceless gift from God and sign of His infinite love for us."[11] Here we can see something of the spiritual and theological orientations that

---

9. Schneiders, *Buying the Field*, 63.

10. See, for example, the following websites: www.holyseemission.org; www.ecojesuit.com; www.oikoumene.org.

11. Pope Francis, Vatican Radio, http://en.radiovaticana.va/news/2014/05/22/pope_francis_warns_against_the_destruction_of_creation_/110078.

strengthen the growing ecological awareness in communicating the gospel message.

Francis of Assisi, declared Patron of Ecology by John Paul II on November 29, 1979, witnesses the sacredness of creation by his life, his choices, and his relations with God and with others. Francis recognized that we humans are called by the Creator to an intimate interrelationship with all creatures.[12] Eloi Leclerc, OFM, points out how Francis, in his "Canticle of the Creatures," explored the genuine kinship that exists between the Creator and each of the creatures, calling them by names that denote a precious relationship: Sister Water and Moon, Brother Sun, Wind, and Fire, and Mother Earth.[13] The relationship denotes a deep awareness marked by the profound respect that shapes Francis's way of seeing. Intuitively, he grasps the love proceeding from a loving Creator, God–Trinity, who holds all in existence and calls all Creation into the communion of the Trinity. Much later, without particular reference to Francis of Assisi, Teilhard de Chardin gives voice to this underlying truth of the canticle: "Love is the most universal, the most tremendous and the most mystical of cosmic forces. Love is the primal and universal psychic energy. Love is a sacred reserve of energy; it is like the blood of spiritual evolution."[14]

There is nothing utilitarian in Francis's way of seeing, and yet utter simplicity characterizes the relationships that spell out his vision. Today international missionary congregations are addressing ecological concerns in direct, hands-on projects that are already showing results that in particular circumstances open new paths to realizations of the gospel. A somewhat random selection of projects undertaken by missionary communities illustrate some of these new paths. In addition, the websites of the missionary congregations, as well as that of SEDOS, offer a wealth of material about other ecological projects.

The continual impoverishment of the rain forest and the plight of the poor in the Amazon region of Brazil came to the attention of the world through the death of Sister Dorothy Stang, SNDN. Dorothy and her sisters lived among the poor in Anapu, Brazil, and set up programs that enabled self-sufficient, independent communities and the sustenance of the rain forest. Several times she requested city, state, and national governments for protection for the people, but her requests were refused. On February 12, 2005, Sister Dorothy was gunned down by two assailants while walking on a lonely road. After Sister Dorothy's death, the Brazilian president put almost 20,000 of the

---

12. See Thomas of Celano, "First Life of St. Francis," in *Francis of Assisi: The Saint, Early Documents* (New York: New City Press, The Franciscan Institute, 1999), 171–357.

13. See Eloi Leclerc, OFM, *Cantique des Créatures: Les Symboles de l'Union* (Paris: Les Editions Franciscaines, 2013).

14. *Human Energy*, trans. J. M. Cohen (London: Collins, 1969), 32.

Amazon's 1.6 million square miles under federal environmental protection. The protected land is in the Anapu region. The people of Anapu and the Sisters of Notre Dame de Namur are encouraged by this action, and human rights defenders and environmentalists are likewise encouraged that Dorothy's work and ministry among the poor and for the sustenance of the rain forest were not in vain.[15] Through giving her life, Dorothy witnessed forcefully to the interrelation between the poor, with whom she lived, worked, and prayed, and the devastation of nature in what has been happening to the rain forest in the Amazon.

In 2005 the Franciscan Missionaries of Mary through the leadership of one of their sisters, Rosemarie Higgins, FMM, became concerned about the disappearance of trees on their property in North Providence, RI, due to age and disease. Local members of the Rhode Island Tree Council shared their concern, and the Tree Project was born. Aged, diseased trees were removed, the trunks ground into chips to use as mulch for the new trees planted. Together with John Campanini, of the Rhode Island Tree Council, the sisters researched the kinds of trees that would grow on the land, and proceeded with a project through which people, individually or in groups, donated a specific kind of tree to be planted. Many persons together with the sisters met to deepen knowledge about the needs of the trees, to train as tree stewards, and to work out ways to realize the Tree Project. Together they found ways to bring much-needed water to the young trees. The tree planting continues. The educational dimension of this project includes students from nearby colleges, who participate in ecological development or who give community service by working on the land and learning about the importance of care for creation.

Likewise, a number of Franciscan Missionaries of Mary from different parts of the world have participated annually in learning how mission includes ecological concerns. The land has become a place where a person can find space for communion with God, the deeper meaning of existence, and one's relationship with the Creator and Creation. Those who attend on the property the Day Center for the Elderly are able, no matter their disability, to absorb the grace that permeates the gardens, trees, and flowers on their walks. The labor-intensive action to improve this space, highlighting the beauty and significance of the earth and its fruits, has strengthened a growing awareness of the place of the sacred in the ongoing action of creation. The many statues that dot the property are reminders of the sacred, and in their own way call forth deeper reflections on the One who is responsible for this beauty. A burning wish expressed by the FMM foundress, Mary of the Passion, for the Institute seems to echo in this context, relating it to the FMM fundamental

15. www.notredameonline.org/en/resources/sister-dorothy-stang.

preference for the poor: "The Gospel! Francis! Truth and Charity! Oh, that I could invite the whole world to understand you!"[16]

Recently, the Maryknoll Sisters in the Philippines have opened the Maryknoll Ecological Center in Baguio City. Originally the sisters had an elementary school. After the school closed, they became more aware of the fragility of the earth. In light of this awareness, they chose to develop an integrated educational program following earth-based values. The dynamic missionary energy, which has led Maryknoll women forward from the time of Mother Mary Joseph, became a vital source of new energy as they chose radically and decisively to dedicate their resources in Baguio to alternative environmental education. "The Maryknoll Ecological Sanctuary was born of the concern that the life-support systems of the whole earth are rapidly being eroded due to environmental destruction."[17] As the sisters recount, it was an earthquake that pushed them toward a deeper assessment of their situation and the radical decision to dedicate themselves to a constructive, missionary response to the earth crisis. The ecological sanctuary has become a resource for many groups in Baguio and the rest of the region. Part of the project includes the development of the Cosmic Journey, an educational experience of how our planet, and all that is part of it, came to be. They note that the journey includes us human beings and attempts to discover our role and mission within the framework of the whole universe. This project opens horizons beyond what we know; it calls for new ways of seeing, new ways of giving ourselves with courage to enter the space of the Other. It calls us into the future with greater awareness of the effects of each one's actions, and the need to explore more deeply the spirituality needed for this action. As they conclude the description of this project they remark, "Indeed the Maryknoll Journey Continues!"[18]

The Society of the Divine Word, together with the Missionary Sisters Servants of the Holy Spirit, formed a Non-Governmental Organization (NGO) that has special consultative status at the United Nations. Under the name VIVAT International, they work with issues of ecology as well as social justice, development, and peace. A few other congregations too have joined this VIVAT International organization. Along with other Catholic and other religious NGOs, they aim to bring ethical and spiritual values to the UN organization and other international groups. The SVD define this mission as follows: "Following in the footsteps of Jesus, one who challenged the economic and social structures of his day by proclaiming the coming of a Kingdom, where the poor and marginalized would have their rightful dignity respected, Divine Word Missionaries today remain committed to build-

---

16. *Spiritual Notes*, 33, published privately by the Franciscan Missionaries of Mary.
17. www.maryknollecosanctuary.org.
18. Ibid.

ing and anticipating that Kingdom through their efforts to promote justice, peace, and the integrity of creation."[19]

Maryknoll Global Concerns represents all those who gather under the name and spirit of Maryknoll: the Maryknoll Sisters, Maryknoll Fathers and Brothers, Maryknoll Lay Missioners, and the Maryknoll Affiliates. Their purpose is education for social justice, peace, and the integrity of creation. They carry out this multifaceted ministry through participating with the United States, the United Nations, and other governmental organizations. They carry out a communications program to give information about advocacy and action for social, economic, and environmental justice. Importantly, they involve Maryknoll missioners in their work by showing the relationships between experience at the grassroots and the systems that create or perpetuate poverty, human rights violations, conflict, and environmental destruction.[20]

The Sisters of Mercy are giving special attention to cosmology and eco-justice. They recognize that in this century environmental degradation is the major issue facing the planet, and this issue most severely affects the poor. Because of their primary work with the poor, the Mercy Sisters have encountered millions of people who live in poverty throughout the world. The great poverty of these people means they depend on degraded ecosystems and natural resources for their survival. From this first-hand experience the sisters state clearly, "It is the poor—especially women and children—who are most at risk, when ecosystems are degraded, as they suffer disproportionately from the health risks caused by inadequate or dirty water and polluted air, and bear the burden of collecting the resources for their daily use, such as water and fuel wood." In their insertions in Nigeria, United States, Philippines, Australia, and Newfoundland, the Sisters of Mercy, through their commitment to work with the poor, are engaged in environmental education and helping poor families develop organic farming.[21]

Many of the missionary societies have set up commissions at the international and provincial levels to develop their missionary commitment related to ecological concerns. At the time of the Thirty-fifth Chapter in 2008, the Jesuits' commitment was made to ecological concerns, and the follow-up has led to development of actions and documents in their various provinces throughout the world.[22] The website vidimusdominum[23] provides information about the various congregations and the activities of the International Union of Superiors General (UISG) and of the Union of Superiors General

19. www.vivatinternational.org.

20. www.maryknollogc.org.

21. http://www.mercyworld.org/mercy_global_action/project-contentpage.cfm.

22. http://www.ecojesuit.com/ecology-documents-from-the-social-justice-and-ecology-secretariat-sjes/.

23. vd.pcn.net/en/.

(USG). The website of SEDOS also gives current information about eco-logical activities among international missionary congregations.[24] The actual commitments of international missionary congregations provides insights into eco-justice, and by concretely connecting the devastation of Creation with the plight of the poor among whom they minister, they also bring about contemporary expressions in mission of communicating the gospel.

Developing a Spirituality of Creation

From the beginning of the universe to the present, we witness the emergence of life through an unbroken series of transformations. Seeing in a new way implies an approach to Creation that is rooted in the contemplative dynamic of the Christian tradition. Sean McDonagh, SSC, drawing on the work of Thomas Berry, invites us to see the emergent universe again and in a new way. He invokes the extraordinary unbroken sequence of events from the initial flaring forth to the beauty, fruitfulness, and diversity of life.[25] Francis of Assisi, the Patron of Ecology, was neither scientist nor theologian. Rather, he was gifted with a profound intuition about the relationship between God the Creator and all of God's creation. Francis was a man profoundly formed by the gospel. One might venture to say that today there are those who, having explored the fields of science, theology, agriculture, philosophy, etc., now recognize that it is formation in the gospel that leads to true contempla-tion, which is sought in prayer and humility. John Polkinghorne, Anglican priest and scientist, describes the importance of cosmological intuition, dis-tinguishing it from cosmological argument: "Achieving scientific success is a specific ability possessed by humankind, exercised in the kind of universe we inhabit. I believe that a full understanding of this remarkable human capac-ity for scientific discovery ultimately requires that our power in this respect is the gift of the universe's Creator who, in that ancient and powerful phrase has made humanity in the image of God (Gen 1:26–27)."[26]

Developing a spirituality from the perspective of ecological justice is indeed a path for mission. Today it is crucial to recognize the relationship between the living memory of Jesus and the catastrophic issues confronting the global community. Ecological action can express a radical commitment to Christ and the practice of faithful discipleship. A deeper formation in the gospel is ultimately the fruit of commitment to eco-justice, sustainability of the earth, and engagement with the poor. This deeper formation in the gospel

---

24. www.sedosmission.org.

25. Sean McDonagh, "The Story of the Universe: Our Story," *SEDOS Bulletin* 41 (2009): 150.

26. John Polkinghorne, *Quantum Physics and Theology: An Unexpected Kinship* (New Haven: Yale University Press, 2007), 8.

is realized through contemplation of the mystery of God–Trinity in relation with the creation. It is contemplation shaped by the Eucharistic mystery that can lead one to see how the God of love is acting continually in creation and the unfolding of the universe. When Christian faith contemplatively holds the constitutive relationships of the evolutionary process in the trinitarian God of mutual relations and events in the life of Jesus, one can experience the God of communion. A trinitarian theology of creation sees the differentiated relationships of creatures as a "limited, creaturely reflection of divine life—a sacrament of communion."[27] God is intimately and deeply present to every aspect of creation: "love revealed in Jesus and poured out in the Spirit is the ultimate guiding meaning of the universe."[28] The trinitarian communion of love is the ground of creation—hence creation takes place within the drama of trinitarian life. The dynamic divine life is the environment in which the universe is brought to life and empowered to unfold.[29] Newness characterizes the mystery of God revealed in Jesus Christ in scripture.[30]

Poverty, suffering, war, and terrorism define the situations of so many persons in the world today. Violence against the human person is constantly in the news, as are reports about devastation and disrespect for other creatures and for creation. In the face of such bleak suffering, we are reminded that God bears the cost of evolution—God hears the cry of the poor. In the passion, death, and resurrection of Jesus we have a microcosm of God's redemptive presence to all creatures facing suffering and death. It is in contemplating the cross of Christ that we discover God's identification with creation. In the death of Christ we have the icon of God's redemptive co-suffering with all sentient life, including the suffering of victims of war, violence, discrimination and all forms of social injustice. By means of deep incarnation, the Christ-event can be understood as God entering into the evolutionary history of life on Earth. God's compassion, through the liberating power of the Spirit, reaches through all time and space, embracing and giving new life to all aspects of the universe's evolution. One may think of God's descent into the deepest layers of the evolutionary process, embracing and suffering with the entire cosmic story. God embraces suffering, and from within the depths of that darkness rises to new life.[31]

Through our involvement in the mystery of the Eucharist we can be led to a new way of thinking, seeing, feeling, acting, living, and praying.[32] Jesus'

---

27. Edwards, *How God Acts*, 6–7.

28. Ibid., 8.

29. Ilia Delio, "Godhead or God Ahead," in Philip Rossi, ed., *God, Grace and Creation*, College Theology Series 55 (Maryknoll, NY: Orbis Books, 2010), 10.

30. Edwards, *How God Acts*, p. 13.

31. Denis Edwards, "Ecological Commitment," *SEDOS Bulletin* 41 (2009): 164–65.

32. Edwards, *Partaking of God*, 163–82.

action in the institution of the Eucharist happens at a meal shared with his friends, and involves the elements of bread and wine, blessed and shared. "Then he took the bread, said the blessing, broke it, and gave it to them, saying, 'This is my body, which will be given for you; do this in memory of me.' And likewise the cup after they had eaten, saying, 'This cup is the new covenant in my blood, which will be shed for you'" (Luke 22:19–20). In this way, and in the continued celebration of the Eucharist, we are drawn into the hospitality, compassion, and action of God expressed in Jesus' life. The release of divine energy reaches its radical expression in the total darkness of Jesus' death, and in the disciples' experience of Jesus as risen from the dead.[33] The dynamic Spirit of God is inherently present in every aspect of creation. Through the Spirit, the disciples understand that their fidelity to God as revealed by Jesus will demand a new universality. Divine compassion is directed to the whole world, and reaches out beyond the human community to embrace "all things" in the reconciliation of Christ (Col 1:15–20). Romans (8:19–24) says the whole of creation awaits redemption. Saint Irenaeus sees all creation, summed up and transformed in Christ, destined to share in his victory over death. Francis of Assisi grasps the intimate relation of all humans to God through the compassion of God embodied in the humble sublimity of Jesus-Eucharist, who reaches out to embrace all his brothers and sisters before God. For Teilhard de Chardin, the whole of evolutionary history is empowered by the Risen Christ, the Omega, source and goal of the whole emergent process. Awareness of our complicity in the destructive effect of our carbon footprint calls for a new way of seeing, and new behaviors of reconciliation and solidarity. Discipleship, marked by reconciliation and solidarity, must be rooted in ecological conversion, in our deep awareness of our relationship to the universe, to the Earth and to all creation. As Christians we are confronted with the need to create in our eucharistic practice a liturgical ethos that will truly realize the incorporation of all creation in the life of God.

There are multiple influences questioning our understanding of discipleship. While these emerge from various sources, there is a growing convergence for a more unassuming participation in "making all things new." For those called into discipleship, the unfolding nature of creation, the mysteries evident in the universe, the pattern of interrelationship in life forms from the simplest to most complicated, the concept of newness present in the New Testament, and new ways of reading scripture from the perspective of the land are some of the challenges presenting us with questions implying radical choices. "The day will come when after harnessing the ether, the winds, the tides, gravitation, we shall harness for God the energies of love. And on that

---

33. Denis Edwards, "Final Fulfillment: The Deification of Creation," *SEDOS Bulletin* 41 (2009): 185–86.

day, for the second time in the history of the world, man will have discovered fire."[34]

Conclusion

Awareness of the challenges of ecology is rapidly assuming greater importance among many persons and a vast number of organizations. This article addresses some of the ways in which ecological justice is increasingly front and center in Catholic missionary congregations of women and men. These examples are indicative of the rapid growth of ecological concerns, and the development of a missionary perspective on the ways in which ecology needs to take its place at the heart of mission. The challenge that emerges now for those engaged in mission is to continue to lead the fruits of these many and diverse energies toward an increasingly dynamic relationship with the mystery of God–Trinity. In other words, we are challenged to discover more fully the spirituality for ecological mission, to discover new insights into the mystery of God and the unfolding creation of the universe, to uncover the eucharistic ethos so central to our prayer and worship. In Romans (8:24–25), Paul reminds us that we are "saved in hope." This hope is in the God who is the absolute, incomprehensible mystery of love. Here we uncover the newness of God as we read in the Book of Revelation:

> I heard a loud voice from the throne saying,
> "Behold, God's dwelling is with the human race.
> He will dwell with them and they will be his people
> and God himself will always be with them as their God.
> He will wipe every tear from their eyes,
> and there shall be no more death or mourning, wailing or pain,
> for the old order has passed away."
> The One who sat on the throne said, "Behold, I make all things new."
> (Rev 21:1–5a)

A disciple cannot be one who follows a static God. God's act of creation is an act of love, a dynamic love permitting the kenosis of freedom in creation.[35] God assumes and embraces the risks of creation, even when costly.[36] Contemplation leads toward awareness of this Trinity of Love, our God who dwells with us. Our insight into God continually unfolds in history through

---

34. Pierre Teilhard de Chardin, *Toward the Future* (New York: Harcourt, 1975), 60–87.

35. See John Polkinghorne, ed., *The Work of Love: Creation as Kenosis* (Grand Rapids, MI: Eerdmans, 2001).

36. John Haught, *Making Sense of Evolution: Darwin, God and the Drama of Life* (Louisville, KY: Westminster John Knox Press, 2010), 84.

the continuity of the Paschal Mystery of Christ, in his incarnation, death, and resurrection. God is not absent from the great tragedies of the present age. The call to discipleship with the One who has realized God's presence among us in the Paschal Mystery is a call to a humility that is far removed from power, control, and domination. We discover God in the place of the poor because this is how God has become incarnate among us. God's presence among us in Jesus of Nazareth reveals to us the humble God, the God who bent low to come to us, to be with us, to live and suffer among us. A new spiritual vision surfaces through scientific discovery and theological imagination.

Through the awakening of missionary congregations to ecological concerns, and through their subsequent commitment to projects on behalf of eco-justice in some of the places that are most bereft of any kind of justice, one can recognize the opening toward a deeper realization of missionary spirituality. This spirituality, while rooted in the concern for eco-justice, will seek to contemplate the mystery of the God–Trinity in relation to the creation. It will do so through commitment to a deeper gospel formation, starting from the living contemplation of the gospels and the mystery of the incarnation and resurrection. The Eucharist, rooted in the symbols of creation, becomes a focus for the contemplative path of ecological justice. The Eucharist obliges us to begin all moments of contemplation, begging God for the grace to sit with those who are little, those who suffer, and those who are poor. One cannot separate contemplation or the way of ecological justice from the lives of the poor, who are loved by God. And it is imperative that missionary men and women carry forward this exploration into new ways of contemplation that eucharistically hold ecological justice and the cries of the poor.

12

The Challenge of Postmodern Culture and Mission

John C. Sivalon, MM

In the philosophical world, postmodernity is most closely related to the thought of Friedrich Nietzsche and those who followed him, including Jacques Derrida. It is seen not as a culture but, rather, as a way of wrestling with the philosophical foundations of truth, morality, identity, and religion. Thus, philosophers tend to limit the meaning of postmodernity to the thought of specific figures.[1]

In the social sciences, the origins of postmodernism are closely associated with François Lyotard and many others, including Zygmunt Bauman.[2]

John C. Sivalon, MM, earned an MA degree in sociology from the University of Dar es Salaam and a doctorate in theology from the University of St. Michael's College in Toronto, Ontario, Canada. After finishing his studies, he was a member of the faculty of the Department of Sociology at the University of Dar es Salaam. In 2002, Sivalon was elected superior general of Maryknoll Fathers and Brothers. After his term, he joined the faculty at the University of Scranton Department of Theology and Religious Studies. He is the author of *God's Mission and Postmodern Culture: The Gift of Uncertainty.*

1. Gerard Mannion, *Ecclesiology and Postmodernity: Questions for the Church in Our Time* (Collegeville, MN: Liturgical Press, 2007), 4. He says, "For some, Nietzsche was both its prophet and its chief intellectual midwife. It is marked by the increasing disillusionment with all overarching explanatory hypotheses for the world in general and human beings and societies in particular. Thus 'grand narratives' such as religion, political ideologies and even science itself are no longer seen to have 'all the answers' to humanity's questions. The postmodern era is thus marked by a shift from belief in certainties and truth claims to more localized and piecemeal factors. The individual is seen as creating his or her own meaning to a certain extent rather than receiving it from without."

2. Its origin, for Lyotard, is found in a reaction to grand narratives or theories that claim to explain everything in the social sphere. He saw these "universalist claims" as being rooted in power and its legitimation. His critique is not against narrative as such but against those narratives that claim a "universal history of humanity." Particular narratives remain important, he said, as a source of dealing with conflicts in the social sphere and maintaining a social bond among particular groups.

Bauman exemplifies the debates associated with the use of the term "post-modern" in the social sciences. He himself moved away from the use of the term to talk, instead, about a "liquid modernity." With others, he is saying that postmodern is really not so much a dramatic break with the past as it is a further development. Hence, for them, the use of the prefix "post" overstates the division.

In this chapter, I will use the term "postmodern culture" and emphasize that we are talking about a culture. It is a culture that has developed over time and guides the behavior of many in North America and Europe. It is significant on a global scale, though, because it articulates with many other cultures around the world. It is a culture that has assimilated in various ways many of postmodernity's deep philosophical issues into an assumed stock of knowledge that guides people's behavior. It also has assimilated into that same stock of knowledge many advances in science over the past century.

Those scientific advances clearly are further developments of the modern scientific method and thus reflect an innate continuity with modernity rather than a radical break. Therefore, when I use the term "postmodern culture," I do so acknowledging a relative continuity with modernity but, also, empha-sizing a real difference from it in terms of how people understand themselves, how they understand truth and knowledge, how they understand their rela-tionship to the other, and how they understand space and time.

Rooted in the enlightenment period, modernity prevailed until the early twentieth century as a paradigm in the West.[3] Enlightenment thinkers looked at two earlier strands of philosophy, rational philosophy and empiri-cal philosophy, and attempted to bring them together. Reason came to be seen as an energy that is brought to observation to yield truth. For them, truth is neither a body of innate ideas nor a slave to simple data, revealed knowledge, or authority. Reason and sensate observation are understood as the cornerstones for knowledge of reality.

Based on this, enlightenment thinkers embraced three principal ideas that fairly well define the spirit of modernity. First of all, they believed in the per-fectibility of humanity by humanity. No longer was perfectibility associated only with God. Rather, it became more and more accepted that humanity's present conditions did not have to be the way they were, and that human beings themselves could change those conditions.

Second, enlightenment thinkers believed that just as the laws of natu-ral movement reside in nature, so must the laws of social movement reside in social reality. No longer was destiny controlled by God or spirits, they believed, but by laws that reside in natural and social life.

---

3. David Harvey, *The Condition of Postmodernity* (Oxford: Basil Blackwell, 1991), 12–14.

Third, philosophy transformed itself into a discipline dedicated to the social critique of existing institutions and the science that would lead to human perfection.[4] It posited that human reason is capable of knowing the inner workings of reality, and thus can manipulate and control reality for human purposes. In this way, the physical and social sciences hijacked religion's rational and explanatory role. Religion, if it had any purpose at all, was reduced to a private, individualistic, affective role.

In differentiating the characteristics of identity, Bauman describes a modern person as one who has a strong sense of being an agent or subject with a unique identity. Modern persons believe that they are authors of their own actions, and thus responsible for those actions. Part of their strong sense of identity is that they also have a strong sense of belonging to a wider group and place through institutions, such as citizenship in a nation state, and a number of wider associations such as unions, religions, professional organizations, and social clubs. They feel rooted, grounded, yet unique. They invest meaning in their journey through life and expect that the rules of the game are stable. Thus, they are willing to delay immediate gratification with the belief that down the road they will be able to enjoy life. They saved for their children, and they also saved for retirement.

After struggling with modernity and the effects of the enlightenment for nearly four hundred years,[5] Vatican II, in its "Pastoral Constitution on the Church in the Modern World," expressed the Roman Catholic Church's compromise most succinctly.

If by the autonomy of earthly affairs we mean that created things and societies themselves enjoy their own laws and values which must be gradually deciphered, put to use, and regulated by men, then it is entirely right to demand that autonomy. Such is not merely required by modern man but harmonizes also with the will of the Creator. For by the very circumstance of their having been created, all things are endowed with their own stability, truth, goodness, proper laws, and order. Man must respect these as he isolates them by the appropriate methods of the individual sciences or arts. Therefore, if methodical investigation within every branch of learning is carried out in a genuinely scientific manner and in accord with moral norms, it never

---

4. As described in Zeitlin Irving, *Ideology and the Development of Social Theory* (Englewood, NJ: Prentice-Hall, 1990).

5. The Roman Catholic Church's struggle with modernity led Roman authorities to label all those who attempted to find the presence of God within modern culture as "modernist." "Modernism" was condemned as the "synthesis of all heresies" by Pius X in his encyclical *Pascendi* (1907). Among the leaders of the Catholic movement were A. F. Loisy in France and George Tyrrell in England. Vital to the Catholic movement were the adoption of the critical approach to the Bible, which was by that time accepted by most Protestant Churches, and the rejection of the intellectualism of scholastic theology.

truly conflicts with faith, for earthly matters and the concerns of faith derive from the same God. (GS 36)

However, while the church was proposing this acknowledgment of modernity, the seed of radical change had already been planted within modernity itself and had begun to grow. This seed has now blossomed into what I call postmodern culture.

Roger Haight describes the culture of postmodernity with the following features:

1. A historical consciousness that is deeper and more radical than that of Modernity; 2. An appreciation of pluralism that is suspicious of all absolute or universal claims; 3. A consciousness of the social construction of self that has completely undermined the transcendental ego of Modernity and encouraged a grasping individualism; 4. A sense of the size, age, complexity and mystery of reality that modern science never even suspected.[6]

In other words, first of all, a growing number of people have come to see how previously unquestioned worldviews and paradigms have been proven wrong. The earth was once accepted as flat. We now perceive it as actually more oval. We once thought that the universe circled around the earth. Then we learned that the earth isn't even the center of our own galaxy, let alone of the universe. We thought the universe would begin to contract, but now see it as potentially expanding forever. Because of this historical consciousness of our knowledge, a very real skepticism has come to permeate how we look upon truth claims and knowledge itself.

This is a very real reinforcement of Nietzsche's claim that all truth is lies. For Nietzsche, all truth statements use words that are conventions created by humans to describe an event or object as it relates to the human and not as it is in itself. Therefore, all statements in a sense are lies. As he says:

The various languages placed side by side show that with words it is never a question of truth, never a question of adequate expression; otherwise, there would not be so many languages. The "thing in itself" (which is precisely what the pure truth, apart from any of its consequences, would be) is likewise something quite incomprehensible to the creator of language and something not in the least worth striving for. This creator only designates the relations of things to men, and for expressing these relations he lays hold of the boldest metaphors.[7]

---

6. Roger Haight, *Christian Community in History: Historical Ecclesiology*, vol. 1 (New York: Continuum, 2004), 57.

7. Friedrich Nietzsche, "On Truth and Lies in a Nonmoral Sense," usu.edu/6890/OnTruth andLies.pdf, p. 3.

Second, as Haight claims, we have come to accept not only that human beings are formed by socialization but that all of our knowledge of reality is socially constructed. This has become even clearer with globalization in all spheres but especially in information technology. People have become increasingly aware of the diversity of the human family. We are able to experience and marvel at all the different cultural and religious expressions to which our brothers and sisters dedicate themselves. Through the ease of transportation, but even without physically traveling around the world, we can celebrate our world's cultures, histories, struggles, and the ways people understand themselves. We can join global social movements through social media and find the global family with all its diversity in our own neighborhoods.

This has led us to become increasingly sensitive to the social construction of knowledge, and how individuals understand the world from their own perspectives. We accept as normal that people from different cultures, ethnicities, ages, genders, sexual orientations, and classes will see the world differently. Coupled with our awareness of how knowledge changes and has changed over time, we sense the impermanence of truth and reality. Just as there is no permanence in the physical world, there is no permanence in the social world. Human knowledge, as much as anything else in creation, is an emerging and an emergent reality.

Therefore, postmodern culture is defined by a sense of pluralism in which the only acceptable metanarrative is that there is no possibility of a metanarrative that can explain all things for all time. Nothing is absolute or set in stone, and everything depends on one's particular frame of reference. These principles were reinforced and moved to a much deeper level by developments in the physical sciences, which began to emerge in the early twentieth century.

Think how dramatically our commonsense understanding of the universe in which we live has changed over the last fifty years. In that time span, we have come to recognize the existence of dark energy and dark matter. We have developed models for understanding the energy states of protons, neutrons, and electrons. Going even deeper into the microcosm, we found quarks to be the building blocks of matter. We have developed a whole new mechanics for dealing with the microcosm of fermions and bosons. We have come to a new appreciation for the age, size, and complexity of the macrocosm, and we have discovered its increasing expansion and the role of inflation in its origins. Most recently, we have been experimenting with the transformation of light into matter. We have killed Pluto as a planet but discovered thousands of others. We have added the strong and the weak forces to our subatomic understanding and developed sophisticated models for seeing into the origins of our universe and the emergence of human life.

In all of this, we have come to accept that probability has displaced certainty. We have realized that the world at all its levels is immensely complex, diverse, emerging, and emergent. And, we have ascertained that everything is relational and intimately tied together through forces and fields. In fact, that relationship can be so intimate at certain levels that we can talk about entanglement as oneness.

In summary, postmodern culture is made up of a radical historical consciousness that tends to make all truth claims relative. It is open to plural understandings and emphasizes the social construction of all reality. Scientific developments in understanding the complexity of the universe and its immensity raise major questions concerning our ability to know anything with certainty.[8]

For Bauman, the implications regarding identity are dramatic. He claims that the postmoderns avoid a fixed identity and, instead, seek to keep their options open. They avoid long-term commitments, and in place of lifelong projects, they prefer a series of short projects. Because the rules of the game are constantly changing, delaying gratification makes no sense. Space or distance is irrelevant as our software universe allows us to traverse space almost instantaneously, canceling the "far away" and the "down here." Fluid lifestyles emerge as the dominant identities of people. They are "strollers," "vagabonds," "tourists," or "players," as Bauman labels the types.[9]

The "strollers" are those who walk gazing at the scenery, including other people, all the while creating their own narratives about its meaning. Malls as promenades and parks were safe havens for "strollers," which eventually led to the shopping malls. The extremes of this type are those who spend a great deal of time gazing at flat screens and two-dimensional reality without having to walk at all or actively engage the other. If they do walk, it is with their noise-canceling headsets, oblivious to the world around them.

The "vagabonds" are those who move at will with no other purpose than to move on. Each place is simply a stopover, and they have no sense of how long they will be at any particular spot. In early modernity, the "vagabonds" were few in number and moved from one settled place to another settled place. In late modernity, their numbers increased dramatically as settled places dis-

---

8. In *Christian Community in History: Ecclesial Existence,* vol. 3 (New York: Continuum, 2008), 244–45, Roger Haight explicitly lays out the problems raised for missionary activity by postmodernity as globalization, historical consciousness, and a pluralist consciousness. Globalization is forcing nations to recognize other nations and cultures in the economic and political spheres as they negotiate their own place in this interdependent globe. Historical consciousness that once was restricted primarily to intellectuals and academics has trickled down to the commonsense understanding of people in general. Universal and eternal truth has been shaken at its bedrock by the sense that particular location, time, and culture all influence what we believe at any particular time. Finally, people, on a large scale, are beginning not only to expect difference but to appraise it positively.

9. Zygmunt Bauman, "From Pilgrim to Tourist—or a Short History of Identity," in Stuart Hall and Paul du Gay, eds., *Questions of Cultural Identity* (London: Sage Publications, 1996).

appeared. Neighborhoods transitioned, factories moved away, certain skills lost their utility, knowledge turned to ignorance, and stable relationships fell apart, leading to this growing number of people who travel out of necessity from one unsettled place to another.

The "tourists" are those who continuously move in search of new experiences. They look for the exotic, but to protect themselves they want to experience it in a domesticated fashion. They want a safe place to which they can return, but, when they arrive there, they often express the need for more space, for a new adventure.

Finally, "the players," or what might now be called "the gamers," view life as a game in which even the world is a player. If you don't like the game you're free to leave it. The object of the game is winning, and therefore, it should have a definite point at which it is over. Everyone should finish the game without grudges or psychological scars and be ready to move on to the next game.

According to Bauman, the consequences of these four identity types of postmodern culture are disengagement and commitment avoidance, which stifle any moral impulse to act toward the other. They all favor and promote distance between themselves and the other and cast the other primarily as an object of aesthetics rather than of moral impulse.

The common initial reaction to postmodern culture is to assume its characteristics have negative implications for Christian faith and Christian mission. With all its talk about the impossibility of truth claims and metanarratives, its emphasis on relativity, and its implicit stoic-nihilistic tendencies, postmodern culture is seen quite naturally to question, at a foundational level, the possibility of revelation, faith, evangelization, and faith-based ethics and morals. This is the context that explains the reaction by many religious followers who view this culture and the changes it is bringing about as a threat.

I propose that postmodern culture, in questioning modernity's claims of certainty, rather than shutting down the possibility of faith, opens up a new and exciting understanding of Christian mission. If we scrutinize postmodern culture from the perspective of the "glass half-full" rather than "half-empty," we discover that its questioning of certainty, its interpretive categories, and its scientific understanding of the universe all open up for us the possibility of moving our understanding of Christian mission beyond the limits of the past fifty years since Vatican II.

The Glass Half-Full

Uncertainty

Among the revelatory elements of postmodern culture, the one that I as a believer think is essential is this "uncertainty" or the scientific shift from certainty to probability. For some, uncertainty denotes ambiguity or confusion, and so is seen as a source of anxiety and tension. But what if, instead, using the lens of our culture, we see uncertainty as a reality that marks the social and physical world and, as such, a gift. For one thing, uncertainty is the ground of questioning. It leads the curious to ask: Why are we doing this; what should we do; or how can we do it better?

More importantly, the gift of uncertainty allows us to share the common table of planet Earth, knowing that no one of us has all the truth, all of us are searching with good will, and that we are searching for answers to the deepest questions about who we are as human beings. It is the gift of uncertainty that moves us to view mission as God's, realizing that the primary agent of mission is God and not us. It requires a renewed sense of the need for contemplation and imagination—listening to the voice of God in creation and culture, including postmodern culture. It is this gift of uncertainty that opens us up to empowering encounters with the other, with a renewed sense of searching together in the "ground" of our culture for our commonness and our survival.

Celebrating Diversity

This naturally leads, then, to the question of how I as a believer understand the "other." And I will offer my conclusion first, that the "other" is not an opponent with whom we Christians need to contend or to negotiate a peaceful coexistence. Rather, the "other" is an intimate and integral part of who we are and who we say our God as Trinity is. Thus, for believers in the Trinity, diversity should be celebrated and nourished.

For a Christian believer, the mystery of the Trinity is not just about unity, it is also about the "threeness." Borrowing from Derrida, the concept he calls "*différance*" can bring a fresh perspective to understanding this "threeness." In describing this concept of "differance," scholars highlight two distinct senses.

"Differance" refers to grasping meaning by way of contrast. For example, we understand tall as not being short, green as not being red, and a chair as not being a table. This is "differance" as difference or contrast. However, "differance" contains an additional idea: that is, that contrast is productive not only for defining what a thing is but also for underscoring its characteristic openness.

"Differance" carries with it the temporal idea of "deferring." "Differance" "defers" closure to a set way of understanding a phenomenon in order to remain open to there "being more." For example, with regard to gender or sexual orientation, "differance" leads us to recognize that while there are real differences in how people perceive themselves, a simple dichotomy between male and female, gay and straight, does not capture the reality of the diversity of genders and sexual orientations that we know today or may know in the future.

Thus, as a believer in God as Trinity, I believe "differance" relates to the mystery of the Trinity. It helps us understand the importance of the persons in defining each as different and in their reaching beyond themselves by deferring closure. This openness to "being more," deferring closure, for us trinitarian believers, is what ushers forth creation with all of its diversity, plurality, and complexity.

This understanding of the Trinity opens to us the possibility of believing in divine life without feeling the need to homogenize creation. In David Cunningham's words, "In the postmodern era, such 'differance' has reemerged as something for which human beings can rejoice and be thankful, rather than something that needs to be subordinated to an all-embracing desire for uniformity." This vision recognizes the absolute necessity of the "other" for me to be who I am. Thus, in mission, we should be searching for our commonness—not our "sameness." Our commonness should not devalue our "otherness" but, rather, celebrate it as essential to who we are and who we understand our God as Trinity to be.

Oneness

In this beautiful mystery of creation, including human histories and cultures, we find the first audible and visible expressions of the Word of God. As Paul said, "Ever since the creation of the world, God's eternal power and divine nature, invisible though they are, have been understood and seen through the things God has made" (Rom 1:19–20). From particle physics, philosophy, social sciences, but, more importantly, through the struggles of everyday life, we know that the universe is made up of elements and forces that are intimately related to one another in a deep, mutual, and intimate fashion. With globalization, as Robert Schreiter says, people have become increasingly aware of the interconnectedness of the human family.[10] All of these insights of the postmodern age combine to reveal the profundity of Jesus' missionary prayer: "so that they may be one, as we are one; I in them and you in me that they may be brought to perfection as one" (John 17:21–23).

And yet, while God reveals in creation and in postmodern culture that we are intimately related to one another, the culture of modern capitalism emphasizes the fundamental lie that we are autonomous individuals. This lie gives birth to a series of other lies that act as forces against our mutuality and oneness. It asserts that competition or rivalry is natural and necessary for the production of social order. Based on the idea that humans are subjects who

---

10. "Mission *Ad Gentes*: Yesterday, Today and Tomorrow," Reflections from Robert Schreiter, CPPS, to the Maryknoll Missionaries, Centennial Celebration of the Maryknoll Society Symposium held at Catholic Theological Union, Chicago, Illinois.

bring into being the meaning of objects, including other humans, it assumes a right to dominate creation and creatures.[11]

This thinking has led to the greatest economic disparity in the United States since before the Great Depression of 1929. It has fostered the continual separation among nations, in terms of wealth, and within nations in terms of ever-increasing economic inequality. It has fostered, as Jimmy Carter and others have highlighted, forms of modern slavery and human trafficking. The notion of ourselves as autonomous individuals who objectify and dominate is further reflected in the number of cases of domestic violence, sexual assault, and rape of minors. This thinking directly relates to our misuse of the environment, leaving Mother Earth scarred with our garbage, our pollution, and our degradation. It is also the basis of ongoing wars throughout the world.

When we ask why this is happening, we find the very heart of the answer in the drive for self-preservation, the modern creation of the autonomous individual, the view of the other as an object or threat, and, most importantly, our failure to listen to the voice of God. God's call, heard through the lens of postmodern culture, is challenging us to an intimate and mutual relationship with one another and with creation.

The Joy of the Cross

Just after the missionary prayer of Jesus in John's Gospel is the narrative of the paschal, or life-through-death, mystery of the cross. It is deemed the fullest, clearest, and most profound window we have into the heart of God as Trinity. While it is commonly claimed that postmodern culture is deeply skeptical of any overarching or metanarrative, one event that postmodern philosophers agree is universal to humans, at least for now, is the centrality of death and, more specifically, our consciousness of it.

Jacques Derrida described the "gift of death" as the foundation for living a truly human life. Even though he makes it clear that Christian revelation is unnecessary for him to arrive at this conclusion, Derrida uses an Abrahamic image to develop his thesis. Reflecting on the story of Abraham in the book of Genesis, he says:

> It is finally in renouncing life, the life of his son that one has every reason to think is more precious than his own, that Abraham gains or wins. He risks winning; more precisely, having renounced winning, expecting neither response nor recompense, expecting nothing that can be given back to him, nothing that will come back to him, he sees that God gives back to him in the instant of absolute renunciation, the very

---

11. Taken from Zygmunt Bauman, *Does the Richness of the Few Benefit Us All?* (Cambridge: Polity Press, 2013).

thing that he had already, in the same instant decided to sacrifice. It is given back to him because he renounced calculation.[12]

Derrida stresses that Christianity itself has neither taken seriously its own central revelation nor the radical implications of it. Derrida's challenge, to all of us who struggle to understand our Christian faith and mission in postmodern culture, is to study more deeply the central message of the narrative we embrace. He forcefully implies that the lens of postmodern culture, which sees death and our consciousness of it as the central mystery of who we are as human beings, will allow us to find in the central Christian mystery of the cross a new richness.

Derrida also answers the critics of postmodern culture who claim it to be a sea of relativism. He insists that meaning, morals, ethics, freedom, and responsibility do have grounding in postmodern culture—in "the gift of death." Meaning comes from learning to live into this mystery or, as the title of the last interview with Derrida manifests, from "Learning to Live Finally," or, as Jesus said, "No one takes my life from me but I hand it over."

All of us are going to die, that is the "ground" of our commonness. Embracing that reality opens us to potentially living our lives by breaking through the fear of death in order to love. The fear of death and the associated fear of vulnerability and uncertainty are expressed in a very real fear of intimacy with one another. At the foundation of our fears and failures in relationships and dialogue is the very real resistance to accept our own mortality, vulnerability, and fragility, and the mortality, vulnerability, and fragility of our institutions. At the foundation of our fears and failures in relating to the "other" is our very real resistance to embrace "learning to live finally," that is, finding our commonness in the "ground" of our creation.

---

12. Jacques Derrida, *The Gift of Death* (Chicago: University of Chicago Press, 1995), 96–97. In *Learning to Live Finally: The Last Interview*, Derrida poetically claimed, "So, to finally answer your question, no, I never learned-to-live. In fact not at all! Learning to live should mean learning to die, learning to take into account, so as to accept, absolute mortality. . . . I live my death in writing. It's the ultimate test: one expropriates oneself without knowing exactly who is being entrusted with what is left behind. Who is going to inherit and how? Will there even be any heirs."

13

Interculturality as a Paradigm of Mission

Roger Schroeder, SVD

The development of the global village over the past fifty years has brought an exponentially expanding number of peoples around the world into contact with one another in the areas of economics, politics, social relationships, and religion. This dramatic phenomenon in the history of humanity is linked to the multidirectional increase in human migration, air travel, international business, and social media. Like the technological inventions of the wheel, printing press, and steam engine in the past, the Internet, computer, and cell phone are reshaping our world today. Men, women, and children of different cultures and contexts have more and more opportunities of interacting with one another.

As for general global trends regarding interactions among different cultures,[1] the mid-sixties in many ways marked the beginning of a sometimes

---

Roger Schroeder, SVD, earned a doctorate degree in missiology from the Pontifical Gregorian University in Rome in 1990. Since then he has taught at Catholic Theological Union in Chicago, where he holds the Louis J. Luzbetak, SVD Chair of Mission and Culture. His publications include *What Is the Mission of the Church? A Guide for Catholics* (Maryknoll, NY: Orbis Books, 2008, 2018) and the following books co-authored with Stephen Bevans: *Constants in Context: A Theology of Mission for Today* (Maryknoll, NY: Orbis Books, 2004), and *Prophetic Dialogue: Reflections on Christian Mission Today* (Maryknoll, NY: Orbis Books, 2011). A member of the Society of the Divine Word (SVD), he worked as a missionary in Papua New Guinea for six years. His recent writing has been in the areas of World Christianity, interculturality, and indigenous peoples.

1. Within the context of rapidly changing societies, "cultures" are no longer defined as static, coherent, and permanent "wholes" that guide thinking and living. Culture is now preferably understood as a dynamic and changing set of beliefs and values that inform common ways of interpreting reality and interacting with one another. Therefore, the term "culture" today would also include social change (due to such factors as globalization, migration, and intergenerational dynamics), social location (i.e., rich/poor; male/female, citizen or not), and particular personal, communal, and local factors. For an in-depth study of the implications of this postmodern understanding of culture for the church and mission, see Michael Rynkiewich, *Soul, Self, and Society: A Postmodern Anthropology for Mission in a Postmodern World* (Eugene,

turbulent transition out of paternalism and explicit racism. This was prompted by political and social movements, such as the civil rights movement in the United States and the decline of colonialism around the world. The social sciences describe the on-going challenge since then as moving toward mutually beneficial relationships between cultures—described as interculturality—in the face of ethnocentrism, de-coloniality, and globalization.[2]

Within this social, political, and economic context, the Roman Catholic Church through the Second Vatican Council, which ended in 1965, officially shifted from a negative to a much more positive theological attitude toward the world and all cultures. In the following five decades, through various aspects of inculturation and by relating to the world today, the church has developed, nuanced, and sometimes struggled with its theology and practice.

During this time, international men's and women's religious congregations have been greatly affected by the above-mentioned global trends in the world, positively and negatively. Congregations form and are formed by the theology and practice of the Catholic Church in terms of their attitude toward peoples of different cultures and contexts. As a case in point, the missionary Society of the Divine Word (SVD) mirrored this development and challenge in its own way. Its primary understanding of itself (*ad intra*) and its relation with others (*ad extra*) can be described as shifting from international to multicultural to intercultural, with the primary goal of this interaction shifting from tolerance to acceptance to mutual enrichment, respectively. The theme of the SVD General Chapter of 2012 was "Sharing Intercultural Life and Mission."[3]

This chapter will develop interculturality as a paradigm of mission. I begin by laying the foundation from the primary mission theologies of the Catholic Church over the past fifty years. Second, the models of contextual theology developed by Stephen Bevans will serve as a framework for interpreting the interaction between Christian faith and culture in each theology. Third, building upon the preceding material, I will present a mission paradigm—theology and principles—of interculturality.

Mission Theology "Building Blocks"

From a number of major mission theologies that have developed around the Christian world over the past fifty years (1965–2015), the focus here will be

OR: Cascade Books, 2011); Gerard Arbuckle, *Culture, Inculturation, Theologians: A Postmodern Critique* (Collegeville, MN: Liturgical Press, 2010).

2. See Roger Schroeder, "Interculturality and Prophetic Dialogue," *Verbum SVD* 54, no. 1 (2013): 9–10.

3. *Documents of the XVII General Chapter SVD, In Dialogue with the Word* (IDW), no. 11 (Rome: SVD Publications, September 2012), 11–30.

on the primary ones within the Catholic Church. Without denying the very significant contributions by theologians, the presentation of each mission theology centers on a key Catholic mission document.

Participation in the Mission of the Triune God (Missio Dei)[4]

Before the Second Vatican Council, the predominant mission theologies and motivations within the Catholic Church, and most other Christian churches, were centered on the salvation of souls and expansion of the church.[5] Two major shifts of perspective, affecting mission theology and practice, occurred with Vatican II. First, the mission of the Trinity was seen as the beginning and the end of the church's mission. As stated in its *Decree on the Church's Missionary Activity* (*Ad Gentes*): "The pilgrim Church is missionary by its very nature. For it is from the mission of the Son and the mission of the Holy Spirit that it takes its origin, in accordance with the decree of God the Father" (AG 2). In the same paragraph, God the Father is presented as a life-giving fountain of love, watering the world and calling all of humanity to share in the fullness of God's life. God has always been in mission through the Spirit, in creation and throughout history. Jesus Christ, as God incarnate and the "face" of the Spirit, called the disciples and the church to continue his mission. In today's terminology, the church doesn't have a mission, but the mission of God has a church.

Second, the church's attitude toward the world changed. The church was seen as a pilgrim people of God and not as a perfect society or as equal to the reign of God (LG 1, 5). Nevertheless, the church is the sacrament of salvation and is to witness to God's reign. Furthermore, the church and the world have both grace and sin. Since the whole world is already graced through the Spirit, the church is not to be a haven from a sinful world but rather a partner with God in bringing salvation and reconciliation. In other words, the embracing and on-going mission of God cannot be contained in or limited to the church, so it must look for God's activity in the world and all of creation in the "signs of the times" (GS 4). Therefore, the church is to be present to all aspects of creation, including other Christian churches and all cultures and religions (GS 22 and see NA).

The following key passage from *Ad Gentes* represents this positive attitude found throughout the council documents toward culture.[6]

---

4. See Stephen Bevans and Roger Schroeder, *Constants in Context: A Theology of Mission for Today* (Maryknoll, NY: Orbis Books, 2004), 286–304.

5. For some of the alternate theologies that were beginning to emerge, see ibid., 244–49, 255–59.

6. Aylward Shorter, *Toward a Theology of Inculturation* (London: Geoffrey Chapman, 1988), 191–205.

The seed which is the word of God grows out of good soil watered by divine dew, it absorbs moisture, transforms it, and makes it part of itself, so that eventually it bears much fruit. So too indeed, just as happened in the economy of the incarnation, the young Churches . . . borrow from the customs, traditions, wisdom, teaching, arts and sciences of their people everything which could be used to praise the glory of the Creator, manifest the grace of the Savior, or contribute to the right ordering of Christian life. (AG 22)

The process, known later as inculturation, would soon be considered relevant and essential for all local churches, not just the "younger" ones.

The rich theology of *missio Dei* did not have an immediate strong impact in the Catholic Church, but since the 1980s, "there has been a genuine renewal in trinitarian theology in Catholic, Protestant, Evangelical, and Pentecostal theology, and it is possible to say that the understanding of mission as rooted in the trinitarian mission of God in the world is once again at the forefront of missiological thinking."[7]

Liberating Service of the Reign of God[8]

Using the reflections of the 1974 Synod of Bishops on "Evangelization," Pope Paul VI published in 1975 *The Apostolic Exhortation on Evangelization in the Modern World* (*Evangelii Nuntiandi*). Rather than starting with the Trinity, he started with the mission of Jesus, of proclaiming, serving, and witnessing to the reign of God, which "is so important that, by comparison, everything else becomes 'the rest', which is 'given in addition'" (EN 8). The church is to continue the holistic mission of Jesus, which touched the spiritual, physical, and social aspects of people's lives. Due to the influence of the Medellin Conference of Latin American Bishops in 1968 and the link between mission and justice in the Synod of Bishops in Rome in 1971, the term "liberation" appears for the first time in an official Catholic Church document, in *Evangelii Nuntiandi*.

In terms of culture, Paul VI, speaking in Uganda in 1969, stated that "you may, and you must, have an African Christianity."[9] In the same vein, *Evangelii Nuntiandi* makes the following affirmation: "evangelization would not be complete if it did not take into account the unceasing interplay of the Gospel and of humans' concrete life, both personal and social. . . . This is why evangelization involves an explicit message . . . about international life, peace, justice and development—a message especially energetic today about liberation" (EN 29).

---

7. Bevans and Schroeder, *Constants in Context*, 291.

8. See ibid., 305–22.

9. Paul VI, "Closing Discourse to All-Africa Symposium," quoted in Aylward Shorter, *African Christian Theology* (Maryknoll, NY: Orbis Books, 1975), 20.

This powerful statement illustrates what this exhortation introduced as evangelizing the very roots of culture (EN 20). While the gospel is not identical with any culture, building up the reign of God "cannot avoid borrowing the elements of human culture and cultures . . . ," which in turn "have to be regenerated by an encounter with the Gospel" (EN 20). This reflects both the incarnation and paschal mystery dynamics necessary for inculturation.

Authors of a wide variety of liberation theologies, as well as other Catholic and Protestant theologians, have continued to develop the reign of God theology.[10]

Proclamation of Jesus Christ as Universal Savior[11]

While affirming these first two mission theologies, Pope John Paul II and some other church officials were concerned that the trinitarian emphasis on the holiness of the world, on cultures and religions and the reign of God, as well as the emphasis on justice and liberation might not give sufficient attention to the role of Jesus as the unique savior and judge of culture, and to the important role of the church in mission. In response, John Paul II issued the 1990 encyclical letter, *On the Permanent Validity of the Church's Missionary Mandate* (*Redemptoris Missio*). "Why mission? Because to us . . . 'this grace was given, to preach to the Gentiles the unsearchable riches of Christ' (Eph 3:8)" (RM 11). Although it is possible to be saved outside the church and explicit faith in Christ, the church still has the obligation to witness to and proclaim Jesus as universal savior. *Redemptoris Missio* includes the trinitarian (chap. 3) and reign of God (chap. 2) theologies, while the Christocentric mission theology is the central theology.

Regarding culture, John Paul II had earlier in 1982 established the Pontifical Council for Culture. He described the link between Christianity and culture in this way: "the synthesis between culture and faith is not just a demand of culture, but also of faith. A faith which does not become culture is a faith which has not been fully received, not thoroughly thought through, not fully lived out."[12] *Redemptoris Missio* provides objective criteria for inculturation, particularly "compatibility with the Gospel and communion with the universal Church" (RM 54).

This encyclical letter highlights the important role of bishops in this process, while also rightly affirming that "inculturation must involve the whole people of God . . . , since the people reflect the authentic 'sensus fidei' which must never be lost sight of" (RM 54). However, underlying the papacy of John Paul II was the sense that he "appreciates the synthesis in the historic

10. Bevans and Schroeder, *Constants in Context*, 310–17.

11. Ibid., 323–47.

12. Pope's communication with the council, *L'Osservatore Romano*, June 28, 1982, 1–8.

cultures of Christian Europe, and fears for the future, while at the same time hesitating to risk the deposit of faith in a dialogue with the cultures of the non-Christian Third World."[13]

A number of Roman Catholic, Evangelical, and Pentecostal theologians have developed this Christocentric mission theology, without being in opposition to the other two theologies.[14] As every theology has its potential weaknesses and dangers, the Christocentric perspective can lead to narrow exclusivism and a very strong distrust of culture. While it "needs to be a vital part of the twenty-first-century theology of mission, it needs to temper and be tempered by the other two perspectives. . . ."[15]

Community of Missionary Disciples

A Synod of Bishops met in 2012 on the theme of "The New Evangelization for the Transmission of the Christian Faith." Before the synod, "new evangelization" focused on a renewed boldness in witnessing to and preaching the gospel, and on doing this primarily in the secularized culture of the West. However, the "calls at the synod for a more open, listening church; the shifts toward spirituality, structured reform, and dialogue; and the insistence on a renewed form of evangelization for the entire church, not just the West, are all features of the remarkable postsynodal apostolic exhortation by the newly elected Pope Francis"[16] entitled *The Joy of the Gospel* (*Evangelii Gaudium*). In comparison with the other Catholic documents treated so far in this chapter, *Evangelii Gaudium* is less theological, and more pastoral or homiletic in tone and style.

In this apostolic exhortation, Pope Francis's key description of the church as "a community of missionary disciples" (EG 24, also see 120) reinforces the understanding from *Ad Gentes* of the church as "missionary by its very nature." He emphasizes that the church grows not from proselytizing but "by attraction" (EG 14), and the words "mercy" and "tenderness" are featured prominently throughout the apostolic exhortation. A review of the 217 endnotes of *Evangelii Gaudium* indicates that Francis drew consistently from the documents of Vatican II, *Evangelii Nuntiandi, Redemptoris Missio,* and other writings and speeches of John Paul II and Benedict XVI. His many references to a number of regional and national church documents highlight his concern for the world church, and the recurring references to the 2007 *Aparecida Document* of the Fifth General Conference of the Latin American and Caribbean Bishops point to the important influence of his social

---

13. Shorter, *Theology of Inculturation,* 231.

14. Bevans and Schroeder, *Constants in Context,* 330–40.

15. Ibid., 331.

16. Stephen Bevans, "New Evangelization or Missionary Church? *Evangelii Gaudium* and the Call for Missionary Discipleship," *Verbum SVD* 55, nos. 2–3 (2014): 169.

and ecclesial location. In developing his mission theology, Francis is drawing from the rich storehouse of the trinitarian, reign of God, and Christocentric theologies from the perspective of the first Latin American pope. The church as a "*mystery* rooted in the Trinity" (EG 111) carries out its mission with "the primacy of the proclamation of Jesus Christ in all evangelizing work" (EG 110), and the "Gospel is about *the kingdom of God* . . ." (EG 180, italics in document).

As for culture, *Evangelii Gaudium* affirms that the Holy Spirit "brings forth a rich variety of gifts, while at the same time creating a unity which is never uniformity, but a multifaceted and inviting harmony" within the church (EG 117). Proclaiming the gospel to cultures includes appreciating popular piety (EG 122–26), engaging "professional, scientific and academic circles" (EG 132–34), and preaching in light of the questions and human experiences of the congregation (EG 154–55). At the same time, inculturation of the gospel implies being in solidarity with the poor (EG 197–201), resolving "the structural causes of poverty" (EG 202–8), and being attentive to the vulnerable, including creation (EG 209–16). Finally, Francis uses the "pillars of the Church's social doctrine" (EG 220) to provide guidelines for the church to engage and dialogue with the state and society in their pursuit of the common good and peace (EG 217–37), and with science, other Christian churches, and other religions (EG 238–58).

Theology and Culture

Having reviewed the primary mission theologies within the Catholic Church as the building blocks for a mission theology of interculturality, I will now briefly describe, and then use models of, contextual theology as a framework for interpreting the types of encounters between Christian faith and human culture within the differing theologies.

Models of Contextual Theology

Stephen Bevans provides us with an excellent study of the models of contextual theology[17] that helps in understanding the theological attitude toward culture, or what he refers to in broader terms as "context" (in line with the dynamic postmodern understanding of culture).[18] First of all, models are streamlined, artificially constructed ways of thinking that can help in identifying current patterns. Bevans's models are not exclusive but rather com-

---

17. Stephen Bevans, *Models of Contextual Theology*, rev. and exp. ed. (Maryknoll, NY: Orbis Books, 2002); Stephen Bevans, *An Introduction to Theology in Global Perspective* (Maryknoll, NY: Orbis Books, 2009), 164–88.

18. See footnote 1.

plementary and inclusive. Second, he describes contextual theology as the dialogue between the experience of the *past*, as found in scripture and church tradition, and the experience of the *present* (context), which includes human experience, culture, social location, and social change.[19] The models reflect the basic perspectives regarding the past and present along this continuum. Third, each model reflects a valid Christian approach.

The *translation model* focuses on the faithful transmission of the gospel, and culture is seen not as something good and revelatory in itself but as a neutral means for doing so. The *anthropological model* focuses on the goodness and possibility of revelation in culture that may offer new richness to Christian faith. The *praxis model* focuses on the dimensions of culture related to social change, and a reinterpretation of Christianity through a process of reflective action for change that embodies Christian principles. The *counter-cultural model* approaches culture with suspicion, and focuses on the confrontation of culture with the culturally specific, yet universally valid, gospel message. The *synthetic model* focuses on the ambiguity of any culture, and looks to other cultures and successful Christian expressions of faith for the most adequate one. The *transcendental model* focuses on the ability of an individual to spark authentic Christian and cultural thinking in dialogue. In terms of the overall continuum, the anthropological and transcendental models give priority to the experience of the present (context), the translation and counter-cultural models to the experience of the past, and the praxis and synthetic models are around the middle.

Interaction of Culture and Faith in Mission Theologies

I shall use these models to situate the perspective toward culture in the four major theologies of mission under consideration. Theology based on the *Trinity* appreciates culture quite favorably. The dogmatic decree *Ad Gentes* describes culture, in its broad sense, as containing "a sort of secret presence of God" (AG 9) and "seeds of the Word" (AG 11). However, the Vatican document also acknowledges that all cultures need to be illumined by the gospel and freed from darkness. The following guidance is offered to missionaries or anyone encountering people of another culture. "Thus they themselves can learn by sincere and patient dialogue what treasures a bountiful God has distributed among the nations of the earth. But at the same time, let them try to illumine these treasures with the light of the gospel, to set them free, and to bring them under the dominion of God their Savior" (AG 11).

In other words, according to trinitarian theology in general, "culture, for eyes of faith, becomes a way of deepening in a fully human and contextual way, human knowledge of and relation with the Mystery," but at the same

---

19. See Bevans, *Introduction to Theology*, 169–71.

time, the gospel confronts "any forms of culture that do not acknowledge human dignity and equality or all of creation's interrelatedness."[20] In summary, the trinitarian theology has a critically positive attitude toward culture and would tend to follow the anthropological and moderate counter-cultural models.

Reign of God theology is primarily positive toward culture. It acknowledges God's presence within human culture and history. In terms of Bevans's framework, *Evangelii Nuntiandi* explicitly addressed the need for maintaining the integrity of cultural adaptation, on the one hand, and the gospel and universal church tradition, on the other.

> Evangelization loses much of its force and effectiveness if it does not take into consideration the actual people to whom it is addressed, if it does not use their language, their signs and symbols, if it does not answer the questions they ask, and if it does not have an impact on their concrete life. But on the other hand evangelization risks losing its power and disappearing altogether if one empties or adulterates its content under the pretext of translating it. . . . (EN 63)

Such adaptation or inculturation by individual or local churches "in a variety of cultural, social and human terrains" (EN 62) "cannot fail to enrich the Church" (EN 63). "Culture, while generally good, can be coopted by the structures of oppression and exclusion, and is often, if not always, in need of prophetic correction in the light of the values of God's reign."[21] Therefore, evangelization includes struggling to eliminate everything which marginalizes people—"famine, chronic disease, illiteracy, poverty, injustices in international relations and especially in commercial exchanges, situations of economic and cultural neo-colonialism sometimes as cruel as the old political colonialism" (EN 30). The reign of God mission theology is primarily positive toward culture, and would tend to follow the praxis and moderate counter-cultural models.

Christocentric theology has a more negative, or at best, a neutral assessment of culture. *Redemptoris Missio* maintains the importance and even the urgency (RM 52) of inculturation, so that the church "becomes a more intelligible sign of what she is, and a more effective instrument of mission," and is "enriched with the forms of expression and values in the various sectors of Christian life" (RM 52). However, as noted above, safeguarding compatibility with the gospel and the universal church is the top priority. At the same time, this encyclical letter opens up the concern of evangelization to broader aspects of society, like urbanization, youth, migration, and poverty, and to

---

20. Bevans and Schroeder, *Constants in Context*, 303.
21. Ibid., 321.

what are called the "modern equivalents of the Areopagus," such as modern communications (RM 37bc). "There are many other forms of the 'Areopagus' in the modern world towards which the Church's missionary activity ought to be directed; for example, commitment to peace, development and the liberation of peoples; the rights of individuals and peoples, especially those of minorities; the advancement of women and children; safeguarding the created world" (RM 37c).

For Christocentric theologies, generally speaking, understanding cultures is essential for communicating the gospel, but cultures are not considered very important as a locus of God's presence. "Cultures are regarded as deeply ambiguous, and need to be either confronted by the gospel or enriched or fulfilled by it."[22] These theologies of mission generally have a more negative attitude toward culture and inculturation, and they tend to use translation or counter-cultural models.

Evangelii Gaudium is quite positive toward culture. Francis fundamentally sees cultures as gifts inspired by the Holy Spirit with the potential for forming a multifaceted and harmonious unity within the church (EG 117, 122). "This means more than acknowledging occasional 'seeds of the word,' since it has to do with an authentic Christian faith which has its own expressions and means of showing its relationship to the Church" (EG 68). This appreciation for culture and human experience touches all aspects of church life, from preaching to popular piety, and it propels the Catholic Church to engage and dialogue with the world and all creation—science, academia, society, and other churches and religions. At the same time, *Evangelii Gaudium* acknowledges that "each culture and social group needs purification and growth" (EG 69). In highlighting a prophetic cry on behalf of the poor, Francis consequently calls for resolving "the structural causes of poverty," which includes "rejecting the absolute autonomy of markets and financial speculation . . ." (EG 202). An example of a critical appreciation and critique of society is Francis's comment that while there is an "innate tension" between globalization and localization, we need both to avoid dangerous extremes (EG 234). In conclusion, *Evangelii Gaudium* appreciates culture fairly favorably, and it would tend to follow moderate praxis, moderate anthropological, and/or moderate counter-cultural models.

Interculturality as a Paradigm of Mission

This review of Catholic mission theologies, from the perspective of contextual theology, has mapped the developing understanding of the intersection of culture with Christian faith over the past fifty years. I will now present a

---

22. Ibid., 346.

mission paradigm with interculturality as its core. This will be done in terms of theology and basic principles.

Theology

The theological framework of *Evangelii Gaudium*, drawing from current mission theologies, offers an excellent foundation for interculturality as a paradigm of mission. It begins with a trinitarian theology. "The Holy Spirit, sent by the Father and the Son, transforms our hearts and enables us to enter into the perfect communion of the blessed Trinity, where all things find their unity. He builds up the communion and harmony of the people of God. The same Spirit is that harmony, just as he is the bond of love between the Father and the Son" (EG 117).

Cultures are gifts through the Spirit and bearers of the "seeds of the Word," echoing *Ad Gentes* (11). They enrich the church and "do justice to the logic of the incarnation" (EG 117). Robert Kisala, in developing the trinitarian foundation for interculturality, states that "the realization of this perfect communion of humanity within the community of the Trinity is the goal of God's mission."[23] In order to participate in God's mission, Francis urges the church to dialogue with the "signs of the times," both within and outside the church. At the same time, each culture also contains "weeds" and needs to be illumined and transformed by the gospel. That is, every culture must face the on-going process of dying and being renewed, as in the paschal mystery. Within this context, interculturality is an essential part of our participation in God's mission, which needs to move beyond mere tolerance and acceptance of other cultures to mutual enrichment. Furthermore, this mutual enrichment includes mutual transformation or conversion.

As its second theological "leg," *Evangelii Gaudium* affirms the reign of God theology found in *Evangelii Nuntiandi* and the *Aparecida Document*. In carrying out the *missio Dei*, Jesus Christ proclaimed, served, and witnessed to God's reign, and he called his disciples to continue this holistic mission. God's reign is already present in human experience, history, and culture, but at the same time, it is not yet present in its fullness.

In that vein, Paul VI emphasized that mission needs to engage the "very roots of culture" (EN 20). As *Evangelii Nuntiandi* pointed out the need to bring a message of liberation to the life situations of "poverty, injustices in international relations and especially in commercial exchanges, situations of economic and cultural neo-colonialism" (EN 30), so *Evangelii Gaudium* calls for the need to resolve the "structural causes of poverty . . . [and] the absolute autonomy of markets and financial speculation" (EN 202). The reign of

---

23. Robert Kisala, "Theological Foundations of Interculturality," *Verbum SVD* 54, no. 1 (2013): 29.

God theology takes culture and human experience very seriously as arenas of God's activity. Interculturality addresses this aspect of the church's mission very intentionally. One also notes the overlap with the work of the social scientists in terms of the goal of interculturality and their broader understanding of culture or context today.

While the important concerns of the Christocentric theology for maintaining the role of Jesus as the savior and judge of culture and the significant role of the church in mission were certainly woven into the fabric of *Evangelii Gaudium*, the predominant theology of *Redemptoris Missio* did not have as much impact on the tone and content of Francis's apostolic exhortation as the other two mission theologies.

Normally, the initial stages of toleration and eventual acceptance among persons of different cultures are based primarily, but not exclusively, on the primary goodness of culture. However, with true interculturality, the individuals or communities acknowledge the gift and, more and more, the need for mutual enrichment and change in presenting the gospel. Another excellent way of describing and elaborating on this theologically (and practically) is the idea of "prophetic dialogue," which Stephen Bevans develops in another chapter of this edited work. Briefly speaking, interculturality is both *dialogical*—acknowledging and engaging God's presence in human experience, culture, history, and all of creation—and *prophetic*—witnessing to and announcing God's reign and the gospel, and denouncing that which is contrary to it.[24]

Principles

The section in *Evangelii Gaudium* on "The Common Good and Peace in Society" (EG 217–36) proposes "four specific principles which can guide the development of life in society and the building of a people where differences are harmonized within a shared pursuit" (EG 221). Using these criteria, based on the church's social teachings, Francis then applies them to specific areas of dialogue, such as with states, societies, Christian churches, and world religions (EG 238–58). They are also very relevant in the area of interculturality, both within (*ad intra*) and outside (*ad extra*) the church or religious congregations. Francis notes that this is beyond simple tolerance—the "mere absence of violence" and maintaining a status quo of inequality (EG 218).

First of all, "time is greater than space" (EG 222–25). An individual or community needs to be committed to steady and often slow progress, not immediate results. "It helps us patiently to endure difficult and adverse

---

24. See Stephen Bevans and Roger Schroeder, *Prophetic Dialogue: Reflections on Christian Mission Today* (Maryknoll, NY: Orbis Books, 2011).

situations, or inevitable changes in our plans" (EG 223). It is a commitment to "*initiating processes rather than possessing spaces*" (EG 223, italics in document). In terms of mission, it "calls for attention to the bigger picture, openness to suitable processes and concern for the long run" (EG 225).

Second, "unity prevails over conflict" (EG 226–30). Rather than ignoring or being paralyzed by conflict or differences, people need to "face conflict head on, to resolve it and to make it a link in the chain of a new process" (EG 227). This requires going "beyond the surface of the conflict, and to see others in their deepest dignity . . ." in order to achieve "a resolution which takes place on a higher plane and preserves what is valid and useful on both sides" (EG 228). "Diversity is a beautiful thing when it can constantly enter into a process of reconciliation and seal a sort of cultural covenant resulting in a 'reconciled diversity'" (EG 230).

Third, "realities are more important than ideas" (EG 231–33). All areas requiring dialogue amid diversity need to be based on reality. "This calls for rejecting the various means for masking reality: angelic forms of purity, dictatorship of relativism, empty rhetoric, objectives more ideal than real . . ." (EG 231). Theologically, this means putting the "incarnation of the word . . . into practice" (EG 233). Interculturality requires engaging the real living situation of people, and not remaining "in the realm of pure ideas" (EG 233).

Fourth, "the whole is greater than the part" (EG 234–36). It is necessary, on the one hand, "to sink our roots deeper into the fertile soil and history of our native place, which is a gift of God," and on the other hand, "to broaden our horizons and see the greater good which will benefit us all" (EG 235). This implies mutual enrichment. Francis uses the image of a polyhedron, "which reflects the convergence of all its parts, each of which preserves its distinctiveness" (EG 236). As for theological wholeness, the gospel has the potential to heal "every aspect of humanity, until it has brought all men and women together at table in God's kingdom" (EG 237).

I would add a fifth element, which is implicit in the above principles. Such openness to dialogue requires a conversion from all forms of egoism, individualism, ethnocentrism, racism, classism, and nationalism. In another section of the apostolic exhortation, Francis calls for "the creation of a new mindset" (EG 188). Of course, this requires a conversion of both the mind and heart. Peter had to confront his ethnocentrism against the Gentiles—repeated three times during his prayer (Acts 10:14–17)—so that, in his encounter with Cornelius and his household, he could more fully participate in God's mission. The rest of the leadership of the early Christian community had to do the same at the Council of Jerusalem (Acts 15:4–21). Michael Amaladoss, writing about the prophetic element of engaging culture and society, insisted on "a call to conversion, *a challenge to change*, an invitation to realize the reign of God, an urge to enter into the creative dynamism of God's action in the world, making all things new."[25]

Conclusion

I have sketched out interculturality as a paradigm of mission by situating it within the rich Roman Catholic mission theologies of the past fifty years, and by focusing particularly on their approach to the interaction of culture and Christian faith. *Evangelii Gaudium* has served as an excellent resource in this process. At the same time, I consider this chapter as only the "tip of the iceberg." A mission paradigm centered on interculturality needs to be developed as well from the disciplines or fields of scripture, history, spirituality, religious life, pneumatology, ecclesiology, theology of culture, intercultural communication, and the social sciences. The other chapters of this volume contribute toward this fuller effort, of developing the paradigm and illustrating the myriad implications and consequences. Interculturality as a paradigm of mission highlights the inspiring and challenging opportunities for contributing to a fuller, but not complete, realization of God's reign around the "banquet table" in our world and in all of creation today.

---

25. Michael Amaladoss, "Mission as Prophecy," in James Scherer and Stephen Bevans, eds., *New Directions in Mission and Evangelization 2: Theological Foundations* (Maryknoll, NY: Orbis Books, 1994), 68.

14

Exploring Primary and New Evangelization
Perspectives from Asia's Multicultural Context

James H. Kroeger, MM

The Federation of Asian Bishops' Conferences (FABC) certainly has been the most influential body in the Asian church since the Second Vatican Council. Worldwide, probably no other church body has given more attention to the multifaceted task of contextual evangelization than has the FABC. In addition, the FABC has strengthened the bonds of communication among Catholic communities and has contributed to the development of a shared vision of the church and her evangelizing mission in Asia. The FABC asserts that the pathway for the church in Asia to truly discover its own identity is to continually engage in a threefold dialogue: with Asian peoples (especially the poor) [integral development], Asian cultures [inculturation], and Asian religions [interfaith dialogue]. This programmatic vision of a "triple dialogue" as a "new way of being Church in Asia" has constructively guided the FABC for over four decades. In a word, one can validly assert that the FABC is truly "Asia's Continuing Vatican II."

An FABC Introduction

Before addressing primary and new evangelization in the pluricultural context of Asia, a brief background contextualization on the FABC appears nec-

James H. Kroeger, MM, is professor of systematic theology and mission studies at Loyola School of Theology, East Asian Pastoral Institute and Mother of Life Catechetical Center in Manila, Philippines. He has served as founding president of the Philippine Association of Catholic Missiologists; he is an advisor to the FABC Office of Evangelization and the Philippine Bishops' Commission on Mission. His Orbis Books publications include *Living Mission: Challenges in Evangelization Today* (1994, 2009), *Once Upon a Time in Asia: Stories of Harmony and Peace* (2006), and *The Gift of Mission: Yesterday, Today, Tomorrow* (2013); he has contributed chapters to several other Orbis books.

essary. The FABC is a transnational episcopal structure that brings together fourteen bishops' conferences from the following countries as full members: Bangladesh, India, Indonesia, Japan, Korea, Laos-Cambodia, Malaysia-Singapore-Brunei, Myanmar (Burma), Pakistan, Philippines, Sri Lanka, Taiwan, Thailand, and Vietnam. FABC has eleven associate members drawn from the ecclesiastical jurisdictions of East Timor, Hong Kong, Kazakhstan, Kyrgyzstan, Macau, Mongolia, Nepal, Siberia, Tadjikistan, Turkmenistan, and Uzbekistan. Thus, in total, twenty-eight Asian countries are represented in the FABC; indeed, the FABC is profoundly a multicultural reality! The FABC grew out of the historic gathering of 180 Asian Catholic bishops with Blessed Pope Paul VI during his 1970 Asian visit.

Aside from a modest central structure, there are nine FABC offices, which are focused on evangelization, social communication, laity and family, human development, education and faith formation, ecumenical and inter-religious affairs, theological concerns, clergy, and consecrated life. Each of these offices sponsors a wide variety of activities that promote the growth of the Asian local churches and its challenging task of integral evangelization.

The supreme body of the FABC is the Plenary Assembly, which convenes approximately every four years. The themes, places, and dates of the eleven plenary assemblies are the following: I: "Evangelization in Modern Day Asia" (Taipei, Taiwan: 1974); II: "Prayer—The Life of the Church in Asia" (Calcutta, India: 1978); III: "The Church—Community of Faith in Asia" (Bangkok, Thailand: 1982); IV: "The Vocation and Mission of the Laity in the Church and in the World of Asia" (Tokyo, Japan: 1986); V: "Journeying Together toward the Third Millennium" (Bandung, Indonesia: 1990); VI: "Christian Discipleship in Asia Today: Service to Life" (Manila, Philippines: 1995); VII: "A Renewed Church in Asia: A Mission of Love and Service" (Samphran, Thailand: 2000); VIII: "The Asian Family toward a Culture of Life" (Daejeon, Korea: 2004); IX: "Living the Eucharist in Asia" (Manila, Philippines: 2009); X: "FABC at Forty Years—Responding to the Challenges of Asia: New Evangelization" (Xuan Loc and Ho Chi Minh, Vietnam: 2012); and XI: "The Catholic Family in Asia: Domestic Church of the Poor on a Mission of Mercy" (Colombo, Sri Lanka: 2016). The emphasis of the FABC and its plenary assemblies consistently centers on the local church and missionary evangelization; for example, note that "evangelization" is the central theme right from the first (1974) to the most recent (2016) of the plenary assemblies.

The basic documents of the plenary assemblies and the initiatives of the FABC offices are available in the six volumes of *For All the Peoples of Asia* [FAPA] (Manila: Claretian Publications, 1992–2017).[1] The *FABC Papers*,

---

1. This continuing series of valuable FABC "source-books" has now reached six volumes. All bear the same title, *For All the Peoples of Asia*, and are published by Claretian Publications

continuously published since 1976, are available in print form and in pdf format on the FABC Central Secretariat website; see numbers 100, 125, and 150 for comprehensive indexes. The six FAPA volumes and the individually numbered *FABC Papers* are indispensable resources for basic FABC material. Due to space limitations, key mission documents of the universal church (*Ad Gentes, Evangelii Nuntiandi, Redemptoris Missio, Ecclesia in Asia*, and *Evangelii Gaudium*) are *not* treated in any depth. A selected bibliography is also presented.

For over four decades, through the FABC the local churches in the multicultural continent of Asia have collaboratively sought to listen to "what the Spirit is saying to the Churches" (Rev 2:7, 11, 17, 29; 3:6, 13, 22). They seek to follow Jesus, the first evangelizer and missionary of the Father, who took flesh as an Asian. With renewed zeal and vigor, Asia's churches accept their missionary vocation! A "new way of being Church" uniquely adapted to the Asian pluricultural context and its diverse challenges has emerged!

Statistical Panorama of Asia

Asian realities surprise and challenge. Approximately four billion people (nearly two-thirds of humanity) are Asians. Both China and India each have a population of over one billion people. Eighty-five percent of all the world's non-Christians live in Asia. Catholics (approximately 115+ million in 2005) represent less than 3 percent of all Asians. Significantly, well over 50 percent of Asian Catholics are found in one country alone—the Philippines; thus, Catholics in most Asian nations are a small—even tiny—minority (frequently less than 1 percent). Islam numbers some 700+ million followers in Asia alone; this means that two-thirds of the worldwide Muslim population live in Asia. The world's four largest Islamic nations are found in Asia and each has over 100 million Muslims: Indonesia (209m), India (176m), Pakistan (167m), and Bangladesh (133m) [2013 statistics].

To capture the minority status of the church in Asia and the ensuing missionary implications, one need only look at various countries and note the percentage of Catholics: Bangladesh (0.27%); Bhutan (0.02%); Burma/

---

in Quezon City, Metro Manila; they are very widely known and quoted by the acronym FAPA. The volumes and their number, years covered, and editors are the following: FAPA I (1970–1991), ed. Gaudencio Rosales and Catalino Arévalo; FAPA II (1992–1996), ed. Franz-Josef Eilers; FAPA III (1997–2001), ed. Franz-Josef Eilers; FAPA IV (2002–2006), ed. Franz-Josef Eilers; FAPA V (2007–2012), ed. Vimal Tirimanna; and FAPA VI (2012–2016), ed. Vimal Tirimanna. For clarity, easy referencing, and economy of printed text, this presentation uses FAPA with volume number and page references; this mode of citation has become standard practice in the Asian theological world.

Myanmar (1.3%); China (0.5%); Hong Kong (4.7%); India (1.72%); Indonesia (2.58%); Japan (0.36%); Korea-North (?); Korea-South (6.7%); Laos (0.9%); Macao (5%); Malaysia (3%); Mongolia (?); Nepal (0.05%); Pakistan (0.6%); Philippines (81%); Singapore (6.5%); Sri Lanka (8%); Taiwan (0.4%); and Vietnam (6.1%).

However, Christians are committed to announcing the gospel in pluricultural Asia. They firmly hold that no Asian church is so small or poor that it does not have something to give, and likewise, no Asian church is so large and powerful that it does not have something to receive. The five local churches generally recognized as having clear mission potential beyond their borders are Philippines, India, South Korea, Indonesia, and Vietnam. It also remains true that, independent of size or numbers, each local church is called to mission in the power of the Spirit.

FABC Perspectives on Evangelization in a Multicultural Context

The Asian local churches are aware, enthusiastic, and committed to the pivotal challenge and obligation of propagating the Christian faith in the Asian milieu. "Asian" church workers, both indigenous Asians as well as expatriate missionaries, view the promotion of the Christian faith as a specific missionary and pastoral commitment.

An FABC statement, made well over three decades ago, validly expresses this vision: "the decisive new phenomenon for Christianity in Asia will be the emergence of genuine Christian communities in Asia—Asian in their way of thinking, praying, living, communicating their own Christ-experience to others. . . . If the Asian Churches do not discover their own identity, they will have no future" (FAPA I, 70). This quote succinctly captures the urgent imperative of both building and strengthening each local church to be, in the words of the First FABC Plenary Assembly in 1974, "a Church incarnate in a people, a Church indigenous and inculturated" (FAPA I, 14).

Capturing the FABC vision of evangelization—and its various dimensions—may be a formidable task. This writer has chosen to identify pivotal themes as his approach to digesting the impressive body of FABC materials that are incredibly rich, amazingly visionary, and deeply inspirational. Each theme will be accorded a separate presentation, introduced by a short caption or title. In addition to the author's brief narrative, the FABC documents themselves will receive pride of place; pivotal quotes will form the bulk of the presentation, thus allowing the fresh, insightful vision of the FABC and the Asian churches to emerge. Readers are encouraged to appreciate the spirit inherent in each of these themes and discover the action of the "befriending Spirit" at work fostering the emergence of genuine Asian evangelizing communities. This writer asserts that because the inculturating Asian churches are discovering their own missionary identity, they have a bright and hopeful future!

An Urgent Imperative

A little known fact is that the word *inculturation* was used for the *first* time in church parlance in Asia. When the Asian bishops met with Blessed Pope Paul VI in Manila in 1970, they reflected, as noted in their final statement, on "the inculturation of the life and message of the Gospel in Asia" (FAPA I, 6). Since that historic meeting from which the FABC eventually emerged, rooting the faith in Asian soil has remained a leitmotif of FABC concerns and reflection. The Christian communities of Asia continue to search for appropriate means to make the church truly Catholic and truly Asian.

This struggle to integrate faith and life—the same task of both primary and "new" evangelization—involves a process of ecclesial self-discovery. As noted above, Asians' desire is to be "Asian in their way of thinking, praying, living, communicating their own Christ-experience to others," because they are convinced that if they "do not discover their own identity, they will have no future" (FAPA I, 70). It is imperative "to deepen the dialogue in Asia between the Gospel and culture, so that faith is inculturated and culture is evangelized" (FAPA III, 27). One must also note that for the FABC the question of the faith-and-culture integration is primarily encountered *concretely and pastorally* as the local churches engage with people and all the life realities of Asia.

For Asian Christians, this is an *urgent imperative* due to the perceived "foreignness" of the church. A 1991 FABC theological consultation stated the challenge quite starkly: "As a social institution the Church is perceived as a foreign body in its colonial origins while other world religions are not. The lingering colonial image survives. . . . The Church remains foreign in its lifestyle, in its institutional structure, in its worship, in its western trained leadership and in its theology" (FAPA II, 195–96).

While honestly admitting the enormity of the challenge, Asian Christians do see significant opportunities emerging. "As Asia comes out of the colonial period, its people have become more aware of their national identity. There is a renewed sense of pride in their religious and cultural values. . . . Reviewing the life of the church in Asia since Vatican II, we find that the churches in Asia recognize the indispensable necessity of inculturation as a path of mission. . . . The emergence of indigenous theology, spirituality, religious life, creativity in liturgical celebrations, etc. are clear evidence of the commitment the Churches have made to achieve this goal [inculturated evangelization]" (FAPA III, 217). Yet, the urgency of the imperative remains.

Already the reader will observe that a hard-and-fast distinction between "primary" and "new" evangelization is of secondary importance in today's Asian context, precisely due to the unique multicultural Asian reality. The observation of Saint John Paul II in *Redemptoris Missio* (34) describes well the Asian reality: "the boundaries between *pastoral care of the faithful, new evangelization* and *specific missionary activity* [primary evangelization] are not clearly definable, and it is unthinkable to create barriers between them or to put them into water-tight compartments."

On the other hand, the admirable, creative initiatives of the FABC and Asia's local churches for the past forty years would reflect the thought of Pope Francis in *Evangelii Gaudium* (11): "Whenever we make the effort to return to the source and to recover the original freshness of the Gospel, new avenues arise, new paths of creativity open up, with different forms of expression, more eloquent signs and words with new meaning for today's world. Every form of authentic evangelization is always 'new.'"

A Descriptive Definition

One looks in vain in the FABC literature to find a consistent definition of culture, interculturality, or inculturation. Yet, this lack of a single term has resulted in a wide variety of descriptions of the inculturation process, some of which boarder on the poetic. While maybe not sociologically or theologically precise, these various descriptions elicit a vision or dream of the mission to be accomplished.

In 1970 the Asian bishops committed themselves to "develop an indigenous theology and to do what we can so that the life and meaning of the Gospel may be ever more incarnate in the rich historical cultures of Asia, so that . . . Asian Christianity may help promote all that is 'authentically human in these cultures'" (FAPA I, 9). The 1974 FABC plenary assembly states: "Indigenization renders the local church truly present within the life and cultures of our peoples. Through it, all their human reality is assumed into the life of the Body of Christ, so that all of it may be purified and healed, perfected and fulfilled" (FAPA I, 16, 23).

The 1979 mission conference in Manila devoted one workshop precisely to inculturation as an Asian missionary task. Precious insights were forthcoming. "Inculturation is not mere adaptation of a ready-made Christianity into a given situation, but rather a creative embodiment of the Word in the local church. In this way they become the Body of Christ in this particular time and place—a local church. . . . The community discovers a new identity, losing nothing of its cultural riches, but integrating them in a new whole and becoming the sacrament of God's liberating love active among men" (FAPA I, 138).

A comprehensive analysis of the copious FABC material shows that through time and experience an integral view of culture and evangelization emerges. Both elements are to be understood in a holistic sense; they incorporate "all the life realities" of a given people; they encompass "whatever truly belongs to that people: its meanings and its values, its aspirations, its thought and its language, its songs and its artistry—even its frailties and failings it assumes, so that they too may be healed" (FAPA I, 14). Because culture is dynamic, evangelization will address "the emergent cultures of Asia, a combination of many diverse elements of modern civilization, yet still rooted in local traditional values" (FAPA II, 198). The dynamic presence of the Holy Spirit is imperative, given the complexity of both "modern" and "traditional" cultures—and the hybrid reality of "culture" today (FAPA I, 73, 130). For these reasons, in Asia it is best to view evangelization holistically—without sharp distinctions between "primary" and "new" evangelization.

A Dialogical Approach

The FABC is eminently clear in stating its conviction about what approach is needed for rooting the faith in pluricultural Asia. "Dialogue is a primary means and way for *inculturation*" (FAPA I, 142). "We perceive dialogue as a necessary condition and instrument for *inculturation*" (FAPA I, 249). These assertions are consistent with the FABC's comprehensive view of mission and evangelization. "Mission may find its greatest urgency in Asia; it also finds in our continent a distinctive mode [dialogue]. . . . Mission in Asia will also seek through *dialogue* to serve the cause of unity of the peoples of Asia marked by such a diversity of beliefs, cultures, and socio-political structures" (FAPA I, 281–82). "The local Churches of Asia will proclaim Jesus Christ to their fellow humans in a dialogical manner" (FAPA I, 346).

A dialogical approach is the only possible avenue, given the multiracial, multilinguistic, multireligious, and multicultural reality of Asia. Such a dialogical approach is not a mere external methodology that the church in Asia will adapt; the church herself is called to be "a community of dialogue. This dialogical model is in fact a new way of being Church" (FAPA I, 332).

As a community of dialogue, the local church "is never centered on itself but on the coming true of God's dream for the world" (FAPA I, 333). Such an engaged church

> will necessarily be transformed in the process. In other words, it will become inculturated—at a level which includes but goes deeper than changes in ritual and symbol. Such a Church may at last become a Church of Asia and not simply a Church in Asia. It may then be perceived as no longer an alien presence. In this model of Church, dia-

logue, liberation, inculturation and proclamation are but different aspects of the one reality. (FAPA I, 333)

The dialogical approach finds its roots in the earliest FABC sources. The programmatic document "Evangelization in Modern Day Asia" from the First FABC Plenary Assembly in 1974 outlined a unique kind of dialogue; it noted that building up a truly local church, one that is "indigenous and inculturated," demands a faith community that is in "continuous, humble and loving dialogue with the living traditions, the cultures, the religions—in brief, with all the life-realities of the people in whose midst it has sunk its roots deeply and whose history and life it gladly makes its own" (FAPA I, 14). In a word, the dynamic of "interculturality" is always at work.

This *operative paradigm* of holistic evangelization (the "triple dialogue" approach) is the *interpretive key* to understanding and appreciating the "rooting of the faith" process in Asia today. This is how the church "lives and breathes" in Asia. Here one finds the Holy Spirit at work. For Asia and the FABC, this is an authentic reception and continuation of the Second Vatican Council! Here, one is reminded of the September 20, 2012, statement of Pope Benedict XVI: "We can say that the new evangelization started precisely with the Council, which Blessed [now Saint] John XXIII saw as a new Pentecost that would make the Church flourish."

Primary Actor: Local Church

Explore any major document that has emerged from the extensive reflection of the FABC and you will probably find several creative insights on the local church in the Asian context. It was the 1970 Asian pastoral visit of Blessed Pope Paul VI with the Asian bishops that gave the impetus for the local churches to begin formulating a vision of church and mission adequate to the "new world being born" in Asia in the postcolonial period. They asked themselves: How would the churches incarnate a decisive "turning to history" and a "turning to the Gospel" within history "for all the peoples of Asia"? How would the FABC articulate an overall vision that captures what "being Church in Asia today" truly means? This is the context for appreciating the role of the local church in the evangelization process.

The Fifth FABC Plenary Assembly, held in Indonesia in 1990, added new clarity and focus by asserting that it is the local church that is "the acting subject of mission." The final document stated: "The renewal of our sense of mission will mean . . . that the acting subject of mission is the *local Church* living and acting in communion with the universal Church. It is the local Churches and communities which can discern and work out (in dialogue with each other and with other persons of goodwill) the way the Gospel is best proclaimed, the Church set up, the values of God's Kingdom realized in their own place and time" (FAPA I, 281). Remarkably, Pope Francis in *Evangelii Gaudium* also emphasizes the need to know "the context in which we all have to live and work" (EG 50) and that it is impossible to have "a uniform and rigid program of evangelization" (EG 75) for the diverse situations all around the world. "It is up to the Christian communities to analyze with objectivity the situation which is proper to their own country" (EG 184).

"Asian Churches then must become truly Asian in all things. The principle of indigenization and inculturation is at the very root of their coming into their own. The ministry of Asian Churches, if it is to be authentic, must be relevant to Asian societies. This calls on the part of the Churches for originality, creativity and inventiveness, for boldness and courage" (FAPA I, 72–73). Indeed, "if the Asian Churches do not discover their own identity, they will have no future" (FAPA I, 70).

An Interfaith Linkage

A previous section of this presentation was devoted to the dialogical approach essential to integral evangelization in the Asian context. It spoke about FABC's "triple dialogue" paradigm and noted that the Asian religions are one of the key "dialogue partners" of the local church.

The FABC is very aware that there is "a strong interrelation in Asia between religion and culture" and often "Asia tends to identify nationality, religion and culture" (FAPA II, 194). "Religion, providing . . . contact of the human with the Divine, is the soul of culture" (FAPA II, 21). "Each culture provides the context for understanding reality and expressing religious faith" (FAPA II, 23).

The FABC takes a positive approach to the religions, promoting constructive collaboration, dialogue, and critical interaction. The presence of the "seeds of the Word" and the action of the Holy Spirit in these religions is affirmed. The First FABC Plenary Assembly, in 1974, gave this orientation toward the religions in its final statement—expressed with poetic elegance. It asserts that building up a truly local church

> involves a dialogue with the great religious traditions of our peoples. In this dialogue we accept them as significant and positive elements in the economy of God's design of salvation. In them we recognize and respect profound spiritual and ethical meanings and values. Over many centuries they have been the treasury of the religious experience of our ancestors, from which our contemporaries do not cease to draw light and strength. They have been (and continue to be) the authentic expression of the noblest longings of their hearts, and the home of their

contemplation and prayer. They have helped to give shape to the histories and cultures of our nations. (FAPA I, 14)

Springing from this positive assessment, the Asian bishops continue:

How then can we not give them reverence and honor? And how can we not acknowledge that God has drawn our peoples to Himself through them? Only in dialogue with these religions can we discover in them the seeds of the Word of God (*Ad Gentes*, c. I, 9). This dialogue will allow us to touch the expression and the reality of our peoples' deepest selves, and enable us to find authentic ways of living and expressing our own Christian faith. It will reveal to us also many riches of our own faith which we perhaps would not have perceived. Thus it can become a sharing in friendship of our quest for God and for brotherhood among His sons. Finally, this dialogue will teach us what our faith in Christ leads us to receive from these religious traditions, and what must be purified in them, healed and made whole, in the light of God's Word. (FAPA I, 14–15; see also: FAPA IV, 215–219)

A truly profound vision of authentic dialogue at the service of evangelization!

Foundations in Spirituality

The Second FABC Plenary Assembly, in 1978, focused on "Prayer—The Life of the Church of Asia"; it was held in Calcutta, India, the land of prayer and pilgrimage centers where the Christian ashram movement has flourished in recent years. The final 1978 statement is a rich resource for appreciating how the church can both give and receive from the spiritual treasury of Asia's venerable religions. This is a fertile ground for inculturated evangelization. Asia's bishops noted:

In keeping with the economy of the Incarnation . . . , the prayer-life of our local Churches should "take over the riches of our nations, which have been given to Christ as inheritance." Important above all, in our present context, are those ways of prayer which have been developed by the native genius of our peoples. . . . We are daily more convinced that the Spirit is leading us in our time, not to some dubious syncretism (which we all rightly reject), but to an integration—profound and organic in character—of all that is best in our traditional ways of prayer and worship, into the treasury of our Christian heritage. (FAPA I, 34–35)

Asia has much to give to authentic Christian spirituality: a richly developed prayer of the whole person in unity of body-psyche-spirit;

prayer of deep interiority and immanence; traditions of asceticism and renunciation; techniques of contemplation found in the ancient eastern religions; simplified prayer-forms and other popular expressions of faith and piety of those whose hearts and minds so readily turn to God in their daily lives. This is Asia's gift of prayer to the Church. (FAPA I, 42)

Discerning the Signs of the Times

Following the Second Vatican Council's injunction to "scrutinize the signs of the times [and] interpret them in the light of the Gospel" (*Gaudium et Spes* 4), Asia's local churches always begin their faith reflection with a respectful attention to Asian realities, statistics, and concrete challenges. This inductive approach (characteristic of contemporary Asian theology) fosters a healthy exploration and discernment of the challenges facing the church and her evangelizing mission on the immense Asian continent, home to 60 percent of humanity.

The Tenth FABC Plenary Assembly, in 2012, explored the theme "FABC at Forty Years—Responding to the Challenges of Asia: New Evangelization." Within the final document one finds an extensive exploration of the present challenges existing in society that demand new perspectives in evangelization. One reads in the section "Mega-trends in Asia and Ecclesial Realities":

> As we thank the Lord, the Spirit calls us again to discern the signs of the times as did our brother Bishops in 1974. . . . Among the signs of the times are positive and negative mega-trends that will shape the evangelizing mission of the Church in Asia. They are pastoral challenges with new faces, new forms, new facets and emphases. In responding to them we note ecclesial realities, both lights and shadows, which in themselves are mega-trends in the Church. We need to view them with the pastoral concern and compassion that Jesus had for the people of his day. (FAPA V, 58)

The document continues:

> The overarching mega-trend that impacts all dimensions of Asian life is globalization. It is an ongoing, inexorable, complex and ambivalent process that impacts as both bane and blessing the world of politics, economics, communications, education, environment, technology, religion, culture, family, and values. Driven as an *economic process* by neo-liberal capitalism . . . , the result is an ever widening gap between rich and poor. As a *cultural phenomenon* using the means of social com-

munication, globalization is quietly and relentlessly disseminating a relatively new culture that threatens cherished cultural values. (FAPA V, 58–59)

The ancient cultures of Asia, once the dominant catalysts of civilizations, are facing the formidable challenge of a globalizing and homogenizing culture that is *secular, materialist, hedonist, consumerist, and relativist. . . .* The post-modern spirit clashes with the pervasive Asian sense of the sacred and transcendent. . . . How the bane and blessings of economic and cultural globalization can be made opportunities of grace through New Evangelization is the over-riding challenge to the Church in Asia. The goal is "globalization without marginalization, globalization with solidarity." (FAPA V, 59–60)

The profoundly reflective FABC X document does an in-depth analysis of several additional signs of the times: poverty, migrants and refugees, indigenous peoples, population, religious freedom, threats to life, social communications, ecology, laity, women, youth, Pentecostalism, and vocations (FAPA V, 60–68; see also FAPA IV, 3–18; FAPA VI, 14–20). The FABC X document asserts: "These mega-trends are the lights and shadows of an Asian world stirred to profound renewal by the Spirit of God. They offer immense possibilities and hope. . . . The call of the Spirit is a call to New Evangelization" (FAPA V, 68).

Conclusion: The "Asian Way" of Being Church

The Fifth FABC Plenary Assembly, in Indonesia (1990), used a phrase that has captured the imagination of many Asian Christians; the bishops' final statement speaks about "a new way of being Church." The phrase is meant to envision "alternate ways of being Church in the Asia of the 1990s"—and beyond. Several key dimensions of this "new" community were noted: the church is to be "a communion of communities," a "participatory Church," a "prophetic sign," a "Spirit-filled community" (FAPA I, 287–88).

For some unfamiliar with the growth of the local churches in Asia after Vatican II, the phrase "new way of being Church" may raise questions. The phrase implies no rejection of essential dimensions of ecclesiology and evangelization; it attempts to capture the aspirations of Asian Christians to live their faith in the Christian community in an "Asian way." This "new way of being Church . . . is nothing more and nothing less than a following of Jesus-in-mission, an authentic discipleship in the context of Asia. . . . For the spirituality of the new way of being Church is the spirituality of those who place their complete trust in the Lord." Their lives are marked by "Gospel values [that] resonate deeply with the cultures of Asia" (FAPA I, 288). In a word, the phrase expresses well the deep desire to be an inculturated Christian community.

Building on the Fifth FABC Plenary Assembly and its vision of "a new way of being Church," the Seventh FABC Plenary Assembly, in 2000, spoke about "the challenge of discerning the Asian way." While noting that "Asia is a cultural mosaic shining with its rich diversity," Asia's bishops stated their position: "We are committed to the emergence of the Asianness of the Church in Asia. This means that the Church has to be an embodiment of the Asian vision and values of life, especially interiority, harmony, a holistic and inclusive approach to every area of life" (FAPA III, 8). This same vision emerges in the Eleventh FABC Plenary Assembly, where it is linked to the family; it is reflected in the very theme of the assembly: "The Catholic Family in Asia: Domestic Church of the Poor on a Mission of Mercy" (FAPA VI, 11–41).

The bishops noted in 2000:

> For thirty years [since the founding of the FABC in 1970], as we have tried to reformulate our Christian identity in Asia, we have addressed different issues, one after another. . . . These issues are not separate topics to be discussed, but aspects of an integrated approach to our Mission of Love and Service. We need to feel and act "integrally." . . . Inculturation, dialogue, justice, and the option for the poor are aspects of whatever we do. (FAPA III, 8)

Rejoicing in the "Asian Way" of being church and seeing it as a gift of the Spirit, the bishops have stated: "We are aware that this Asianness, founded on solid values, is a special gift the world is awaiting" (FAPA III, 9). Here one finds a genuinely comprehensive vision of integral evangelization, integrating the "old" and the "new," the contemplative and active, the spiritual and practical, a vision truly adequate to the multireligious and pluricultural reality of Asia in the third millennium. This is Asia's gift to the entire Church.

Other References

Barron, R., *Catholicism: The New Evangelization* (Print and Video) (Skokie, IL: Word on Fire, 2013).

Benedict XVI, "Pontifical Council for Promoting New Evangelization Established," *Origins* 40, no. 25 (November 25, 2010): 394–96.

———, "Address to Pontifical Council for Promoting New Evangelization," *Origins* 41, no. 6 (June 16, 2011): 90–91.

————, "The New Evangelization Started with Vatican II," *L'Osservatore Romano* (English) 45, no. 39 (September 26, 2012): 5.

Dulles, A., "John Paul II and the New Evangelization," *America* 166, no. 3 (February 1, 1992): 52–59, 69–72.

————, "John Paul II and the New Evangelization," *Studia Missionalia* 48 (1999): 165–80.

————, *Evangelization for the Third Millennium* (New York: Paulist Press, 2009).

FABC Central Secretariat, *FABC Papers 1–154* (Hong Kong: Central Secretariat, 1976–2017).

Fisichella, R., "Jesus and the Year of Faith: Impelling the New Evangelization," *Origins* 42, no. 14 (September 6, 2012): 217–21.

————, *The New Evangelization: Responding to the Challenge of Indifference* (Herefordshire, UK: Gracewing, 2012).

For All the Peoples of Asia: I-VI, series published by Claretian Publications, Quezon City, Philippines. The specific volumes and dates of coverage, editors, and publication dates are as follows: I (1970–1991), ed. Gaudencio Rosales and Catalino Arévalo, 1992; II (1992–1996), ed. Franz-Josef Eilers, 1997; III (1997–2001), ed. Franz-Josef Eilers, 2002; IV (2002–2006), ed. Franz-Josef Eilers, 2007; V (2007–2012), ed. Vimal Tirimanna, 2014; VI (2012–2016), ed. Vimal Tirimanna, 2017.

Francis (Pope), *Evangelii Gaudium* (Rome: Vatican Press, 2013).

Kroeger, J., *Asia-Church in Mission: Exploring Ad Gentes Mission Initiatives of the Local Churches in Asia in the Vatican II Era* (Quezon City, Philippines: Claretian Publications, 1999).

————, "A Church Living to Evangelize: Recent Popes and Integral Evangelization," in *Becoming Local Church: Historical, Theological and Missiological Essays* (Quezon City, Philippines: Claretian Publications, 2003): 55–86.

————, *Once Upon a Time in Asia: Stories of Harmony and Peace* (Maryknoll, NY: Orbis Books, 2006) [ten translations].

————, "FABC: Asia Needs Renewed Evangelizers," *East Asian Pastoral Review* 50, no. 2 (2013): 171–88.

————, *Asia's Dynamic Local Churches: Serving Dialogue and Mission* (Quezon City, Philippines: Claretian Communications and Jesuit Communications, 2014).

Martin, R., and P. Williamson, *John Paul II and the New Evangelization* (Cincinnati, OH: Servant Books, 2006).

Menamparampil, T., "What is New about the New Evangelization?" *Vidyajyoti Journal of Theological Reflection* 61, nos. 6–7 (June-July 1997): Part I: 361–71; Part II: 436–45.

Routhier, G., "Vatican II as the Point of Departure for the New Evangelization," *Doctrine and Life* 62:3 (March 2012): 21–39.

United States Conference of Catholic Bishops (USCCB): Committee on Evangelization and Catechesis, *Disciples Called to Witness: The New Evangelization* (Washington, DC: USCCB, 2012).

Wang, S., *The New Evangelisation: What It Is and How to Do It* (London: Catholic Truth Society, 2013).

Wuerl, D., "Pastoral Letter on the New Evangelization," *Origins* 40, no. 16 (September 23, 2010): 241–51.

_____, "What Is the Synod on the New Evangelization," *The Priest* 68, no. 10 (October 2012): 10–13.

15

Prophetic Dialogue and Intercultural Mission

Stephen B. Bevans, SVD

Practicing Prophetic Dialogue

Thomas, a Divine Word Missionary priest working in the state of Odisha on India's east coast, received a telephone call from his bishop. The bishop counseled Thomas to leave his parish for a few days: rumor had it that a band of radical Hindus were planning to attack Catholics in the area, and if they did, Thomas's life would be in danger. This had happened several times before in the state, and each time several Catholics were killed, and several parish churches had been burned. This was one more instance of the strong anti-Christian and anti-missionary sentiment that had killed Australian missionary Graham Staines and his two sons in the neighboring state of West Bengal. Thomas, the bishop warned, could suffer the same fate.

Thomas thought and prayed about his options long and hard, and finally decided to stay put. After all, he thought, he was the local pastor. If he left, what would happen to his small but flourishing Catholic community? He would stay with his people, he decided, no matter what the consequences. If necessary, he thought with considerable fear and trembling, he would lay down his life for his sheep. And so he and his community prayed for their persecutors and prayed that they be spared. Perhaps it was a miracle, but they

Stephen B. Bevans, SVD, is professor emeritus of mission and culture at Catholic Theological Union in Chicago, and he serves as the faculty advisor for the CTU program, "Catholics on Call." He is a commissioner on the World Council of Churches' Commission on World Mission and Evangelism, a member of the Society of the Divine Word's Arnold Janssen Spirituality Team, and a member of his SVD Chicago Province's Provincial Council. He is an editor of the Brill series Theology of Mission in Global Christianity and on the editorial board of the *International Review of Mission*. His current work includes research into Pope Francis's thinking on inculturation and on Francis's signature phrase, "the culture of encounter."

were. The attack never came, and life gradually moved toward normalcy. But rather than turn inside themselves, Thomas and the community continued to work, as before, to develop better relations with their Hindu neighbors, trying to show them that they had nothing to fear from Christians, that Christians indeed could be authentic participants in Indian culture and social life.[1]

Robert Schreiter, my colleague at Catholic Theological Union, Chicago, and member of the Missionaries of the Precious Blood, traveled several years ago to the Southern Philippines to give, to bishops and members of the clergy in several dioceses on the island of Mindanao, a workshop on peace-making and reconciliation. Tensions between Muslims and Christians had been strong in the past several years, and violence had broken out on both sides. Schreiter's task, at the bidding of several local bishops, was to convince church members that only an attitude of dialogue, forgiveness, and reconciliation could break the cycle of growing hatred. For Schreiter, practicing reconciliation and peacemaking in particular contexts of violence is a powerful way to practice mission in today's world.[2]

Another colleague, Claude Marie Barbour, is a French Presbyterian and former missionary to Lesotho in Southern Africa, but for the last several decades she has developed a close relationship with Native Americans of the Lakota People of South Dakota in the United States. Over the years, she and her friends and colleagues Eleanor Doidge and Roger Schroeder have mentored thousands of ministry students as they traveled to the Pine Ridge and Rosebud Reservations in that state, and she has developed an understanding of mission as "Mission in Reverse," a stance of openness, listening, and dialogue, allowing the people among whom one ministers to first minister to and even evangelize them with their culture and experiential wisdom. Through her, these students have made their own the powerful wisdom of John V. Taylor: "Our first task in approaching another people, another culture, another religion, is to take off our shoes, for the place we are approaching is holy."[3]

---

1. This incident is based on a true narrative told by a participant in a workshop I conducted at a renewal course for Divine Word Missionaries at the Ad Gentes Center in Nemi, Italy, in 2012. Fr. Thomas is not the person's real name.

2. Among Schreiter's many writings on reconciliation, see his "Reconciliation as a Model of Mission," in Stephen Bevans, ed., *A Century of Catholic Mission* (Oxford, UK: Regnum Books, 2014), 232–38; Robert J. Schreiter, "The Emergence of Reconciliation as a Paradigm of Mission: Dimensions, Levels and Characteristics," in Robert J. Schreiter and Knud Jorgensen, eds., *Mission as Ministry of Reconciliation* (Oxford, UK: Regnum Books, 2014), 9–29; Robert J. Schreiter, Scott Appleby, and Gerald F. Powers, eds., *Peacebuilding: Catholic Theology, Ethics, and Praxis* (Maryknoll, NY: Orbis Books, 2010).

3. See John V. Taylor, Preface to *The Primal Vision* (London: SCM Press, 1963), 10. See Claude Marie Barbour and Eleanor Doidge, "Mission as Accompaniment," in Bevans, ed., *A Century of Catholic Mission*, 275–83.

Jonny Baker is a lay Anglican who lives in London and works with British young adults, many of whom are unchurched and basically ignorant of Christianity. His task, as he describes it, is to find grace in this highly secularized and sometimes even anti-religious youth culture rather than condemn it outright. He is convinced that, by patient listening and sympathetic observation, the Holy Spirit's presence can be discovered, and a way to preach or at least witness to the gospel in this particular context can be gradually developed.[4] To do this "may mean a different newspaper, listening to dubstep, joining in karaoke, developing a dark sense of humor, sharing stories through asking about tattoos, going to the fish and chip shop on a Thursday night, playing bingo, doing yoga or whatever it is in the local culture, and all the while prayerfully asking to see rumors of glory, hints of God at work, noticing when the sacred is being mediated in and through the everyday stuff of the local culture."[5]

All four of these thinkers about and practitioners of mission are practicing prophetic dialogue, the topic of this essay, as they engage in intercultural mission, also the topic of this book. Thomas, in choosing to remain with his parishioners, is performing a dramatically prophetic act, while recognizing that mission still needs to be profoundly dialogical, as is so necessary in his Indian context. Schreiter, in working for dialogue, is also encouraging a prophetic stance—one of openness and peacemaking in a hostile and violent situation. Claude Marie Barbour emphasizes that the only way to adequately preach the gospel is to first develop an attitude of dialogue and respect for those with whom one wants to share the good news. And Jonny Baker advocates the same thing in his search for God's presence amidst what he calls an "unpopular culture" of tattoos and rap music.

Sometimes mission can only be done as a prophetic act. In a situation, for example, of gross injustice or inhuman oppression, the annunciation of the gospel can only be done by a denunciation of such evil.[6] But when Christians pay close attention to the unjust situation and analyze it closely, they will be able only to denounce and not offer alternative life-giving ways. Sometimes a particular context—for example in a country and culture where preaching the gospel and conversion to Christianity is forbidden or almost impossible—demands of Christians a stance of listening and trying to appreciate that context. But such respect for the context is itself a silent witness of God's patience and presence in that context. For the sake of clarity, this essay will

4. See Jonny Baker, "Contemporary Culture and Prophetic Dialogue," in Cathy Ross and Stephen Bevans, eds., *Mission on the Road to Emmaus: Constants, Context, and Prophetic Dialogue* (London: SCM, 2015), 201–14.

5. Ibid.

6. See Gustavo Gutiérrez, *A Theology of Liberation* (Maryknoll, NY: Orbis Books, 1973), 265–72.

focus first on mission as dialogue and then on mission as prophecy, before putting them together in kind of creative and tensive synthesis. But mission is always carried out in prophetic dialogue, sometimes more dialogical than prophetic, sometimes more prophetic than dialogical. This is what is revealed when we understand mission as rooted in the prophetic and dialogical mission of the triune God, and when we reflect on mission's biblical foundations in the New Testament.

Mission as Dialogue

In a recent interview in the Argentine weekly *Viva*, Pope Francis spoke of "Ten Secrets" for a joyful life. Number 9 of the ten was "Don't proselytize." "The worst thing of all," the pope said, "is religious proselytism, which paralyzes: 'I am talking with you in order to persuade you.' No. Each person dialogues, starting with his and her own identity. The Church grows by attraction, not proselytizing."[7] Thirty years ago, the Vatican body that was then called the Secretariat for Non-Christians spoke of dialogue as "the norm and necessary manner of every form of Christian mission, as well as of every aspect of it, whether one speaks of simple presence and witness, service or direct proclamation."[8]

Dialogue in this sense is more than a practice, as in the practice of interreligious or ecumenical dialogue. It is a basic attitude, indeed, a kind of spirituality that underlies every aspect of mission. My colleague, of whom I spoke above, Claude Marie Barbour, speaks of "Mission in Reverse," a way of doing mission that is convinced that the Spirit is present before the arrival of the missionary. Because of this, mission is first being open to be evangelized by those we have come to evangelize. Mission is about allowing the women and men among whom we work to teach us first—about their questions, their hopes, their dreams, their cultural values, their own sense of God. Our basic stance is openness, an attitude of respect and listening.[9] It is about a profound "letting go" before "speaking out."[10]

In one of the most striking interventions at the 2012 Synod of Bishops

7. "In Latest Interview, Pope Francis Reveals 10 Secrets to Happiness," *Catholic News Service*, July 29, 2014, http://www.catholicnews.com.

8. Secretariat for Non-Christians, "The Attitude of the Church towards Followers of Other Religions: Reflections and Orientations on Dialogue and Mission," *Bulletin. Secretariatus pro non christianis* 56, no. 13 (1984/2), paragraph 29.

9. See Claude Marie Barbour, "Seeking Justice and Shalom in the City," *International Review of Mission* 73 (1984): 303–9. See also Stephen Bevans, Eleanor Doidge, and Robert J. Schreiter, eds., *The Healing Circle: Essays in Cross Cultural Mission* (Chicago: CCGM Publications, 2000).

10. Stephen B. Bevans and Roger P. Schroeder, *Prophetic Dialogue: Reflections on Christian Mission Today* (Maryknoll, NY: Orbis Books, 2011), 88–100.

on the New Evangelization, Luis Antonio Tagle, now Cardinal Archbishop of Manila, called for the church to listen first before speaking. "The Church must discover the power of silence," he said. "Confronted with the sorrows, doubts and uncertainties of people she cannot pretend to give easy solutions. In Jesus, silence becomes the way of attentive listening, compassion and prayer."[11]

This basic attitude or spirituality of dialogue, of course, is the sine qua non of intercultural mission. Only when those engaged in mission are open to the women and men among whom they work, only when they allow themselves to learn from and be challenged by those among whom they minister, can the full impact of intercultural mission be experienced and profited from. On the other hand, only when those among whom missionaries work are open to the contributions and challenges of their ministers can the powerful mutuality on intercultural ministry have effect. Intercultural mission, by definition, is a two-way street, so to speak, and an attitude of dialogue is what helps the easy flow of traffic on it.

Mission as Prophecy

But if an attitude of dialogue is foundational to any kind of mission today, without the cultivation of the spirit of prophecy it lacks any direction or purpose. Prophecy, like its specific form in verbal proclamation, must always employ a "dialogue method";[12] but mission is more than "being nice," or learning from others, or even developing relationships and making friends, as essential as these latter three are for its identity. Mission is ultimately about sharing the good news of God's reign with the peoples of the world. Christians believe that this reign has been already inaugurated in the life, death, and resurrection of Jesus of Nazareth, is present in the church as its sacrament (LG 1), and is present in secret ways (AG 9) beyond the borders of the Christian community. The way that the church communicates this good news is through the practice of prophecy.

Prophecy is a many-faceted reality. On the one hand, it is nonverbal, incarnated in the witness of an individual Christian or a Christian community. Think, for example, of Jeremiah walking through Jerusalem with a yoke on his shoulders (Jer 27–28), Isaiah speaking of God's Servant (an individual and corporate personality) as a "light to the nations" (Isa 49:6), or Jesus' healings and exorcisms. On the other hand, prophecy literally means "speaking forth," speaking the Word of God. "To whomever I send

---

11. Intervention of Luis Antonio Tagle, http://www.vatican.va/news_services/press/sinodo/documents/bollettino_25_xiii-ordinaria-2012/xx_plurilingue/b07_xx.html.

12. Marcello Zago, "The New Millennium and the Emerging Religious Strategies," *Missiology: An International Review* 23, no. 1 (2000): 17.

you, you shall go," God tells Jeremiah, "whatever I command you, you shall speak. . . . See, I place my words in your mouth!" (Jer 1:7, 9); Jesus preaches in parables and offers words of wisdom in pithy phrases, as in the Sermon on the Mount (Matt 5–7).

In both wordless gestures and witness, and in powerful spoken and written messages, prophets offer comfort and hope in times of persecution and afflic-tion (e.g., Isa 40:1–11); a vision of a God of unsurpassable love, mercy, and compassion (e.g., Isa 49:14–18); and a denunciation of every form of injustice and oppression (e.g., Amos 8:4–8). Christians in mission create communities of hope, where life together, the quality of liturgical celebrations, commit-ment to education, and openness to other Christians and other religions give witness to how the gospel message can give life to women and men in any situation, no matter how difficult or hopeless. Such communities are signs of the presence of the reign of God already present, and give testimony to the mercy, life-giving nature, and truth of the God revealed by Jesus. They are also powerful communities of counter-witness in an unjust, individualistic, or life-denying society, and bear witness to the justice of God's reign in the face of oppression and injustice.

Christians in such communities of "missionary disciples" (EG 24) also speak forth a message of encouragement and hope. They dedicate themselves to developing ways of communicating the gospel message that is clear and focused, relevant and powerful, one that engages people's lives and the cul-tures in which they live. They speak out as well in all sorts of ways against evil in society. Individuals do this in daily encounters, in editorials, in blogs and tweets; communities in statements of opposition to oppressive laws or cultural elements; and the institutional church in statements that condemn political injustice, ecological destruction, economic exploitation, or religious intolerance.

Living out mission as prophecy can be as dramatic as an Oscar Romero protesting the death squads of El Salvador, or the peace efforts of the San Egidio community in Africa, an Amish community offering forgiveness to the person who had killed several of its children in a shooting rampage, or the earth-keeping ministry undertaken by a number of African Initiated Churches in Zimbabwe. It can, on the other hand, be as simple and everyday as a mother telling stories of Jesus to her young child, a community that consistently welcomes visitors and strangers at its liturgies, a priest preaching a well-prepared homily, or a march for clean water in a poor urban barrio in the Philippines.

Mission as prophecy has intercultural dimensions as well. A prophetic call for hope, for example, might make use of some of the deepest resources and values in a particular context or culture. In the wake of the devastating typhoon that hit the Philippine island of Leyte in October of 2013, Filipino Christians might have been reminded of their deep value of Bayanihan, or community spirit. All the painstaking effort of inculturating the gospel is ultimately for the sake of a clearer, more intelligible, more challenging preaching and proclamation of the Christian message. There will always be something counter-cultural in gospel proclamation. It needs to be presented, however, in a way that, if it is rejected, it is rejected for the right reasons—not because the proclamation is irrelevant to culture and context.[13] Any denunciation of injustice can only be authentic if it is rooted in a deep understanding of the cultural and contextual resources of a culture. Martin Luther King's prophetic challenge to U.S. American racism pointed to the fact that the denial of equal rights to African Americans was in fact a betrayal of the vision of democracy on which the United States had been founded.[14]

Mission as Prophetic Dialogue

As I have written in the introduction to this chapter, authentic mission is always—or nearly almost always—carried out in prophetic dialogue, whether missionaries are aware of it or not. Thomas's prophetic act of staying with his people is coupled with his continuing commitment to dialogical openness. Schreiter's call for dialogue in the context of Christian–Muslim tensions in the Philippines is itself a call for a prophetic act in that particular context. Claude Marie Barbour's insistence on mission in reverse is itself a profound witness to the God who comes to people where they are—and thus prophetic. Jonny Baker's prophetic act is founded on a deep respect for the young adult culture within which he attempts to preach the gospel. Intercultural living and mission, both *ad intra* and *ad extra*, need to be open to the intercultural nature of community as women and men learn from each other's cultures and social locations. But, if it is to move beyond mere toleration, Christians in mission need to develop skills by which they can offer a prophetic word of critique or encouragement to one another when such a word is needed.

In some situations, more dialogue will be necessary. In others, more prophecy will be needed. For several years now I have begun to think of the practice of mission as a contextual practice, much akin to doing theology contextually.[15] Like contextual theologizing, the first thing needed is to discern the context and the particular model of theologizing that would be most appropriate for a particular situation or context. Roger Schroeder has dem-

---

13. See Darrell L. Whiteman, "Contextualization: The Theory, the Gap, the Challenge," *International Bulletin of Missionary Research* 21, no. 1 (1997): 2–7.

14. See, for example, Martin Luther King's "Letter from the Birmingham Jail," http://www.africa.upenn.edu.

15. See my article "Prophetic Dialogue and Contextual Theology" in Ross and Bevans, eds., *Mission on the Road to Emmaus.*

onstrated in his chapter in this volume how particular situations would be served by various contextual models. I have imagined a kind of continuum with dialogue on one side and prophecy on the other. In each context it needs to be determined where the emphasis will be placed as Christians engage in missionary work. Will it be a stance more of listening and dialogue, or will it be one of prophetic witness or proclamation? Will the decision to dialogue be a prophetic action, as Thomas and Schreiter advocated? Or will the prophecy be rooted in respect, openness, and dialogue, as Barbour and Baker advocate? These are the kinds of questions that always need to be asked as we engage in intercultural mission.

Trinitarian Foundations

A stance of prophetic dialogue as Christians engage in mission is no arbitrary one, nor is it a mere strategy better to justify it. Much more deeply, practicing prophetic dialogue is to participate most fully in God's trinitarian mission itself. Christian faith came to explicit trinitarian faith as Christians reflected on the saving action of God in the world. That action is perceived first in the gentle presence of the Spirit as she patiently encouraged, persuaded, and cajoled the emergence of the various elements after the Big Bang into gases, stars, galaxies, elements, as life slowly emerged on planet Earth (and most probably on other planets in our vast universe), as plant and animal life began to flourish, as creation became gradually conscious of itself in homo sapiens, and as humanity tried to express the wonder of creation in various religious expressions. The Spirit's work in creation was one of dialogue, and still is, as she whispers truth in women's and men's hearts and consciences, and brings them together in a communion that is a sacrament of the new creation to come.[16] But especially in the history of one people, Israel, the Spirit raises up prophets to speak words of hope to an oppressed people, to call them back to fidelity to the covenant, to speak in powerful images about the identity of the God whom Israel worships and who chastises the rich among the people who oppress the poor.

In "the fullness of time" (Gal 4:4), in the second place, God's pervasive, persuasive, and prophetic spirit took on a human face in Jesus of Nazareth. Jesus was a man filled with God's Spirit, the Spirit that fell upon him at his baptism in the Jordan and anointed him with the prophetic mission of bringing good news to the poor, proclaiming liberty to captives, healing to those who suffer, freeing those who are oppressed, and proclaiming God's mercy—

---

16. See Denis Edwards, *Breath of Life: A Theology of the Creator Spirit* (Maryknoll, NY: Orbis Books, 2004), 33–49; Elizabeth A. Johnson, *Ask the Beasts: Darwin and the God of Love* (London: Bloomsbury, 2014), 122–53. On the probability of intelligent life in many parts of the universe, see Thomas F. O'Meara, *Vast Universe: Extraterrestrials and Christian Revelation* (Mahwah, NJ: Paulist Press, 2012).

the mercy of a loving and forgiving father—to those who had sinned (see Luke 4:18–19). His prophetic ministry was expressed in his beautiful, consoling, yet challenging parables and pithy sayings, in his healings and exorcisms, and in his practice of including everyone, especially in the context of table fellowship.[17] At the same time, Jesus is remembered as a man of dialogue, open to the requests of others (Luke 7:1–10), gentle and humble of heart (Matt 11:29), asking people about their needs and wants (Matt 20:32; Mark 10:51), ready to listen, even learning from others (Matt 11:21–28). In his words and deeds Jesus bore prophetic witness to the coming reign of God, revealing a God who rules the world in overflowing mercy, patience, vulnerability, and generosity (see Luke 15; Matt 20:1–6). This dialogical nature of God was revealed especially in Jesus' death and resurrection, where God's love for the world was poured out "unto the end" (John 13:1), and then shared abundantly with Jesus' disciples as they are called to share in God's very mission through the pouring forth of God's Spirit upon them (see the whole movement of Acts, and especially Acts 2).

As Christians—challenged by various misunderstandings of Jesus' and the Spirit's identity—reflected further, they gradually realized that God's deepest identity is revealed in God's saving activity in creation and history. As Kathleen Cahalan puts it, "who God is and what God does is one divine life."[18] As Edward Hahnenberg has expressed it, the God who works in dialogue and for human communion is, in God's self, dialogue and communion.[19] That communion, as Thomas Aquinas groped for words to express it, is spoken forth in the Word, and breathed forth in the Spirit,[20] whom Augustine called the bond of love or the "friendship" between Father and Son, Holy Mystery and spoken Word.[21] God, then, is a community of prophetic dialogue, a God who shares the divine mission with women and men, who are called as well to be a community "in the unity of the Father, the Son and the Spirit," (LG 4) a community that witnesses and works in prophetic dialogue. The church is God's people, the body of Christ, the temple of the Spirit, a sacrament of the divine communion and self-giving that is an instrument of God's dialogical and prophetic saving activity in the world.

It is to this dynamic of God's presence in creation through the Spirit, through the creating Word (John 1:3) and Christ's cosmic presence (Eph

---

17. See Edwards, *Breath of Life*, 66–86; Bevans and Schroeder, *Prophetic Dialogue*, 101–14.

18. Kathleen A. Cahalan, *Introducing the Practice of Ministry* (Collegeville, MN: Liturgical Press, 2010), 150.

19. Edward P. Hahnenberg, *Ministries: A Relational Approach* (New York: Crossroad, Herder and Herder, 2003), 85.

20. Thomas Aquinas, *Summa theologica* I, 27, a. 1; 34, a. 1 and 2; 37, a. 1.

21. See Augustine, *De Trinitate*, 6.5; see Justo L. González, *A History of Christian Thought, I, From the Beginnings to the Council of Chalcedon* (Nashville, TN: Abingdon, 1970), 332.

1:20–23; Eph 1:15–17), coupled with the Spirit's speaking through the prophets, lavishing the Spirit of prophecy upon Jesus of Nazareth, and continually gifting and challenging the church, that the church is called to participate in intercultural mission. On the one hand, those engaging in mission are called to recognize the "seeds of the Word" and God's "secret presence" (AG 11; AG 9) in all cultures and contexts. On the other, there is the need to recognize that all cultures are shot through with imperfections and evil, and so need to be ennobled and purified (AG 9). Intercultural mission, grounded in trinitarian practice, engages in prophetic dialogue.

Scriptural Foundations

Reflecting on the trinitarian foundations of prophetic dialogue certainly leads to an understanding of the rich scriptural foundation of this attitude and practice. The scriptures bear clear testimony both to God's loving dialogue with humankind and God's prophetic communication of the divine identity, the nature of God's saving work, and God's opposition to all evil and injustice. The ministry of Jesus in particular, as we have seen, illustrates this dynamic and creative tension between dialogue and prophecy. More work in the biblical foundations of prophetic dialogue needs to be done. In this section, however, I would like to focus briefly on two passages, one from Luke's Gospel, and one from the writings of St. Paul.

Our first passage is from Luke 24:13–35: the story of the disciples on the road to Emmaus. As the disciples discussed and commiserated with each other as they left Jerusalem three days after Jesus' death, Jesus appears to them, but they do not recognize him. He appears, as he had appeared to Mary Magdalene earlier in the day (John 20:11–18), as a stranger. As he joins the two on the road, the stranger asks the disciples what they had been discussing, and listens intently as they tell him. But then, having listened, he interprets the scriptures for them in a way that begins to make sense to them, and sets their hearts on fire. When the disciples reached their destination they invite the stranger to stay with them, for it was getting too late for further travel, and so he accepts their invitation and becomes their guest. But then, as he breaks bread, blesses it, and gives it to them, they recognize who he really is—the guest has become the host, the stranger has become the friend. And then, when he disappears, the two disciples hastily run back to Jerusalem to share the news of the resurrection with their sisters and brothers.

The pattern is one of prophetic dialogue. They recognized Jesus in the breaking of the bread, surely. But perhaps they also recognized him in the pattern of his ministry—openness, listening, accompaniment, accepting of hospitality, and yet bearing a message and a relationship that is saving and transforming.

A second passage is from what is considered the oldest of the New Testament writings, the First Letter to the Thessalonians. In chapter 2 Paul talks about the beginnings of his ministry in the city of Thessalonica. He speaks about how, after being mistreated in Philippi, he found such hospitality in the city that he once more summoned the courage to preach the gospel plainly. Paul talks about how God had entrusted him with this precious message, and so he proclaimed it boldly, "not trying to please human beings, but rather God, who judges our hearts" (1 Thess 2:4). This is prophetic witness. Nevertheless, the way Paul did this, he recalls, was not to pull his weight as an apostle. Rather, as he puts it, "we were gentle among you, as a nursing mother cares for her children" (2:7). He goes on to talk about the relationship that he had built up with his new Thessalonian friends—he shared with them not only the gospel but his very self, treating them as a father treats his children. It is in this mode that Paul preached: exhorting and encouraging them to conduct themselves worthy of the God who called them into God's reign (see 2:10–12).

The dynamic of prophetic dialogue is particularly evident here, and in the intercultural context of an Asia-Minor-born, Jerusalem-trained apostle, preaching the gospel in northeastern Greece in the context of Hellenistic culture within the Roman Empire. Paul paints a picture of himself as the persecuted prophet who boldly preaches the gospel, but at the same time as the friend whose manner of presentation is couched in deep gentleness and relationship. Once again we see traces of God's own action in ministry through the Spirit and the Word, through the ministry of Jesus as Jesus embodies and proclaims a tender, gentle Father. Paul is only imitating his Lord in his boldness and gentleness for the sake of the gospel.

The Path Ahead

I have constructed the narrative of this chapter in a way that is rather opposite from usual theological discourse. Usually, in other words, theological reflection begins with the scriptural basis of an issue, then proceeds to the doctrinal and other wisdom of the tradition, and ends in laying out some implications for practice. Here I have started with examples of the practice of prophetic dialogue and moved through theological reflection to its doctrinal and biblical foundations.

My point in doing this is twofold. First, it is an attempt to help the reader see that the attitude and practice of prophetic dialogue is no mere theoretical construction but something going on in our everyday world of missionary service and ministerial life. A more intentional practice of prophetic dialogue, especially in the practice of intercultural mission, would therefore serve only to enhance the way we do mission.

Second, ending this reflection with a scriptural investigation points us to the sources of reflection on our missionary lives and hopefully will lead us to further scriptural reflection on the practice of prophetic dialogue. We participate in the work of a God whose persuasive triune presence in the world can transform and heal our lives. Searching God's Word will help us not only be transformed and healed more fully, but more worthily join God in that transforming and healing work.

16

More or Less in the Divine Image?
Gender Justice in an Intercultural Context

Toni Harris, OP

One of the sisters with whom I lived in Rome was a professor in one of the pontifical universities there. She taught students from all over the world; the classes were racially and ethnically diverse; the students were religious sisters, priests, and laity. One day when this sister-professor came home, she was quite upset. Something was happening in her classes that she never anticipated. She discovered that some of the sister-students from Africa were in fact doing the class assignments for some of the priest and seminarian students from Africa in the same class. The sisters were writing papers that the priests and seminarians then submitted as their own work. When the sister-professor confronted the problem, students involved were quite surprised. The men assumed that it was the role of the women to do this for them and the women seemed unable to object.

What questions does this experience raise? What does the situation reveal about culture? What assumptions does it demonstrate about gender roles? Or is this simply an example of a few misguided individuals engaged in questionable behavior that has little to do with culture or gender?

Effective efforts to promote the reign of God—God's dream for the world—in our globalized reality must recognize the importance of gender and culture. Beginning in centuries past, persons committed to proclaiming the gospel traveled mostly from the Global North to the South and from the Global West to the East. In this twenty-first century, men and women from

---

Toni Harris, OP, has been a Dominican Sister of Sinsinawa (USA) for more than forty-six years. Based in Rome, Italy, she served as the International Promoter for Justice and Peace for Dominican Sisters International (2007–2013). Sister Harris lived and worked among both reservation and urban Native American (indigenous) communities for sixteen years. She served as superior general of her congregation (2000–2006), and prior to that she was a general council member (1986–1994). Currently, she lives at her motherhouse in Sinsinawa, WI, USA.

this Global East and South have increasingly moved into significant roles in mission efforts in the Global West and North, as well as in their own countries of origin. Our current, intercultural reality demands that we seriously examine assumptions about gender and culture.

The Meanings of Key Terms

As we begin this reflection, let's consider the meanings of key terms involved:

Sex and Gender: Sex refers to physical or physiological differences between males and females, including both their primary and secondary sex characteristics. Gender, on the other hand, refers to social or cultural distinctions associated with being male or female. Scholars generally regard gender as a social construct—meaning that it does not exist naturally but is instead a concept that is created by culture and societal norms.[1]

Gender Roles: As we grow, we learn how to behave from those around us. In this socialization process, children are introduced to certain roles that are typically linked to their biological sex. The term gender role refers to a society's concept of how men and women are expected to act and behave. These roles are based on norms, or standards, created by society.[2]

Gender Justice: Gender justice means equal treatment and equitable value of the sexes. Therefore, gender equality is a fundamental human right that is guaranteed in international and regional treaties, conventions, and national legislation. Achieving gender equality means that men and women are able to share equally in the distribution of power and knowledge and have equal opportunities, rights, and obligations both in their private and public lives.[3] In addition, gender justice exists when all people—especially women, girls, and gender-variant people—are able to identify and express their gender and sexual orientation without fear, discrimination, or harm and have the economic, social, and political power and resources to make healthy decisions for themselves, their families, and their communities in all areas of their lives.[4]

LGBTQIA: Younger generations in some parts of the world are seeking to upend gender roles beyond male and female. They believe that the essential question is not whom they love but rather who they are—that is, identity as distinct from sexual orientation. While in the past, "gay and lesbian"

---

1. Sarah White, "Gender Roles and Differences," *Boundless Psychology. Boundless,* Nov. 14, 2014. https://www.boundless.com/psychology/textbooks/boundless-psychology-textbook/gender-and-sexuality-15/introduction-to-gender-and-sexuality-75/gender-roles-and-differences-296-12831/.

2. Ibid.

3. United Nations Population Fund (UNPFA), "Frequently Asked Questions about Gender Equality," 2005, https://www.unfpa.org/resources/frequently-asked-questions-about-gender-equality.

4. Social Justice Fund NW, Seattle, WA 98101, www.socialjusticefund.org.

were used to describe various sexual minorities—and more recently LGBT to include bisexual and transgender—a broader, more inclusive acronym is now proposed. LGBTQIA includes these additional elements: "Q" can mean "questioning" or "queer," an umbrella term itself, formerly derogatory before it was appropriated by gay activists in the 1990s; "I" is for "intersex," someone whose anatomy is not exclusively male or female; "A" stands for "ally" (a friend of the cause) or "asexual," characterized by the absence of sexual attraction.[5] Therefore, LGBTQIA stands for Lesbian, Gay, Bisexual, Transgender, Queer/Questioning, Intersexual and Asexual/Ally persons.

Scriptures and Social Teaching

For those of us who claim to be followers of Jesus, our efforts to promote gender justice in an intercultural context are grounded in the scriptures and in our Church's Social Teaching (CST). "So God created humankind in his image, in the image of God he created them; male and female he created them" (Gen 1:27). The foundational principle of CST is the dignity of the human person. Every human being is created in the image and likeness of God and therefore has inherent dignity. However, our words and actions sometimes reveal an assumption that certain human beings are created more in God's image than are others. This seems to be especially true related to matters of gender. Otherwise, why would basic human rights be denied to women and girls? Or to those who are LGBTQIA?

Let us first consider gender justice as this relates to women and girls. "Pre-Vatican II, women covered their heads, were considered impure after the birth of a child, could not enter the sanctuary in the Church, never had a chance to read or study scripture, could not study theology, and in general were looked upon as second class in the church and a source of temptation and sin. Pope John XXIII . . . helped to change all this. He created a consciousness in the Church of the 'signs of the times' with regard to women" (PT 41). As early as 1963, Pope John XXIII acknowledged: "Since women are becoming even more conscious of their human dignity, they will not tolerate being treated as inanimate objects or mere instruments, but claim, both in domestic and public life, the rights and duties that befit a human person."[6]

Developing this theme, Professor Mary Martone states,

> *Gaudium et Spes* is a pastoral constitution that puts a great deal of emphasis on the dignity of the human person and the solidarity of the entire human family. It encourages us to support this dignity and

5. Michael Schulman, "Generation LGBTQIA," *New York Times*, January 9, 2013.

6. Virginia Saldanha, "Vatican II Brought Wholeness to Life," *Just Good Company: A Cyberjournal of Religion and Culture* 1, no. 3 (September 2003), http://www.westcoastcompanions.org/jgc/1.3/saldanhatext.htm.

solidarity in the context of the modern world, to scrutinize the "signs of the times," and to interpret these signs in the light of the gospel. It recognizes the shift from a static concept of reality to a more dynamic and evolutionary one, and highlights various concerns that have arisen as a result of this shift. One of the concerns that the document highlights is the social relationships between men and women. *Gaudium et Spes* recognizes discrimination as an evil that is to be overcome, and encourages us to work towards the elimination of discrimination.[7]

Specifically, in the document we hear the following challenge:

Nevertheless, with respect to the fundamental rights of the person, every type of discrimination, whether social or cultural, whether based on sex, race, color, social condition, language or religion, is to be overcome and eradicated as contrary to God's intent. For in truth it must still be regretted that fundamental personal rights are still not being universally honored. Such is the case of a woman who is denied the right to choose a husband freely, to embrace a state of life or to acquire an education or cultural benefits equal to those recognized for men. (GS 29)

Likewise, the *Catechism of the Catholic Church* also underscores this teaching: "Every form of social or cultural discrimination in fundamental personal rights on the grounds of sex, race, color, social conditions, language, or religion must be curbed and eradicated as incompatible with God's design."[8]

Our church announces these principles for the universal church. Therefore, inequality and discrimination are unacceptable—no matter the cultural context. However, "[Fifty] years after the publication of *Gaudium et Spes*, women around the world are still struggling to be treated with dignity, to be afforded basic human rights, and to live free from the threats of violence and injustice, despite attempts that have been made to legislate rights and protections."[9]

Unjust Conditions for Women

Whether women live in less developed countries or in wealthy, industrialized countries, data reveal that inequality continues for women. Consider the following facts:

- Every year, more than one million children are left motherless because of preventable deaths of women in childbirth. More than 350,000 women

---

7. Marilyn Martone, "*Gaudium et Spes* Suggests a Change in Moral Imagination to Ensure the Just Treatment of Women," *Journal of Catholic Social Thought* 3, no. 2 (2006): 373.

8. *Catechism of the Catholic Church* (Vatican City: Libreria Editrice Vaticana, 1993), #1935.

9. Martone, "*Gaudium et Spes* Suggests a Change," 373.

die annually from complications during pregnancy or childbirth, almost all of them (99 percent) in developing countries. The maternal mortality rate is declining only slowly, even though the vast majority of deaths are avoidable. In South Asia and sub-Saharan Africa more than half of births are not attended by skilled staff.[10]

- Recent data show that in sub-Saharan Africa, North Africa, and the Middle East, women account for more than half of people living with HIV/AIDS. The toll exacted by HIV/AIDS on the lives of women extends beyond their physical health to the families and communities that depend on them.[11]

- The majority of children not in school are girls, due to cultural mores that favor boy children. Seventy-two million children—54 percent of them girls—are out of school. However, measurable progress has been made toward greater gender parity in primary enrollment.[12]

- Two out of three of the world's illiterate adults are women. Women account for two-thirds of the world's 774 million illiterate adults—a proportion that is unchanged over the past two decades.[13]

- Women continue to bear most of the responsibilities for the home: caring for children and other dependent household members, preparing meals and doing other housework. In all regions, women spend at least twice as much time as men on unpaid domestic work.[14]

- Over the years, women have entered various traditionally male-dominated occupations. However, they are still less frequently employed in jobs with status, power, and authority. Women are more likely than men to work as unpaid family laborers or in the informal sector. Women farmers tend to farm smaller plots and less-profitable crops than men. Women entrepreneurs operate in smaller firms and less-profitable sectors. As a result, women everywhere tend to earn less than men.[15]

- Women continue to be underrepresented in national parliaments, where on average only 17 percent of seats are occupied by women. Only 7 of 150 elected heads of state in the world are women, and only 11 of 192 heads of government.[16]

---

10. UN Department of Public Information, "We Can End Poverty—2015 Millennium Development Goals. Goal 5: Improve Maternal Health," DPI/2650 E/Rev. 1, September 2010.

11. amfAR, The Foundation for AIDS Research, New York, NY 10005–3908.

12. UN Department of Economic and Social Affairs, Statistics Division: Demographic and Social Statistics, "The World's Women 2010: Trends and Statistics," United Nations, New York, 2010, viii.

13. Ibid.

14. Ibid. ix.

15. Ibid.

16. Ibid. x.

- Of the 500 largest corporations in the world, only 24 have a female chief executive officer.[17] In many countries, women—especially poor women—have less say over decisions and less control over resources in their households.
- Female genital mutilation/cutting affects an estimated 130 million women and girls. Each year, two million more undergo the practice.[18] Violence against women also takes the form of other harmful practices: rape and sexual abuse of girls; forced and early marriage; stalking; crimes in the name of "honor"; acid burning; dowry-related violence; and widow inheritance and cleansing (both of which increase HIV risks); trafficking and sexual exploitation; sexual harassment and domestic violence.[19]
- Throughout the world, one in three women will be raped, beaten, coerced into sex or otherwise abused in her lifetime. Violence against women (VAW) is a violation of women's fundamental human rights and is both a cause and a consequence of women's inequality. Systematic rape, used as a weapon of war, has left millions of women and adolescent girls traumatized, forcibly impregnated, or infected with HIV.[20]
- 884 million people worldwide do not have access to safe drinking water. More than half of rural households and about a quarter of urban households in sub-Saharan Africa lack easy access to drinking water. In most of those households, the burden of water collection rests on women. Poor infrastructure and housing conditions as well as natural hazards disproportionately affect women from the less-developed regions.[21]
- Lack of access to clean energy fuels, and improved stoves in sub-Saharan Africa and parts of Southern and Southeastern Asia, continue to have a major impact on health. Women are more exposed than men to smoke from burning solid fuels because they spend more time near a fire while cooking, and more time indoors taking care of children and household chores.[22]
- Women and children make up more than 70 percent of the poorest people in the world. Continuing gender inequity means poverty hits women and their children the hardest.[23]

---

17. Caroline Fairchild, "Number of Fortune 500 Women CEOs Reaches Historic High," http://fortune.com, June 3, 2014.

18. UNICEF, "Three million girls undergo female genital cutting every year," https://unicef.org, November 24, 2005.

19. End Violence Against Women, United Kingdom, www.endviolenceagainst women.org.uk.

20. Ibid.

21. UN Department of Economic and Social Affairs, "The World's Women 2010," x.

22. Ibid.

23. The Borgen Project, "Top 10 International Poverty Statistics," https://borgenproject.org, August 1, 2013.

- Half the migrants around the world are female, and numbers are increasing. Currently 104 million women, 48.4 percent of the global migrant population, are away from their homes, fleeing persecution, poverty, and economic and political instability.[24]
- More than one-half of the victims of human trafficking are women and girls. It is estimated that victims of human trafficking (adults and children in forced labor, bonded labor, and forced prostitution) around the world are 12.3 million (only 0.4 percent are identified), and at least 56 percent of those victims are female.[25]
- The statistical phenomenon of "missing women and girls" does not refer to female runaways. Rather, it is the shortfall in the actual number of women relative to the number that would be expected if there were no sex-selective abortion or female infanticide or if the newborn of both sexes received similar levels of health care and nutrition. Globally, about four million girls and women "go missing" each year due to prebirth discrimination or excess mortality at birth. Nearly all (85 percent) are in China, sub-Saharan Africa, and India. About two-fifths of the missing are never born; one-fifth "goes missing" in infancy and childhood, and the remaining two-fifths do so between the ages of 15 and 59.[26]

Responses: Civil and Ecclesial

During recent decades, the United Nations has attempted to respond to injustices affecting women and girls in particular. Such actions include the following:

1946 The Commission on the Status of Women (CSW or UNCSW) was established by the United Nations to promote, report on, and monitor issues relating to the political, economic, civil, social, and educational rights of women.

1979 The UN General Assembly adopted the Convention on the Elimination of All Forms of Discrimination against Women (CEDAW).

2000 The Millennium Development Goals of the UN identified several objectives to improve conditions for women and girls.

2008 UN "Security Council resolution #1820" recognized sexual violence in conflict as a matter of international peace and security.

2010 In July 2010, the United Nations General Assembly created "UN Women," the United Nations Entity for Gender Equality and the

---

24. The United Nations Population Fund, "Migration," www.unfpa.org.

25. United Nations Office on Drugs and Crime, "Global Report on Trafficking in Persons 2012," https://unodc.org, p. 7.

26. The World Bank, World Development Report 2012: Gender Equality and Development, https://openknowledge.worldbank.org.

Empowerment of Women. This new structure came about as part of the UN reform agenda, bringing together existing resources and mandates for greater impact.

Additionally, it is helpful to recognize that the Delegation of the Holy See to the United Nations has been a strong advocate concerning some significant realities affecting women worldwide. Consider the following formal interventions of the Holy See in recent years:

1988 "The rights of women are a natural consequence of the fundamental and inalienable equality of all persons flowing from the dignity of the human nature which they share."[27]

2010 "Women and girls must be guaranteed their full enjoyment of civil, political, economic, social, and cultural rights, including equal access to education and health."[28]

2010 "The wellbeing of the future of the human community depends to a great extent upon the ability of governments and civil society to truly respect women, their dignity and worth."[29]

2011 "Taking up the issue of human trafficking, my delegation cannot stress enough that this form of modern slavery must end and it must end now!"[30]

2012 "Poverty and hunger are brought about to a large degree by unfair social and political systems that perpetuate inequality, where women are deprived of legal rights and a voice in decisions that affect them."[31]

2014 "Reports show that, in many parts of the world, women and children form the majority of the poor and are affected by the burden of poverty in very specific ways. . . . The Holy See believes that much is still to be done to effectively address the inequalities between men and women, girls and boys."[32]

Although the church stands firm on the principle that all human beings are created in the Divine image and promotes justice for women and girls in

27. Suzanne Scorsone, "The Church Has Defended Women's Rights for 2,000 Years," *L'Osservatore Romano* 31, no. 17, April 29, 1998.

28. Celestino Migliore, Statement of the Permanent Observer Mission of the Holy See to the United Nations, https://holyseemission.org, July 1, 2010.

29. The Holy See Delegation, 23rd Special Session of the General Assembly, New York, October 12, 2010.

30. The Holy See Delegation, 55th Session of the Commission on the Status of Women, February 28, 2011.

31. The Holy See Delegation, 56th Session of the Commission on the Status of Women, March 6, 2012.

32. Bernardito Auza, Statement of the Permanent Observer Mission of the Holy See to the United Nations, https://holyseemission.org, October 14, 2014.

international venues, it is ironic, therefore, that the church has not incor-
porated in its own structures and systems the values to which it calls other
institutions in society. This problem was recognized by the church itself in
the 1971 Synod of Bishops document Justice in the World:

> While the Church is bound to give witness to justice, she recognizes
> that anyone who ventures to speak to people about justice must first
> be just in their eyes. Hence we must undertake an examination of the
> modes of acting and of the possessions and life style found within the
> Church herself. Within the Church rights must be preserved. No one
> should be deprived of his ordinary rights because he is associated with
> the Church in one way or another. . . . We also urge that women should
> have their own share of responsibility and participation in the com-
> munity life of society and likewise of the Church. We propose that this
> matter be subjected to a serious study employing adequate means: for
> instance, a mixed commission of men and women, religious and lay
> people, of differing situations and competence. (JW 41–43)

Related to this point, the World Union of Catholic Women's Organizations
(WUCWO), which represents Catholic women's groups with a combined
membership of thirty million, made this important observation in the mid-
1980s: "the way we understand humanity, the way we understand what it
means to be a human being created in the image and likeness of God, conditions the roles of people in private and public life, both in society and in
the church. It is now clear that anthropology is responsible for much of the
existing stereotyping, discrimination and conflictual divisiveness that exists
in the world and in the church."[33] The report expressed concern that many
women leave the church because the church is insensitive to their desire to
"participate fully" in her life and mission.

In one of the countries of Asia where there are several Dominican congregations, there is a continuing concern about religious congregations who are
under the authority of particular local bishops (diocesan right), rather than the
authority of the Holy See. For example, rather than encouraging small congregations of the same charism to come together and explore the advantages of
becoming a united, larger congregation—perhaps of pontifical right—, some
bishops have urged congregations of sisters in their dioceses to separate from
their "mother" congregation in a neighboring diocese. Sometimes manipulating ethnic differences, a bishop may pressure a congregation to place itself
under his jurisdiction and to distance itself from other congregations that
share the same charism. This phenomenon has been happening for decades

---

33. Mary Luke Tobin, S.L., "Women in the Church since Vatican II," *America*, November
1, 1986, https://www.americamagazine.org/issue/100/women-church-vatican-ii.

around the world. It is an effort to undermine the autonomy and strength of religious congregations. Rather than supporting the development and solidarity of congregations of the same charism for the sake of their shared mission, a bishop may prefer to keep a congregation local, dependent on himself and under his control. This action can be an abuse of local women religious.

During my travels over the past several years, I had many opportunities to witness the status of women in local churches around the world. One of the experiences that was most significant for me happened while I was visiting our Dominican Sisters in Mozambique, a country on the southeastern coast of the African continent. As we prepared to go to Mass on a Sunday while I was there, the sisters told me we would need to leave thirty minutes early in order to get a seat in the church. Now the church was on the same compound as the sisters' house—less than a five-minute walk. Yet, the church was nearly full when we arrived. When it came time for the gospel, a local woman stepped into the pulpit. And the priest stepped to the center of the main aisle and—like everyone else in the church—turned his attention to the woman. The woman proclaimed the gospel loudly in the mother tongue of the assembly. After the gospel, the priest began to preach his homily in the country's official language, Portuguese. He paused periodically so that the woman in the pulpit could interpret his sermon in the local language of the people. I was moved by the way she announced glad tidings in that assembly with a powerful, emphatic voice. I was delighted to learn later that she was a member of the Dominican Laity.

Although the status of women is improving in some areas, gender justice for women in society and in the church has not been achieved. "The call of *Gaudium et Spes* is that women must be respected and appreciated. All discrimination against women must end. For this to happen, however, there needs to be a change of hearts as well as laws put into place that protect women."[34]

LGBTQIA Persons and Gender Justice

As we next consider LGBTQIA persons and gender justice, it is helpful to recall an attitude that appears to have been a reality in many North American indigenous cultures—prior to colonization by Europeans. In many Native American cultures, persons who exhibited cross-gender roles (the male female; the female male) were called "two-spirited." In most cases, such persons were valued in the culture because they were blessed with two spirits, both male and female. Two-spirited people were often the visionaries, the healers, the medicine persons, the nannies of orphans, and the caregivers in

---

34. Martone, "*Gaudium et Spes* Suggests a Change," 13.

indigenous communities. However, with colonization and the influence of Christianity, two-spirited persons increasingly lost their dignity and place in society.[35] Nevertheless, this historical reality reveals the importance of culture in the shaping of gender roles.

Previously, it was stated that the term "gender role" refers to a society's concept of how men and women are expected to act and behave. Gender-variant persons whose actions and behaviors do not conform to society's norms for heterosexual men and women are frequently victims of injustice.

> Deeply embedded homophobic attitudes, often combined with a lack of adequate legal protection against discrimination on grounds of sexual orientation and gender identity, expose many LGBT people of all ages and in all regions of the world to egregious violations of their human rights. They are discriminated against in the labor market, in schools and in hospitals, and mistreated and disowned by their own families. On the streets of towns and cities around the world, they are singled out for physical attack—beaten, sexually assaulted, tortured and killed. And in some 76 countries, discriminatory laws criminalize private, consensual, same-sex relationships—exposing individuals to the risk of arrest, prosecution, and imprisonment.[36]

Our Catholic Social Teaching does not qualify the basic principle that all persons are created in the Divine image and, therefore, have inherent dignity. Therefore, no persons are created in a lesser Divine image. We are all daughters and sons of God, and every person is a revelation of God. Consider again the mandate from *Gaudium et Spes*: "With respect to the fundamental rights of the person, every type of discrimination, whether social or cultural, whether based on sex, race, color, social condition, language or religion, is to be overcome and eradicated as contrary to God's intent" (GS 29). Doesn't it follow, then, that the principles enumerated in the preceding paragraphs necessarily apply to persons who are lesbian, gay, bisexual, transgender, questioning, intersexual, or asexual?

In its final message in October 2014, the Synod on the Family stated the following:

> Some families have members who have a homosexual tendency. In this regard, the synod fathers asked themselves what pastoral atten-

35. Sandra Laframboise and Michael Anhorn, "The Way of the Two-Spirited People," www.dancingtoeaglespiritsociety.org.

36. Office of the High Commissioner, "Born Free and Equal: Sexual Orientation and Gender Identity in International Human Rights Law," www.ohchr.org, United Nations Human Rights, Geneva and New York, 2012, p. 7.

tion might be appropriate for them in accordance with the Church's teaching: "There are absolutely no grounds for considering homosexual unions to be in any way similar or even remotely analogous to God's plan for marriage and family." Nevertheless, men and women with a homosexual tendency ought to be received with respect and sensitivity. "Every sign of unjust discrimination in their regard should be avoided."[37]

The teachings of the Catholic Church regarding "gender-variant" persons do not presently emphasize equal rights in the same way that many other religious and civic institutions do. However, the church denounces discrimination and calls for "respect and sensitivity."

The United Nations began to directly address the human rights of LGBT persons around 2008. Resolutions related to this issue were adopted during the ensuing years. In 2012, the Office of the High Commissioner on Human Rights published "Born Free and Equal," with five key recommendations to member states regarding sexual orientation and gender identity. Careful consideration of the entire resource would be useful to all who hope to promote a more just world. The summary of the five recommendations is as follows:

• Protect people from homophobic and transphobic violence. Include sexual orientation and gender identity as protected characteristics in hate crime laws. Establish effective systems to record and report hate-motivated acts of violence. Ensure effective investigation and prosecution of perpetrators, and redress for victims of such violence. Asylum laws and policies should recognize that persecution on account of one's sexual orientation or gender identity may be a valid basis for an asylum claim.

• Prevent the torture and cruel, inhuman, and degrading treatment of LGBT persons in detention by prohibiting and punishing such acts and ensuring that victims are provided with redress. Investigate all acts of mistreatment by state agents and bring those responsible to justice. Provide appropriate training to law enforcement officers and ensure effective monitoring of places of detention.

• Repeal laws criminalizing homosexuality, including all laws that prohibit private sexual conduct between consenting adults of the same sex. Ensure that individuals are not arrested or detained on the basis of their sexual orientation or gender identity, and are not subjected to baseless and degrading physical examinations intended to determine their sexual orientation.

• Prohibit discrimination on the basis of sexual orientation and gender identity. Enact comprehensive laws that include sexual orientation and gen-

37. Synod of Bishops, "The Pastoral Challenges of the Family in the Context of Evangelization," *Relatio Synodi*, October 2014, #55, available at http://www.vatican.va.

der identity as prohibited grounds of discrimination. In particular, ensure nondiscriminatory access to basic services, including in the context of employment and health care. Provide education and training to prevent discrimination and stigmatization of LGBT and intersex people.

- Safeguard freedom of expression, association, and peaceful assembly for LGBT and intersex people. Any limitations on these rights must be compatible with international law and must not be discriminatory. Protect individuals who exercise their rights to freedom of expression, association and freedom of assembly from acts of violence and intimidation by private parties.[38]

On September 26, 2014, the Human Rights Council of the United Nations adopted another resolution (A/HRC/27/L.27/Rev.1) on sexual orientation and gender identity and expressed grave concern at acts of violence and discrimination, in all regions of the world, committed against individuals because of their sexual orientation and gender identity. The council also requested the high commissioner to update the report entitled "Discriminatory laws and practices and acts of violence against individuals based on their sexual orientation and gender identity," with a view to sharing good practices and ways to overcome violence and discrimination. (Vote: 25 in favor; 14 against; 7 abstentions)

As is apparent from the vote distribution on UN resolutions related to this issue, there is no universally shared conviction concerning what constitutes gender justice for LGBTQIA persons. Cultural norms or standards vary greatly on this issue. However, the movement for recognition of the human rights of "gender-variant" persons is growing around the world.

Concluding Remark

The population of our world is currently about 7.6 billion people. Of that population, 50.4 percent are men and 49.6 percent are women.[39] There are thousands of peoples (cultural groups) in our world today. Many around the globe recognize at least seven categories of sexual orientation and gender identity. In light of all this, diversity is a significant global reality that has implications for any efforts to promote the reign of God—God's dream for the world.

If we take seriously the foundational principle of CST—the dignity of the human person—then this principle will affect our attitudes, words, and actions in the intercultural context today. As was stated earlier, CST is directed to the universal church. Therefore it must not be diluted or dis-

---

38. Office of the High Commissioner, "Born Free and Equal," 13.
39. Country Meters, http://countrymeters.info/en/World.

regarded depending on the cultural context. When persons of a particular culture genuinely incorporate the principles of CST as their own, then those persons may be able to influence their own cultural practices with the values of CST. It is unlikely that persons who are guests in a particular culture are able to effectively exercise such influence.

Gender justice requires everyone's effort. Change is not only the responsibility of those who seem to have power in particular situations, e.g., men over women, straight over gay. Rather, those who have been victims of injustice must also claim their dignity and rights. Women and "gender-variant" persons must assert that they, too, are created in God's image. Such struggles for justice always face the challenge of maintaining mutual respect in the process, without "returning evil for evil" (Rom 12:17).

Respect for human dignity must be in the forefront of our intercultural exchanges. The experience of intercultural living is enhanced to the extent that every person is respected and treated equally. The dream of God for the world includes "peace, justice and joy in the spirit" (Rom 14:17) for all God's children. May we recommit ourselves to promoting gender justice in every cultural context.

17

"Drinking from the Same Calabash"
Resources for Reconciliation in African Spirituality

Laurenti Magesa

Human Nature and the Reality of Conflict

Reconciliation is an exercise, or rather process, of conflict transformation. One thing that cannot be easily disputed is that conflict is part and parcel of human existence. If history is a record of anything, it generally appears to be dotted by conflict, often violent, among human beings—individuals, groups, and nations. To be sure, the traditions and records of various peoples and nations also say something concerning seasons of planting and harvesting, of hunting and fishing, or of buying and selling. But these do not feature with the same frequency and intensity in the chronicles of history as the narratives about war, conquest, and defeat. Accounts of peace and tranquility exist, but they appear less often than those of people killed in raids, of hostages captured, property looted, and buildings destroyed in combat. History generally, therefore, seems to consist of accounts of empires built viciously by the sword and of material gain established by force, for the benefit of some and at the expense of and by the subjugation and economic deprivation of others. So much so that we find that even in some otherwise innocuous activities in human interaction, like commerce, there are frequently instances of misunderstandings, giving rise to hostilities between and among peoples. Indeed,

Laurenti Magesa is a priest of the Catholic Diocese of Musoma in Tanzania. He teaches African theology and Christian ethics at Hekima College, Jesuit School of Theology and Tangaza University College, both constituent colleges of the Catholic University of Eastern Africa (CUEA) in Nairobi, Kenya. He has authored many books; the latest is *What Is Not Sacred? African Spirituality* (Orbis Books, 2013). His main areas of research include African religion and culture and their historical and current interface with Christianity.

this situation, unfortunately, continues to prevail. The story of human relations is, in fact, essentially no better today than it was yesterday. Given the technological capability of destroying one another and even the entire earth that contemporary humanity has acquired, this precarious situation may actually be worsening.[1]

Conflict between and among religions resulting in "religious wars" is, similarly, also not new. Often, the various "holy books" that different faiths have do, in fact, contain narratives of violent subjugation of one faith by another or others based on certain conceptual principles. Without exception, these concepts are glorified in the original narratives, but much more so, and more ominously, by their interpreters throughout the ages. Oftentimes they are taken as they stand to represent the divine will. On this account, even forcible "conversions" of people from one faith allegiance to another have sometimes been lauded as the godly thing to do.[2] Time and again, these interpretations, to some degree or another, still direct the lives of some religious adherents. This, for example, is true of sections of contemporary Christianity and Islam. True, many contemporary leaders and scholars of these

---

1. By comparison, in terms of ways used and the number of lives involved, ancient conflicts come nowhere near to the devastation modern and contemporary wars cause. For example, between 60 and 85 million people died during the Second World War alone. In 1945, on August 6 and 9 respectively, atomic bombs—the only ones to have been employed in warfare before or since—were dropped by American war planes on the Japanese cities of Hiroshima and Nagasaki. Of a total population of 350,000 in the city of Hiroshima, the explosion killed about 70,000 instantly while another 70,000 died within five years from the bomb's effects. This constituted approximately a third of the city's population. See http://history1900s.about. com. The numbers of casualties in any modern conflict thus generally exceed by far those of premodern times. In the wars of the late twentieth and early twenty-first centuries, most of the victims, especially civilians, who are today euphemistically called "collateral damage," and are mostly from the vanquished sides, have gone unaccounted for. This is the case, for example, with the invasion of Iraq in 2003.

2. In his 1994 apostolic letter *Tertio Millennio Adveniente* (35), Pope John Paul II recognized the folly of this perception and publicly requested for forgiveness on behalf of the Catholic Church whenever this had happened in the past. The pertinent passage is worth quoting in full for its forthrightness: "Another painful chapter of history to which the sons and daughters of the Church must return with a spirit of repentance is that of the acquiescence given, especially in certain centuries, to intolerance and even the use of violence in the service of truth." Even "considerations of mitigating factors" of sincerity and limited vision and knowledge on the part of the perpetrators, the pope wrote, cannot totally "exonerate the Church from the obligation to express profound regret for the weaknesses of so many of her sons and daughters who sullied her face, preventing her from fully mirroring the image of her crucified Lord, the supreme witness of patient love and of humble meekness. From these painful moments of the past a lesson can be drawn for the future, leading all Christians to adhere fully to the sublime principle stated by the Council: 'The truth cannot impose itself except by virtue of its own truth, as it wins over the mind with both gentleness and power.'" See also The International Theological Commission, "Memory and Reconciliation: The Church and the Faults of the Past," December 1999. See www.vatican.va.

religions have largely learned to interpret these narratives in a way that is not destructive of human unity. On the contrary, they see these narratives as symbols for just the opposite spiritual and religious message of peace and harmony. However, too many others remain unable or unwilling to see this point. This is exemplified in our day by the intermittent acts of interreligious brutality occurring around the world. Although, of course, there are many people who would refute the claim, several reputable scholars such as Hans Küng,[3] Paul F. Knitter,[4] and Samuel P. Huntington[5] have advanced the not implausible thesis that if there were to be another global tragedy in the future similar to that of the two World Wars in the last century, chances are that it will break out not as a result of differences of political or economic ideologies but on account of religious-cultural antagonisms.

Küng, a Catholic theologian, ecumenist, and scholar of interfaith dialogue, has long argued for mutual understanding and tolerance among religions. As a member of the Parliament of the World's Religions, he sees the only way to avoid universal conflagration lies in the realization by every human being, but especially by religions, of the interconnectedness of the human race, regardless of ethnic or religious affiliations. Along the same lines, Knitter analyzes Christian claims of religious-epistemological "superiority" and shows how they can lead to intolerance. However, interfaith harmony is possible, according to Knitter, and a particular religious belonging need not be a source of strife in the world, something which, given present trends, Huntington, a political theorist, foresees.

As Huntington argues, "in the emerging era, clashes of civilizations are the greatest threat to world peace, and an international world order based on civilizations is the surest safeguard against world war."[6] Huntington notes the view of Lester Pearson that, in the interests of global peace and to avoid inevitable "catastrophe," different cultures must now be willing to live side by side and learn from one another's positive values.[7] In Küng's view, "one cannot repeat often enough the thesis ... [that] there can be no peace among the nations without peace among the religions. In short, there can be no world peace without religious peace."[8] Knitter understands this interreligious dialogue to include its basic sense of people merely living together and cooperating with one another, even without verbal or doctrinal philosophical

---

3. Hans Küng, *Global Responsibility: In Search of a New Global Ethic* (New York: Crossroad, 1991).

4. Paul F. Knitter, *One Earth Many Religions: Multifaith Dialogue and Global Responsibility* (Maryknoll, NY: Orbis Books, 1995).

5. Samuel P. Huntington, *The Clash of Civilizations and the Remaking of World Order* (New York: Simon & Schuster, 1996).

6. Ibid., 321.

7. Ibid.

8. Küng, *Global Responsibility*, 76.

articulation of the principles behind the dialogical endeavor. He calls this "the broad but hidden liberative dialogue."[9] At any rate, from the religious experience and basic faith of human beings, religion must become a major player in the process of reconciliation and world peace. This is absolutely necessary in our day when, although the technological and information revolution is in many respects turning the world into a "global village," this process of globalization is paradoxically at the same time pitting cultures against one another, increasingly in religious terms. So, as Huntington, Knitter, and Küng have argued—correctly in my opinion—resources for conflict transformation, understanding, and peace—in a word, reconciliation—should be sought from the religions of the world themselves. This is why, to the necessity of interreligious dialogue in the interests of interreligious and world peace, Küng adds a third requirement: research into the resources for peace within the various religious traditions. "There can be no dialogue between the religions without research into theological foundations," he writes.[10]

Many religious faiths with written traditions and histories of theological speculation have tried to indicate in a systematic way the moral and spiritual resources for dialogue embedded in their traditions. Again this is true of Christianity and Islam, among several others. In the oral religious traditions, such as in African religions, the ethical foundations for individual and social behavior were largely transmitted by word of mouth from one generation to another. Though no less methodical overall, this mode of communication made them much less amenable to academic analysis, and therefore facilitated and encouraged the tendency—actually the error—by outsiders, particularly those raised on and accustomed to written traditions, to dismiss oral traditions. Literary traditions have invariably described oral traditions as lacking in divine inspiration (nonrevealed) and having no ability to provide serious social guidance. However, following Küng's intuition about the importance, for the sake of world peace, of research into the theological foundations of religious faith, the present contribution reflects on the assets that African religions or African spirituality hold and can offer for the process of reconciliation.

God's Kingdom Comes Only as a Result of Reconciliation

The hermeneutic key for building God's kingdom on earth can be said in one word to be conversion (*metanoia*). This was John the Baptist's message announcing the arrival of the physical, historical embodiment of that kingdom, Jesus the Christ (Matt 3:1–12). It was, moreover, Jesus' personal message identifying himself early on in his ministry (Matt 4:17). As the Gospel

---

9. Knitter, *One Earth*, 178–79.
10. Küng, *Global Responsibility*, 105.

according to Matthew puts it: "From that time on Jesus began to preach, 'Repent, for the kingdom of heaven has come near'" (Matt 4:17). Perhaps even more significant in terms of ecclesiology and pastoral theology, this was the task bequeathed by Jesus to the disciples whom he designated to carry on his work (Matt 10:7). The command to love and its theological elaborations that we find in various places in the New Testament are explanations of this fundamental principle of conversion. Empirically, it translates into reconciliation. For, what else can love be in a world characterized by conflict and strife, as we have described it in the preceding paragraphs? The injunction of St. Paul to the Corinthians explains this point:

> Therefore, if anyone is in Christ, the new creation has come: The old has gone, the new is here! All this is from God, who reconciled us to himself through Christ and gave us the ministry of reconciliation: that God was reconciling the world to himself in Christ, not counting people's sins against them. And he has committed to us the message of reconciliation. We are therefore Christ's ambassadors, as though God were making his appeal through us. We implore you on Christ's behalf: Be reconciled to God. God made him who had no sin to be sin for us, so that in him we might become the righteousness of God. (2 Cor 5:17–21)

This perception might at first sight suggest a pessimistic, almost Manichaean view of the world, where the primary understanding of reality is that of evil almost incapable of "redemption." This impression, which the Bible—especially in its creation myths—suggests is, however, false. The original goodness and beauty of the human creature and the entire universe are not in question in this approach. On the contrary, they are affirmed as the foundational reality of divine will. Conversion or *metanoia* is a task that implies the sustained effort of reviving and reintegrating within us humans and in the universe the original nature of creation as the reflection of the face of God. Thus, prevailing events notwithstanding, the foundational principle of Christian thought and action should not be the power of evil but goodness, not destructiveness but constructiveness, not divisiveness but integrity and wholeness. We might apply the prayer of Jesus for unity of everything in Christ to the process of reconciliation as the true meaning of conversion: "That all of them may be one, Father, just as you are in me and I am in you" (John 17:20–26). Obviously, it would be reductionist and a serious mistake to restrict this prayer to what today goes under the label of "Christian Unity." Its intention, as Paul shows in the passage we have quoted above, is much wider and deeper; it embraces the entire universe as the divine reign,[11] in other words, Jesus prays that the universe should be "reconciled in God."

---

11. For example, see *The New Interpreter's Bible* (Nashville: Abingdon Press, 2000), 95–96.

A powerful illustration of this in Christian theology is the doctrine of the Trinity when it is understood not as theoretical construct ("Trinity *in se*"), as Elizabeth A. Johnson notes, but as an active "symbol in the religious experience of salvation" in human history ("Trinity *pro nobis*").[12] The dynamics of the Trinity involve an endless process of a faith vision of perfect integration, or unity in difference, for *the world*.[13] The Trinity cannot be well understood apart from society, Johnson insists. In her own words, "What is particular to . . . [the Christian] faith is that . . . [the] one God has graciously reached out to the world in love in the person of Jesus Christ in order to heal, redeem, and liberate—in a word, to save."[14] In this process, the trinitarian symbol, that God is one-in-three, is not without significance. "To say that God is *one* is to negate division, thus affirming the unity of the divine being: there is only one God," Johnson explains. "To say that the 'persons' are *three* is to negate solitariness, thus affirming that the divine being dwells in living communion." God is "a living fecundity of relational life that overflows to the world" "with gracious compassion."[15] This is, of course, the call of Christian and human living that recognizes the other as oneself.

We have to be realistic, however, as Johnson warns. The Trinity as a practical and active symbol of communion is precisely an appeal. It does not imply the automatic end of conflict in the day-to-day world, an accomplished reconciliation or kingdom achieved. "Rather," she says, the Trinity "functions as a source of vision to shape our actions in the world, a criterion to measure the fidelity of our lives, and a basis for resisting every form of oppression that diminishes community."[16] In human experience, the most serious situation that militates most fundamentally against community is absence of reconciliation or refusal to transform conflict into mutuality. As the letter to the Ephesians says: "'In your anger do not sin': Do not let the sun go down while you are still angry" (Eph 4:26). There is similar counsel elsewhere in the scriptures.[17] African spirituality likewise holds this as a cardinal point.

---

12. Elizabeth A. Johnson, *Quest for the Living God: Mapping Frontiers in the Theology of God* (New York: Continuum, 2007), 206 and 210.

13. Because there is no conflict in the triune God, the image of "reconciliation" does not quite fit here unless it is understood—which it ought to be—in the sense of integration or, in the expression of Johnson, *Quest*, 214, "coinhere[nce] . . . in a communion of love."

14. Ibid., 202.

15. Ibid., 213 and 222.

16. Ibid., 223. Taking into account the distinction that sociologist Ferdinand Tönnies made between "community" and "society" (Gemeinschaft and Gesellschaft), we should understand here, at least theologically, the latter as a desirable internal extension of the former.

17. For example, see Jesus' teaching in Matt 5:21–48.

Foundations in African Spirituality for Conflict: Transformation and Reconciliation

One distinctive feature of African spirituality is its strong centripetal perspective for all reality. In the final analysis, the dynamics of the energies of creation that make all existence and particularly human life possible are, in this view, not binary but single. All vital energies tend toward the core, which is life in its totality and fullness.[18] Of course, African spirituality is not naïve; it recognizes the reality of evil influences in the universe. These are centrifugal, destructive forces that tend to split life asunder. But they are considered to be only a necessary element in the process of the unity of life, making the reintegration effort of the vital powers all the more urgent. Religion and spirituality consist precisely in this human struggle of bringing together and placing all of the existential forces (good and bad) at the service of the good life. In other words, the final goal, or what in Christian theology we call the salvation of humanity and the universe, is reconciliation, wholeness or holiness. This makes the sense and reality of harmony the most desired quality of human and universal existence. Anything that threatens harmony, that is, any centrifugal force threatening consonance of any kind in life, must be brought and made to serve wholeness. This is why destructive forces—typically death and everything associated with it—must be treated with the same seriousness as, or even with more attentiveness than, the benevolent ones.

Everything possible must be mustered to keep at bay suffering and death at a young age. Elderhood is something desirable and is held in great esteem and respect when it has succeeded in integrating (or reconciling) together in the individual elder all the various forces so that they serve positively his or her life. But beyond that, through the elder in question, vital forces must also, conspicuously and positively, serve the good life of the family, clan, and the entire community. This link between the elder's positive accomplishments and the life of the community is essential in African spirituality: by his/her integrated, whole, or holy life, the elder achieves "salvation" for him- or herself and also, in a way, for the entire community, the elder being part and parcel of it. To be complete, one's personal holiness must be reflected by a similar holiness in the community, fostered in one way or another by the (example of the) elder through his/her solidarity with it. As Felix Mabvuto Phiri explains "Solidarity and service towards one another in the community are [the] ways through which life is propagated, increased and protected."[19] And this cohesion is realized through reconciliation. Reconciliation in

---

18. See Charles Nyamiti, "The Incarnation Viewed from the African Understanding of Person," *African Christian Studies* 6, no 1 (1990): 3–27.

19. Felix Mabvuto Phiri, *Reconciliation: A Scandal of Divine-human Self-emptying Love* (Nairobi: CUEA Press, 2014), 281.

African spirituality, according to Phiri, serves unity in the threefold dimension of community: "the self," "the visible world of humanity and nature," and "the invisible world of God, spirits, and ancestors."[20]

We have just discussed the dimension of the self in the process of reconciliation, where the self-integrated elder is the epitome. Phiri, referring to other African scholars, warns that self-integration of the individual should not be mistaken for selfishness or "narcissism," because genuine self-integration is always directed outward toward and for the individual members of the community, and ultimately for the entire community so that they may enjoy abundant life. In a word, genuine self-integration is for service. Authentic elderhood reaches its culmination in ancestorship, and since the primary responsibility of the ancestors is to see to it that their descendants living on earth enjoy the good life, they must constantly stay close to and in communion with them.[21] In these dynamics, the responsibility of the living to the ancestors—also referred to as "the living-dead"—is crucial. To deserve ancestral solidarity, the living must strive to remain reconciled and maintain harmonious communion with the ancestors and other invisible powers as well as the rest of visible creation. Disharmony with any of these elements destabilizes the entire social and religious fabric of society at all these levels.[22] The outward-going process of each dimension is, in fact—even if apparently paradoxical—centripetal, as each dimension seeks the good life of the other, and consequently of the entire community. By being in solidarity with the community of the living, the elders represent it before the other dimensions of existence.

Thus Phiri accurately observes that, according to African spirituality, the most damaging breach of order "does not come from outside the family or the community" but from within it. Loyalty to the community in all of its dimensions is of the essence. Phiri makes clear, in agreement with Desmond Tutu, that any breach of harmony must be repaired at the earliest opportunity and as thoroughly as possible. "The insider's treachery destabilizes the whole system which binds the family [and community] together." Reconciliation in the sense of "healing of breaches, the redressing of imbalances, the restoration of broken relationships" is, therefore, the only approach toward a comprehensible and acceptable remedy. Reconciliation in African spirituality seeks "to rehabilitate both the victim and the perpetrator, who should be given the opportunity to be integrated into the community he [/she] has injured."[23] This is so in order to make it possible for the perpetrator of disharmony to again share life together with the community, to "drink from

---

20. Phiri, *Reconciliation*, 281.

21. See Charles Nyamiti, *Christ as Our Ancestor: Christology from an African Perspective* (Gweru: Mambo Press, 1984).

22. Phiri, *Reconciliation*, 281–85.

23. Ibid., 282–83.

the same calabash," as the saying goes. The goal, as always, is total healing, making the community whole. It is a goal that is ideally inclusive of the entire community. When it becomes necessary that an obstinate individual is excluded—or more correctly, excludes him/herself—from social communion, the pain is felt by the community for a long time, or even indefinitely, and forever cries out for rectification, for such exclusion is a negative lesson for the ideal, primary, and positive intent of inclusion.

"Drinking from the Same Calabash": Structures of Reconciliation in African Spirituality

If there is any one overriding need in the African psyche, it is not power or success or glory, but the need to belong. Now as in the past, it controls the social existence of black African peoples everywhere. Practical expressions of this need have, of course, changed, and do not appear as they did in older generations; individualistic tendencies are more prevalent today and are oftentimes peddled as desirable virtues. The preference for large families, however, and the urge to form associations to further communal assistance in the eventuality of adverse or even propitious situations, such as funerals or weddings, for example, indicate that belonging is still a strong and driving criterion in the African person's life. Another indication is attachment to ancestral land, and this even among the elite, particularly when burial space for oneself or a dear one is the issue. Admittedly, in urban areas, these associations are now more class- than family-based, and the demands they place on a member can be much more easily be evaded. Still, the class in these scenarios substitutes for family (often mistakenly described by observers from outside Africa as "extended family"), since the latter is today much more geographically dispersed than was the case previously.

"Drinking from the same calabash"[24] or "eating together"[25] is the meta-

---

24. A calabash or calabash gourd is a dried and hollowed-out part of the fully grown fruit of a ground vine (Lagenaria siceraria). In the olden days, it was the preferred container for storing and serving certain foods and drinks such as rice, water, gruel, wine, or beer, or for making hats, musical instruments, or pipes. Even today when calabashes have been largely replaced in many African homes by industrial products such as glass, melamine, tin, and iron table utensils, older people still avow that drinks and food tasted better when served in a calabash rather than in these modern utensils.

25. This is the essence and meaning of the "mato oput" ritual as practiced among the Acholi people of Uganda, in which parties in a conflict are invited to drink some healing herbal concoction from the same calabash believed to cool down anger, or share a meal of a roasted lamb as "a final act of reconciliation." See Richard N. Rwiza, "Opportunities for Reconciliation in Africa," in Agbonkhianmeghe E. Orobator, ed., *Practising [sic] Reconciliation, Doing Justice, Building Peace* (Nairobi: Paulines Publications, 2013), 35–36. Also Elias O. Opongo, "Between Violence, Reconciliation Rituals, and Justice in Northern Uganda: The Church in Africa and the Challenge of Post-Conflict Reconstruction," in ibid., 25–26.

phor that is used by peoples across the sub-Saharan region to depict this family- or class-based social bonding, expressing reconciliation and peace within the group. It stands for the reality of friendship, unity, participation, and communion in genuine community. In the African view, there is neither theoretical nor practical community when food and drink are not shared on a regular basis. This is the case from the most basic to the most complex of social groupings, as well as in a variety of occasions—from the most joyous to the most sorrowful. Sharing food and drink both expresses and creates solidarity, the most desired conditions of living together. No wonder, then, that food and drink feature prominently at reconciliation ceremonies, weddings, and funerals. The more the food and the participants in the meal at any of these occasions, the better is the hope for the success of the purpose of the occasion. When this happens, the conflicting parties, for example, seal their agreement to permanently cast away anger, the newlyweds stand a better chance of success in their marriage union, or the deceased, because this particular event contributes to the sustenance of their memory among the living, are set on a sure path toward ancestorship.

The basic intent or ideal of communion, community, cooperation, and participation constitutes the structure of reconciliation embedded in African spirituality. In Richard Rwiza's words, it implies "walking together." Reconciliation as conflict transformation means "a restoration of broken relationships," Rwiza explains. It is "an act of coming together of those who have been alienated or separated from each other by conflict."[26] Social alienation endangers the community at its very core, at the level of disturbing the congruence or harmony of the vital energies that assure not only personal vitality (I exist because we exist) but communal well-being as well (because we exist, I exist). It is crucial to point out in this regard that, ordinarily, "structures" of reconciliation in African spirituality are not extraneous to the whole process of day-to-day life. Rather, they are systemic, ideally embedded in the very fabric of daily living.

"This is why," as Achieng A. C. Oyier, notes, "working on social relationships is critical." It is here where "hospitality has the greatest potential to serve as a source of practical, immediate action . . . to sustain . . . peace."[27] According to Victor B. Adangba, hospitality as an integral part of the African conception of community, where everyone is a (prospective or actual) guest or host, "offers a hermeneutic for drawing a theology of peace leading . . . towards reconciliation and peace."[28] Hospitality, as portrayed even in

---

26. Rwiza, "Opportunities," 36.

27. Achieng A. C. Oyier, "Context of Peace: Transformation of Human Relationships and Peace Education," in Orobator, ed., *Practising Reconciliation*, 113.

28. Victor B. Adangba, "God Writes Straight Lines of Peace: A Theological Perspective for Peace in Côte d'Ivoire," in Orobator, ed., *Practising Reconciliation*, 103.

greeting formulas,[29] builds trust, perhaps the axial attitude that relieves the community from the burdens of the past and gives it hope for a harmonious existence for the present and future. Hospitality and trust are components of love in practice, love as "the real, concrete attachment of one being for another," as Jonathan Sacks has explained the concept.[30] They are visible signs of integrity. Here, what Frans Wijsen and Ralph Tanner portray in a different context as "the eyes and tongues of the neighborhood"[31] is of consequence for behavior. While individualistic ethos does not give much weight or attention to public opinion about one's personal conduct, African ethos places premium consideration on it because upon it depend the life and well-being of the community.

Some are more than skeptical about what sometimes seems like romanticism or idealization in Africa of values such as hospitality. How do we account for ethnic divisions and wars in the past and today, between and among African peoples who are reputably so hospitable? How about present-day xenophobia, not least in the birthplace of the Ubuntu philosophy (which is based on this idea) of South Africa?[32] We must note on this issue, however, that the skeptics are erroneous on two counts. First, they are anachronistic, looking at African traditional life with today's spectacles. The scope of community, as perceived by African spirituality then (as in other spiritualities), was by necessity geographically very limited, yes, in fact "clannish," lacking a global vision of humanity. Second, they forget that social ideals describe simply that, ideals (or "ideologies," according to M. E. Kropp Dakubu) and not necessarily practice. "Like the Ten Commandments, the rules would not have to be expounded so emphatically if people always obeyed them." In any society, despite the ideal one will find "under-handedness, dissatisfaction and rebellion, turbulence and lack of social cohesiveness."[33]

Pragmatism about the human condition has necessitated in African spirituality what we might call "extrinsic" or "extraordinary" patterns of reconciliation, structures that interrupt the everyday pattern of living to correct aberrations besetting it. From time to time there is drastic and public rupture of communion in society which brings about negative consequences, and these may even have natural causes, such as droughts, floods, general ill health, and lack of prosperity. In other words, there is an absence of the

---

29. For example, for the Ga people of Ghana, see M. E. Kropp Dakubu, "Creating Unity: The Context of Speaking Prose and Poetry in Ga," *Anthropos* 82 (1987): 507–27.

30. Jonathan Sacks, *The Dignity of Difference: How to Avoid the Clash of Civilizations* (London/New York: Continuum, 2002), 180.

31. Frans Wijsen and Ralph Tanner, *Seeking a Good Life: Religion and Society in Usukuma, Tanzania, 1945–1995* (Nairobi: Paulines Publications, 2000), 82.

32. Questions put to me by Kpanie Addy on March 23, 2014.

33. Dakubu, "Creating Unity," 520.

good life. Hospitality and trust are broken, a situation that threatens their replacement with destructive emotions of anger, retaliation, and revenge. Witchcraft and murder are such instances of public and drastic breach of harmony that bring with them anti-life effects. As a metaphysical condition, witchcraft can bring about the practical careless handling of nature, such as deforestation or senseless consumerism at the expense of Mother Earth. Both require, as a consequence, similar public attention for amendment. Both call for performance of some rituals in which significant signs and symbols of forgiveness are expressed. In extreme cases, such as that of obdurate witchcraft, purification by expurgation from social communion is required. However, in these instances and in most cases, forgiveness is the desired spirit of reconciliation rituals.

There is a fundamental understanding in African spirituality that, because human nature tends toward retaliation for wrongs suffered or perceived, forgiveness, to use the apt explanation of Jonathan Sacks, becomes a "counter-intuitive" force, a "stunningly original strategy" for a return to normalcy. As he clarifies:

> In a world without forgiveness, evil begets evil, harm generates harm. . . .[But] Forgiveness breaks the chain. . . . It represents a decision not to do what instinct and passion urge us to do. It answers hate with a refusal to hate, animosity with generosity. . . . Forgiveness means that we are not destined endlessly to replay the grievances of yesterday. It is the ability to live with the past without being held captive by the past. . . . [F]orgiveness is the most compelling testimony to human freedom. It is about the action that is not a reaction. It is the refusal to be defined by circumstance. It represents . . . [human] ability to change course, reframe the narrative of the past and create an unexpected set of possibilities for the future.[34]

In addition to the material symbols and signs of conciliation required in rituals of reconciliation, the word, spoken from the heart and before the community, plays a central role there. Many African scholars have noted this.[35] Ultimately, in the African context, forgiveness is not concerned with winning or losing an argument or case, as in contemporary forms of litiga-

---

34. Sacks, *The Dignity of Difference*, pp. 178–79. See also Matt 5:38–48.

35. Specifically, Bénézet Bujo, *Foundations of an African Ethic: Beyond the Universal Claims of Western Morality* (Nairobi: Paulines Publications, 2003), 68–88, 184–94; and Fabien Eboussi-Boulaga, *Les conferences nationales souveraines: Une affaire a suivre*, 2nd ed. (Paris: Karthala, 2009 [1992]), 154–56. See also Paul Bere, "The Word of God as Transformative Power in Reconciling African Christians," in Agbonkhianmeghe E. Orobator, ed., *Reconciliation, Justice, and Peace: The Second African Synod* (Maryknoll, NY: Orbis Books, 2011), 48–58.

tion, but with uniting, with restoring the wholeness of and in, the community constituted by its fourfold dimension of the living, the living-dead, the unborn, and the togetherness of goods. The word, concretized by and uttered in the context of the institution of the palaver, an institution that brings these dimensions together in a very intensive way, has a profoundly sacred character. Formalized by sharing a meal or drink together, it carries weight for conformity that few people would dare to ignore or carelessly counteract. The word is a sacred "performance" intended ideally for openness, sincerity, and unity. In the encounter between two people among the Ga people, for instance, "visitor and host must allay each other's fears that the speaker is not acting in a perfectly open manner, and so assure him of his good will."[36]

> In repeatedly asking after each other's towns, households, and families, host and visitor create a social universe, for the purpose of that visit, that contains and unites the two of them in their social selves, which in the process are identified and made known to each other and all present. The speeches simply amplify this knowledge and make it more explicit. Whatever is not included in this way, that is, is not identified as relevant and related to these two social persons and made socially known and included, is not merely left in social limbo, but excluded, as threatening to the group, an attitude which becomes more obvious at the next stage [of the greeting], when super-natural persons are addressed.[37]

This is not to say that there are no differences of opinion in the community, but this is precisely where the word of the elders (representing that of the ancestors and ultimately that of God) comes in. In spite of whatever differences there may be, a key principle in African spirituality is that God and the ancestors desire the communion of hearts of the community. This is necessary for it to function holistically and smoothly, and this is what the word, to which everyone must adhere, of the elders of the community transmits as the summation of the palaver structure.

Drinking from the Same Calabash as Restoration of the Ideal of Community

Already in 1963, participants in the eighth Congress of the African Catholic Student Union (l'Union des Étudiants Catholiques Africains, UECA), at

---

36. Dakubu, "Creating Unity," 510.

37. Dakubu, "Creating Unity," 510. "The sequence of speeches and prayers [in Ga greeting] is always accompanied by something to drink: traditionally, water before the speeches, water or more often alcohol (palm wine or gin) after the prayers." Ibid., p. 508.

Weremme, Belgium, observed that despite the ridicule until then heaped upon Africans and African social institutions, perhaps Africa had something crucial to tell the world after all. As they pointed out:

> Our own institutions have for long been insolently condemned as factors of social backwardness and economic stagnation. But as long as we can see the so-called "evolved" peoples of the world torn desperately between a rugged and speculative individualism, on the one hand, and an excessive collectivism, on the other; as long as we can observe both sides tread timidly the path towards a more human equilibrium and a more acceptable social order—the happy synthesis and balance created by the communitary spirit of our ancestors begins to appear to us no longer as an out-moded proposition discarded by modern times, but rather as the genuine pointer and solution for the future.[38]

Whether resources for reconciliation in African spirituality, as noted in summary above, are merely naïve romanticism is therefore, even today, an objection not totally unforeseen. As we have already noted above some people may argue that Africa has not been in the past, nor is it now, a model of reconciliation and peace to emulate. There were intra- and inter-tribal wars in former times, and strife within and between nations today. And practical examples for these situations may be adduced by name: Rwanda, Burundi, Congo, Côte d'Ivoire, Central African Republic, South Sudan . . . the list of major and minor internecine conflicts on the continent is apparently endless. Does not reality like this render any claim meaningless that the continent can and does offer resources for reconciliation and peace?

It is important to reiterate in response that Christians, and indeed all religious believers, should not ask that question in skepticism. Only hardcore empiricists may be excused the cynicism. Every religious faith and every social organization, in fact, presents its adherents and members with a certain ideal to emulate, and it is not nullified if it is not completely attained. In fact, this is all the more reason for retaining and revisiting the ideal for further inspiration and sustenance. Should a religious or social ideal be abrogated, the raison d'être for the entity in question and the entity itself cease to exist. What I have tried to present in this reflection is that there are in the African spiritual ideal resources for conflict transformation that, if studied seriously and implemented, could lead to understanding between peoples and nations and world peace.

---

38. Quoted in Bede Onuoha, *The Elements of African Socialism* (London: Andre Deutsch, 1965), 19.

18

Intercultural Communication in a Digital World

Franz-Josef Eilers, SVD

Intercultural encounters and communication exist since the beginning of humankind. Human history is full of meetings between different cultures such as the Babylonian, Persian, Greek, Roman, Germanic, Jewish, and Arab cultures. Interactions of cultures were taking place among various cultures in India and China, and also between Mediterranean cultures. Similarly, on other continents cultures were in intensive contacts and mutually influenced one another. In fact, even the whole Old Testament is to quite an extent, especially in the historic books, a report on the meeting of different cultures and their positive and negative interchanges. The whole First Testament is full of the Jewish people's relationship and exchanges with other cultures and the influence of these on their life and faith.

Intercultural communication developed in the United States after the Second World War as a special academic field of communication studies. Edward T. Hall, a government officer for the U.S. Indians, was the first to realize the importance of comparative studies, and developed, from his own experiences as a field officer working with American Indians like the Hopi and Navajo, the concern for intercultural understanding and communication, which made him somehow the "Father of Intercultural Communication." In his *The Silent Language* of 1959, with chapters on "What Is Culture," the "Vocabulary of Culture," "Culture Is Communication," he reports and reflects on his studies in nonverbal communications and

Franz-Josef Eilers, SVD, is professor of social communication and missiology at the Divine Word School of Theology in Tagaytay City, Philippines, and Santo Tomas University, Manila. He is executive director of the Asian Research Center for Religion and Social Communication at St. John's University in Bangkok and former secretary for the Office of Social Communication of the FABC. He is the founder of the journal *Communicatio Socialis* and was consulter of the Pontifical Media Council at the Vatican.

their organizing patterns. In further chapters on "Time Talks" and "Space Speaks" he reflects on their respective organizing patterns. This first study was later followed by his books *Beyond Culture, The Hidden Dimension,* and *The Dance of Life.*

Thomas Ohm, OSB, the immediate successor of the founder of Catholic missiology Joseph Schmidlin at the Theological Faculty of the University of Münster (Germany), became quickly aware of Hall's publication, and, underlining the strong relation between Hall's concern and missiology, recommended it already in 1961 to his missiology students. He felt that both fields had important common concerns and should be related to each other. Unfortunately, however, this joint concern and interest was not continued by his successors. In fact the field of intercultural communication developed slowly on its own in the United States, and in such a way that today with growing globalization it is almost a discipline in itself.

SVD Origin and Developments

The importance of culture and cultural studies, including communication, can be seen already quite early in the history of the Divine Word Missionaries (SVD). Right at the beginning of the first community in Steyl (Netherlands), there was a certain intercultural dimension, and Arnold Janssen's insistence on academic studies further contributed to this vital interest.

The very first community in Steyl was already a kind of *intercultural* grouping, albeit on a small scale. It had people from different cultural areas of Europe such as Bavaria (Johann Baptist Anzer), Tyrol (Joseph Freinademetz), and Luxembourg (Franz Xaver Reichart, Peter Bill). Janssen himself hailed from the Rhineland and was also looking for cooperators in the Netherlands and Belgium (Leuven). One might say that in a European context, this first community in Steyl already was something that can be called *intercultural.*

As a former teacher, Janssen had a special concern for academic studies. Therefore he selected the Dominican Third Order as the first rule for his house. The silver jubilee book of 1900 gives as a reason: "The Dominican Order is according to his rule a teaching and mission order and still does accomplish excellent work in this field till today." Because of this and already at an early stage of the Mission House, many of the young members were sent not only for philosophical and theological studies, but also for seemingly more secular subjects such as linguistics, ethnology, and anthropology. Father Wilhelm Schmidt, who later became famous through his twelve-volume work *Der Ursprung der Gottesidee* (The Origin of the Idea of God), was one of them. Along the same lines, Janssen also encouraged all his missionaries to collect, from the culture of people they were working with, data in these fields and related subjects.[1] This, and early studies by Fr. Wilhelm Schmidt in different fields of culture toward the end of the nineteenth century, led Janssen, three years before his death (1909), to encourage and support Schmidt in the foundation of the scientific journal *Anthropos*. The main purpose of this publication, which still, together with an institute of the same name, exists today, was to publish reports and studies of missionaries on the people with whom they worked and on their cultures.[2] Ethnology, anthropology, and linguistics soon became a trademark of the Steyl society. This shows a strong relation and concern about the cultures of people right from the early days of the SVD.

In a review for the second volume of *Anthropos*, a reviewer wrote: "In this voluminous tome with over 1,100 pages, one finds more about the culture of foreign people than in all other publications of this kind together in the whole of Germany."[3] Between the two world wars, a whole group of recognized SVD anthropologists augmented the Anthropos team, with names like Martin Gusinde, Paul Schebesta, George Hoeltker, Wilhelm Koppers, Damian Kreichgauer, and Michael Schulien, who also became the founder and first director of the Ethnological/Missiological section of the Vatican Museum, founded in 1925 as a Mission Museum in the Lateran.

All this proves that right from the beginning of the SVD, different cultures were of an utmost concern of the society. One can say that at the initial stage of the society itself, importance was given for intercultural communication for the SVD living and doing mission on all continents of the world, although it was not named like that those days.

Development of the Field of Intercultural Communication

There are a number of reasons why, since the Second World War, intercultural communication developed as a special field in academic studies. Here are some of them:

• Although in the earlier days it took quite some time to travel to other countries and continents, now it is only a question of hours because "now everybody can fly" and the world shrinks through travel and new means of communication.

---

1. Hermann Fischer, *Arnold Janssen, der Gründer des Steyler Missionswerkes: Ein Lebensbild* (Steyl: Missionsdruckerei, 1919), 241.

2. Wilhelm Koppers, "Das Anthropos-Unternehmen in St. Gabriel," in Hermann Fischer, ed., *Im Dienste des Göttlichen Wortes: Jubiläumsschrift der Gesellschaft des Göttlichen Wortes 1875–1925* (Steyl: Missionsdruckerei, 1925), 23–26; see Franz-Josef Eilers, "Interculturality, Communication and the SVD," *Verbum SVD* 54 (2013): 48–49.

3. Koppers, "Das Anthropos-Unternehmen in St. Gabriel," 24.

- A growing number of foreign students came and are coming to the United States for specialized studies. Migration from other continents also increased considerably.
- The growing insight that communication is a cultural process has to be applied especially in so-called developing countries. So-called development projects for them called for a proper understanding of people and their cultures. They often did not proceed because the cultural implications were not sufficiently recognized.
- There was also a growing awareness of the "ethnography of language," which considers not only grammar and words but also the cultural background from which people originate.
- A growing globalization and internationalization of business and economics demanded a proper and culturally adjusted way of dealing with one another.
- In Christian circles there was a growing conviction for the need of proper theologically determined intercultural approaches, responsive to different cultural situations in many parts of the world (e.g., liberation theology and others!).
- Intercultural theology became a special field of studies, which builds on the difference in cultures and the need to respond to this fact in a proper way.
- Also the ethnic changes in church leadership must be considered. While at the Second Vatican Council most bishops representing Africa and Asia were of European or American origin, this is almost exactly the opposite today with the growing number of young churches and their local leaders: A world ("kat-holón"!) church must also be an intercultural church!
- The change, with modern technical developments in communication to a digital world, became with its 24/7 access a special challenge for everybody all over the world.

Intercultural communication as a *field of special studies* started small but has developed rapidly in recent times. While in 1971 only five universities in the United States offered courses or programs in intercultural communication, the numbers are expanding today by the hundreds. Further, the field is no longer confined to the United States but grows now in Europe and has started growing in Asia and Africa as well. For the first time, in 1981, the Gregorian University in Rome offered, in cooperation with the newly established Interdisciplinary Center for Communication, a course on intercultural communication in their missiology faculty. This offering continued till 1996; after this time it slowly faded because of lack of qualified professors. In general, Catholic universities are not in the forefront of this development. The awareness of the field apparently has not yet developed, and the urgency to address it in a digital world does not yet seem to be very present.

Inter-cultural versus Cross-cultural Communication

Very often the expressions "cross-cultural" and "inter-cultural" communication are used in an identical way. In reality, however, these expressions do not have the same meaning. While cross-cultural communication *crosses borders* into other cultures, intercultural communication is based on a *participatory* understanding. Many business people wish to sell their goods in other cultures, and that is the reason why they study and develop the field under the perspective of how best to sell their goods. They "cross" into other cultures similarly to how, in the past, missionaries "crossed" into other cultures to bring their "faith." Opposed to this is the intercultural approach, which is based on a participatory understanding of the process. In such an understanding, one shares and becomes one with the other in the attempt to mutually understand and cooperate.[4]

The immediate purpose of studying intercultural communication is to develop a deeper understanding of other cultures. This is basic for proper living in intercultural communities and social networks. Because of this, it should be an obligatory subject especially for all departing "missionaries" and those living in intercultural communities. Many tensions arise because participants in a community are not disposed to, or have not learned to approach, other cultures in a proper and respectful way. Over the years, we have experienced returning confreres who, because they were not prepared for situations of intercultural communication, were not able and prepared to respond to and live in other cultures. Proper emotional and even spiritual abilities were missing to understand and act in a positive way in the other culture. Beside IQ and the EQ [intelligence quotient; emotional quotient] in the selection of candidates a sufficient CQ ("cultural quotient"!) is needed to respond in a proper way to the needs of ministry! In the Philippines, it seems that only one theological school and seminary offers a course on intercultural communication that is obligatory for all students: "Maryhill School of Theology" (MST) of the CICM Missionaries in Manila.

Intercultural Communication—The Field

The study of intercultural communication usually begins with clarification of the concepts and understanding of culture, communication, and intercultural communication. An overview and treatment of the exciting field of *nonverbal communication* follows. Ray Birdwhistell[5] says that up to 80 percent

---

4. Franz-Josef Eilers, *Communicating between Cultures. Introduction to Intercultural Communication,* 4th ed. (Manila: Logos, 2012).

5. Ray C. Birdwhistell, *Kinesics and Context: Essays on Body Motion Communication* (Philadelphia: University of Pennsylvania Press, 1970).

of our communication, from our body language (*kinesics*) to *proxemics* (space and distance), is nonverbal. *Chronemics* studies and reflects the use of time in different cultures. Audio expressions, like *sound*, music, but also *silence* are other important fields as well. Nonverbal communication further includes *haptics*, the field of touch, as well as *olfactory communication* (smell) and *taste communication* with food and drink. All expressions in nonverbal communication are heavily determined and influenced by culture and need special attention in intercultural community living. The seemingly same "sign" does not necessarily have the same meaning as, for example, head nods, gestures, or even smiles. The same holds for the concept of time, space and even taste. *Haptics*, the field of touch, is especially delicate, but also smell communicates as much as does food.

Verbal communication is essential for mutual understanding. If one is not able to use or even apply a proper level of language, one will have difficulties in communication. Language is determined and shaped by culture. Thus, without a proper knowledge, one will not be able to appreciate and understand the culture of the other person, and thus will be easily isolated from others.

Social structure is another important field of study for intercultural communication. The structure and relation within families, and similar groups in society, determine to quite an extent the understanding and living together in another culture. The role of parents, and also the relation with siblings, is determined by this, and often has a special emphasis, such as the role of the "Kuya," the eldest brother, within a family in the Philippines. Communication happens within social structures, first in families and similar communities, but also in political and other social groupings, each with its own way of communicating. Social structure influences our communication with one another, and also the way we live. Newcomers can be effective only if they find their proper place and ways of expression, corresponding to the specific social realities. A strong relation within family and a strong role of an extended family need special awareness from those who come from other social realities. A European man marrying a Filipina is often not aware that he not only marries "his" lady but also the whole of her clan and extended family. With the Internet and social networks, these experiences and needs are not diminished but rather heightened when we "share" with "unknown" persons from other parts of the globe!

Similar things can be said about the different *value systems* of different cultures and societies. What is considered a *primary value* in my own culture might only be a tertiary and even nonvalue in another culture. Value systems are also influenced by a differing worldview of societies and people which need a proper understanding and adjustment. In fact the value systems might be already different between rural people and those coming from bigger cities.

All these and many more related insights of the broad field of intercultural communication should be applied and considered by international/intercultural communities, but very often they are neither seen nor addressed. People involved often lack proper understanding of the process of intercultural communication. This holds also in social networks in a digital world and is often the deeper reason for difficulties in mutual understanding and intercultural living, even via the Internet. The so-called interculturality is only one aspect of a broader field and process.

In practical perspective, experts like Milton J. Bennet[6] see that to be able to properly communicate interculturally six steps are needed to move from *ethnocentrism* to *ethnorelativism*. The process starts (Step 1) with a *denial* of any difference between cultures: There are no differences, everybody is the same. In Step 2 small differences are acknowledged, but played down in *defense* of oneself ("Is it bad to be 'American'?"). In Step 3, differences are *minimized* ("We are all God's creatures"). This is considered the last step under ethnocentrism. The first stage toward ethnorelativism is (Step 4) *acceptance* of differences between cultures, which are seen as necessary and "normal." Step 5 is the processing of this acceptance and this leads into *adaptation*. I accept differences and adjust accordingly. Finally, Step 6 in this process is *integration*. I am able to live in one or the other culture without any prejudice, can easily shift from one to the other without any prejudice, and can comfortably live and move between two or more cultures, feeling at home in the process. Only if this level is reached and practiced can intercultural persons live and grow into a mature society. In fact, any Divine Word Missionary should be ready for such a development. Arnold Janssen's advice to missionaries, "to study and adjust to other cultures," goes exactly in this direction, which we could today also classify under intercultural communication—something we require also in context of the digital revolution.

A recent study from China[7] goes beyond the usual general terms in proposing a "dialogic" intercultural communication. The study addresses the quality of the intercultural process and notes that while in past studies similarities and differences between cultures and their historical or structural adaptation to each other are examined, dialogue is demanded in such a way that both parties stand on an even "ground." Based on philosophical insights from Martin Buber ("I and Thou"), Emmanuel Levinas, and others, this approach calls for a dialogic process between equals, that is to "be dialogic, to celebrate differences, otherness, and plurality." Such an approach also points

---

6. Milton J. Bennet, "A Developmental Approach to Training for Intercultural Sensitivity," in *International Journal of Intercultural Relations* 10 (1986): 179–96; Franz-Josef Eilers, *Communicating between Cultures*, 133ff.

7. Kaibin Xu, "Theorizing Difference in Intercultural Communication: A Critical Dialogic Perspective," in *Communication Monographs* 80, no. 3 (September 2013): 379–97.

toward the development of a proper *intercultural communication spirituality*, which should be an essential part of SVD spirituality.

Global Intercultural Communication

The recent (2014) second edition of a *Global Intercultural Communication Reader*, which is edited by an African scholar (Molefi Kete Asante) and two Asian scholars (Yoshitaka Miike and Jing Yin), is a good example for an overview of the field beyond the Western world. The volume presents, under five different headings, some thirty-two academic articles that should be of interest to anybody working in the field, especially members of intercultural communities. The book treats culture in historical and actual perspectives, and respective theories. African and Asian communication paradigms are presented in intercultural perspective. The intercultural dimensions of competence in certain cultures, such as silence in India or "the two faces of Chinese communication" and Confucian principles, are presented in intercultural perspective. Also, the ethical issues for intercultural relations and living are discussed. All these are, however, only a few indicators of the importance of intercultural communication in the modern and digital world. They should be an essential part of any formation for intercultural living and mission. A quotation of the Japanese Buddhist Zen scholar Daisetzu Suzuki in the same volume indicates the disposition needed for all this: "*Outwardly be open; inwardly be deep.*"[8]

Yoshitaka Miike has pointed to the need for proper intercultural communication ethics, which for him allows one's own culture to become central in linguistics and in religio-philosophical, historical, and aesthetic perspectives, but also leads to five Asian concerns: (1) recognition and respect; (2) reaffirmation and renewal; (3) identification and indebtedness; (4) ecology and sustainability; and (5) rootedness and openness. He thus expects the "ethical intercultural communicator" to "(1) remain rooted in his or her Culture and open to other cultures with the local knowledge in mind; (2) situate and envision locality in the global context and globality in the local context; and (3) learn to speak a local language for intercultural interactions with insiders and a global language for intercultural interactions with outsiders."[9]

---

8. Molefi Kete Asante, Yoshitaka Miike, and Jing Yin, *Global Intercultural Communication Reader*, 2nd ed. (New York: Routledge, 2014), 213.

9. Yoshitaka Miike, "Between Conflict and Harmony in the Human Family: Asiacentricity and Its Ethical Imperative for Intercultural Communication," in Xiaodong Dai and Guo-Ming Chen, eds., *Conflict Management and Intercultural Communication: The Art of Intercultural Harmony* (Milton Park: Routledge, 2017), 57.

Intercultural Communication and Theology

Intercultural communication is theologically very much related to concepts such as inculturation, interreligious and human dialogue.[10] Steve Bevans's *Contextual Theology* (1997) and Louis Luzbetak's *Church and Cultures* (1963, 1988) are excellent examples for a deeper SVD study and approach, and would also be for intercultural communication. Examples from Protestant missiology that address the field are Charles Kraft's *Christianity in Culture*, Eugene Nida's *Message and Mission* (1960, 1990), and David J. Hesselgrave's *Communicating Christ Cross-Culturally* (1979, 1984). Finally, there is also the book of Lyman E. Read, *Preparing Missionaries for Intercultural Communication* (1985), which is hardly known but of great value. These last publications are from the William Carey Library in Pasedena, California.

When around the year 600 AD, Pope Gregory the Great told his confreres when they went as missionaries to England they should not destroy the heathen temples but rather convert them into Christian churches, he already applied an important rule for intercultural communication: Accept what you have found, evaluate and apply it for the kingdom of God.

Formation in Intercultural Communication

There is a difference between training and formation. Training refers to skills, e.g., how to use technical devices, how to make a good radio program, mix it, or how to operate a television set, cellphones, and their applications. All this is training, and the practical use of media for catechesis and ministry is part of media training and media education.

Most of this, however, does not directly apply to intercultural communication, which deals with people and their cultures. The ability to communicate interculturally demands from persons and communities a proper inner disposition, which is expressed in outside behavior. A spirituality of pastoral and evangelizing communication responds to this by demanding and developing a specific openness to God, to self, and to others.[11] Only if somebody is well disposed and open to other persons and cultures, including new technical possibilities, can s/he properly communicate and build up relationships.

When Ignatius of Loyola was asked to send some Jesuits to the Council of Trent in 1546, he did not tell them what to do in the sense of concrete proposals of "how to do" but rather pointed to the inner dispositions needed

---

10. An extensive bibliography on intercultural communication, including aspects of theology and missiology, is to be found in Franz-Josef Eilers, *Communicating between Cultures*, 201–18.

11. Franz-Josef Eilers, *Communicating in Ministry and Mission*, vol. 3, 3rd ed. (Manila: Logos, 2009), 33–40.

for such a task. He gave them seven rules, or rather dispositions,[12] which are basic to pastoral and also intercultural communication: "He wants them to be open and to value dialogue, to be considerate and attentive not only to words but also to the feelings and the whole manner of communicating of others; they should try not to be biased but clear in their presentations. They should take time, value silent and attentive listening as much as well-reflected speaking; they should not 'hide' unnecessarily behind authority." Following a Spanish proverb, they should "Enter through the other's door."[13]

All these dispositions are basic. They are needed and expected for proper intercultural communication. There are textbooks, with a how-to-do approach similar to books on media training, on how to communicate with people from this or that culture. But such books are very narrow, and far from sufficient. A proper intercultural-communication formation must rest on adequate dispositions based on a specific spirituality. In order to be able to also enter through "the other's door," what Pope John Paul II presents as missionary spirituality, in the last chapter of his encyclical *Redemptoris Missio* (87–91), has to be repeated here as basic for proper formation in intercultural communication. He affirms that we have to be led by the Spirit who transformed the apostles into "courageous witnesses." They are challenged to "make themselves everything to everyone" in deep apostolic charity, stand under the universal call to holiness, and become "contemplatives in action." Only if someone grows in this direction will s/he be able to properly communicate interculturally without any useless bias. S/he will be open to the treasures of other cultures. Once again, intercultural communication is not about skills development—how to *use* the media. It is about a disposition that is deeply engrained in the personality. It is as essential in a digital world as it has always been in the past, though seldom sufficiently recognized.

Digital Communication

In the age of digital communication with social media and social networks, intercultural communication assumes an additional meaning. Today, digital cultures exist and will further determine our life in many ways. These cultures not only are accessible worldwide but are also interacting permanently in a 24/7 environment with "total" communication. Social networks have existed since the beginning of humankind,[14] but now there is a new situation: Places and people who were far away before are now near and instantly "avail-

---

12. Willi Lambert, *Directions for Communication: Discoveries with Ignatius of Loyola* (New York: Crossroad, 1999), 28–43.
13. Cf. Eilers, *Communicating in Ministry and Mission*, 75.
14. See Tom Standage, *Writing on the Wall: Social Media—The First 2000 Years* (New York: Bloomberg, 2013).

able" through social media and networks from all over the globe. This brings about a new missionary situation.[15] Religion has become an important area in the modern digital world.[16] Arnold Janssen definitely would have embraced this situation, which has a strong intercultural dimension. So-called digital natives, born after the beginning of the World Wide Web (1991), have been right from the beginning of their lives in an environment where everything is available anywhere at any time. But they also admit that, on the other hand, they need their family, friendship, and the bonds of culture![17] How do we react to such a situation from the missionary perspective? Where are the interculturally prepared "cyber-missionaries"?

---

15. See Pierre Babin and Angela Ann Zukowski, *The Gospel in Cyberspace* (Chicago: Loyola, 2001).

16. Heidi A. Campbell, ed., *Digital Religion: Understanding Religious Practice in New Media Worlds* (London: Routledge, 2014), 4.

17. Philipp Riederle, *Wer wir sind and was wir wollen: Ein digital Native erklärt seine Generation* [What we are and what we want. A digital native explains his generation] (Munich: Knauer, 2013), 10ff.

19

Postmodern Youth
Challenges and Connectivity

Isabelle Jonveaux

Christian mission is a kind of communication between a group that aims to spread a religious message and a public that can be converted to it. Yet this message has to be understood by the public, and for this reason missionaries and their public target have to speak the same language. When the target of the mission is young people, missionaries have to adapt their communication to them by speaking their language and using their means of communication. But does this translation of the religious message not risk an alteration of the original message? To what extent do the missionaries have to use the communication codes of youth if they want to speak to them? To take into account the expectation of the young generation also means understanding the general context, religious or not, of this generation, and what makes it different from the preceding one. For the present young generation, we can underline three main aspects: internal mutations of the Catholic identity of young people, the integration of a religious market, and the changes due to the advent of new technologies in almost all dimensions of life.

This paper is divided into three parts. I will first briefly deal with the main characteristics of the new generation, and especially with those that have consequences for religious affiliation or the way religion is practiced. Then I will present the challenge for the church to speak to the young generation in a context of religious pluralism and the religious market where authorities become redefined. Finally, I will spell out the implications of the new media for communication between the church and the new generation of Catho-

Isabelle Jonveaux is from France. She completed her PhD in sociology with a dissertation on the economic systems of monasteries. She now works at the Institute of Religions, Karl Franzens University, Graz, Austria. Her publications include *Le monastère au travail* (Paris: Bayard, 2011), and *Dieu en ligne: Expériences et pratiques religieuses sur Internet* (Paris: Bayard, 2013).

lics. This article will synthesize some observations of religious sociology, but the empirical approach will also enrich these observations. Field inquiries in monasteries were conducted in seven countries[1] from 2004 until now, and the issue of using the Internet[2] and the recruiting of young people were also part of this research. Moreover, in May 2014, in France and Austria, two quantitative inquiries with a questionnaire about religious activity on online social networks were conducted. The results of these different inquiries will therefore be used to answer the questions.

The Religion of Young People in Modern Society: Decline or Redefinition?

The French sociologist Pierre Bourdieu entitled one of his articles "Youth is just a word."[3] With this provoking title he means that youth is not a homogeneous group but can cover extremely different realities. Even within the same society, the lives of people between eighteen and thirty-five (youth lasts longer and longer!) can be very different. What is the common point between a twenty-two-year-old young man who is studying and living with his parents and a coeval young person who already works and maybe married with a child? Before we present the main characteristics of present-day youth, it is therefore important to keep also in mind the different conditions young people are experiencing. As this book deals with missiology, we will tackle three important characteristics here, although these are not the only ones needed to understand the context of youth: the characteristics of young Catholics for the practice and the transmission of the faith, the global context of religion nowadays in an age of religious pluralism, and the influence of new technologies.

Disruption in the Transmission of Religious Identity

In Western societies we can observe two main evolutions of Christian religion among young people. The first one is an important quantitative decline in affiliation and practice, and the second one is the set of mutations in the way young people live their religion.

First of all, if we are considering at this point only the quantitative factor, the young generation of Western Europe is now practicing less than the

---

1. In France, Italy, Germany, Belgium, Austria, and, since 2013, Togo and Kenya. These communities were Benedictines, Trappists, Cistercians, Carmelites, Dominicans, Franciscans, and Brothers of the Christian Schools.
2. Results of the inquiry about the Internet and consecrated life are published in Isabelle Jonveaux, *Dieu en ligne: Expériences et pratiques religieuses sur Internet* (Paris: Bayard, 2013).
3. Pierre Bourdieu, "La jeunesse n'est qu'un mot," in Pierre Bourdieu, *Question de sociologie* (Paris: Éd. de minuit, 1984).

generation of its parents or grandparents. For instance in France, only 8% of young people aged between 18 and 29 are considered as "churchgoers," which means that they are going to church at least once a month, whereas 18% of the 45–59 age group and 33% of people older than 60 do. The percentage of Catholic baptisms among the births of the year went down from 77.8% in 1975 to 52% in 2000.[4] One of the explanations for this is the disruption in the transmission and the decline of religious socialization. According to the German sociologist Hubert Knoblauch, "It was only their generation who actually detached the individual choice of religion from traditional institutions—the family, neighborhoods, villages, classes, milieus and regions. The generation of baby boomers turned against Church authority and established religion as a matter of the autonomous individual."[5] As a consequence, this generation of parents has privileged the free choice of religion for their children rather than their compulsory religious socialization, and the result is a rupture in the transmission of religious socialization.

Changes in the Religious Practice of Young Catholics

It is often taken for granted that young Christian people practice their religion less and less in Western countries. But parallel to this quantitative aspect, we have to pay attention to some qualitative evolutions in the Christianity of young people today, who also show great commitment. As already said, religious affiliation nowadays is more of a personal choice that as a consequence has to be affirmed. That is why the authenticity of the practice plays an important role for this generation, which will alternatively accept or refuse some practices in the name of authenticity. As an example, we can cite this case of a young woman at the World Youth Days in Paris (1997) who declared: "I am Catholic, I go to church on Sunday. Well, not always: sometimes I don't feel like it says anything to me."[6] Young Catholics nowadays are proportionally fewer than the preceding generation, but often have a high commitment where the authenticity of the practice is more important than norms and duties. Philippe Portier speaks about "identity Catholicism," for which the personal commitment holds the highest value.[7] This reflects important mutations in the way of believing and practicing. D. Hervieu-Léger draws up six identification modalities for Christianity among young

4. Céline Béraud, Denis Pelletier, Philippe Portier, "Portrait du catholicisme en France," in A. Pérez-Agote, ed., *Portraits du catholicisme: Une comparaison européenne* (Rennes: PUR, 2012), 107–61.

5. Hubert Knoblauch, *Populäre Religion: Auf dem Weg in eine spirituelle Gesellschaft* (Frankfurt-am-Main: Campus Verlag, 2009), 39.

6. Danièle Hervieu-Léger, *Le pèlerin et le converti* (Paris: Champs Flammarion, 1999), 95.

7. Philippe Portier, "Pluralité et unité dans le catholicisme français," in C. Béraud, F. Gugelot, and I. Saint-Martin, eds., *Catholicisme en tensions* (Paris: EHESS, 2012).

people, which show that the religious life of young Catholics is nowadays less marked by a proselytizing militancy than by actions (humanitarian aid for instance) and strong emotional experiences. Hervieu-Léger speaks about the "exaltation of the collective gathering." The identity is based on the emotional community, which, if we take the concept of Zygmund Bauman, can also be ephemeral or "liquid," such as for the time of an event rather than the constancy of a stable parish. To emphasize that extraordinary religious events have more success than the traditional Sunday Mass, an Italian adage says that Italy would be the country "of empty churches and full squares."[8] It may be noted that the young generation is more present at such events than at the Mass.

Challenges for the Church on the Global Religious Market: The Marketing Imperative?

The new generation moves on in a context of a global religious market. How can the church make its voice heard in such a context? Does it have to use marketing tools as evangelical churches do? And in what way can the church use these tools of communication to spread its religious message without distorting it?

To Be a Catholic in an Age of Religious Pluralism

In Western society, young Christians nowadays are living in the context of a "religious market." This term defines the new religious pluralism in which people can theoretically choose between different religious propositions. Peter Berger speaks about a "heretical imperative."[9] The decline of religious socialization in the family or in the village, combined with this context of a religious market, favors the individualization of the religious path. Each individual can, therefore, theoretically choose his or her religion, and inside the religion choose the element they want to believe in or not. A good example of that is the growing number of Christians who also believe in reincarnation.[10] Sociologists denote this phenomenon with the term "bricolage of beliefs." It represents a challenge for the church to try to reduce this bricolage and to justify all elements of its system of belief. Moreover, the question of a religion's truth is being put into a perspective of pluralism. According to the European Values Survey 2008, only 7 percent of young Catholics between

---

8. Franco Garelli, *Religione all'italiana: L'anima del paese messa a nudo* (Bologna: Il Mulino, Collana "Contemporanea," 2011).

9. Peter L. Berger, *The Heretical Imperative: Contemporary Possibilities of Religious Affirmation* (New York: Doubleday Anchor, 1979).

10. Hervieu-Léger, *Le pèlerin et le converti*.

eighteen and thirty-five consider their religion to be the only true one. On the one hand, the challenge is, therefore, for the church to affirm why its truth is different, and to justify this difference, but, on the other hand, relativism also helps interreligious dialogue. Nevertheless, in order to distinguish it from other religions young people expect clear positions from the church.

The Catholic Church and the Challenge of Marketing to the Young

This logic of market entails the necessity for each church to become known, and that means to use tools of communication and marketing. Evangelical megachurches use these strategies with music, CDs, and youthful language; and theological content is relegated to second place.[11] Can the Catholic Church do the same, and, if it does not enter into this dynamic, can it still have a place in this religious market? Lionel Obadia asks, "Is it conceivable to 'sell' religious products utilizing the techniques of marketing and business?"[12] On the one hand, religion is a free commodity that cannot be sold, and the goal of the Catholic Church is not to gain the most believers and become the first on the market, but to spread the "Good News of the gospel," to give people the possibility of being saved. In this sense, the definition of marketing would be contrary to the aim of the church. People do not have to go to church because it is attractive, or more attractive, than another one but because they believe in the message of the church.

This equation is particularly difficult for young people, who are used to choosing what is the most attractive, and to being spoken to in the language of marketing and publicity. But as Olivier Roy says, "Codifying religious fact into the language of youth implies without doubt staying within the transitory and ephemeral. Moreover, that is often the argument of the religious persons in question, for whom it is important to attract the client but not to adopt his worldview."[13] The difference between the language used for the communication—or, we can say, the means of communication—and the content of the message has to be taken into account. The message and truth of the church cannot be changed in order to translate it into a new and more attractive language, but the church can use the means of communication of its time, such as the Internet, as we will spell out later. As we already know from advertising, the attractiveness of marketing lasts only for the time of discovery and surprise.

Appeals by the church for young people are more and more diverse, with

---

11. Knoblauch, *Populäre Religion*, 92.

12. Lionel Obadia, *La marchandisation de Dieu: L'économie religieuse* (Paris: CNRS Editions, 2012), 82.

13. Olivier Roy, *La sainte ignorance: Le temps de la religion sans culture* (Paris: Seuil, 2008), 27.

websites, apps, and events going as far as Christian rock 'n' roll festivals. Do such propositions really spread the profound message of the gospel? In a way, a part of the religious message can be lost, but, on the other hand, such events play a relevant role for the identity of young people as Catholics. As we saw before, the identity sentiment during large meetings is important for the young generation to feel "Catholic." A right balance has therefore to be found between attractive marketing to speak to young people and, to keep those people in the church, faithfulness to the original religious message.

Crisis of Religious Authorities and Institutions?

Sociologists of religion speak of modernity as a crisis of religious authorities and religious institutions. This can be illustrated first of all by the loss of confidence in the ecclesial institution, and, second, by the evolution of religious authorities, for instance on the web. In France, only 11 percent of Catholic people say they really trust the church. Among eighteen tested institutions, the Catholic Church arrives in the fourteenth position. One well-known explanation for that is the position of the church on sexual and familial questions. Only 29 percent of Catholics think the church is delivering good and helpful answers to these questions. The same can be observed for social problems, as only 22 percent of French Catholics say the church is delivering the right answers to those problems. This last question is especially interesting when we speak about the young generation. We say that the social and humanitarian commitments are important for the way to define oneself as a Catholic. The young generation expects the church, therefore, to take clear positions on and to show concrete behavior about these questions. The success of the new Pope Francis among the young generation can be explained by his commitment to social problems, which are so important for young people. But the question about confidence in the institution concerns not only the positions of the church but also the way the church shows that it is taking into consideration the expectations of the faithful and especially of young people. The young generation is also the generation of interactivity, which is used as a means to express their minds and views (for instance on digital social networks or forums). That is why it is important for the church to show concretely how it is listening to what the young generation has to say. In this sense, the opinion poll in preparation of the bishops' synod of 2014, to find out the position of Catholics on questions of family, sexuality, and life, was a good attempt, through using new ways of communication and governance, to take into account the opinion of the faithful.

New Media: A New Chance for the Church?

As we have already said, another characteristic of the young generation is its connectivity through new media and technologies. Online activity of young people is especially concentrated on social networks. Does that mean that the church also has to be present on these social networks, even though their codes of communication do not correspond with the classical communication and values of the church?

Do Young People Use Online Social Networks for a Religious Purpose?

A second big change, which concerns the majority of people in society nowadays, is the digital revolution, which is changing some ways of life and ways of communication. The young generation between eighteen and thirty-five years is the most involved in online activities. Although the gap is reduced now, ten years ago young people under the age of thirty-five were clearly the biggest users of the new technology. It would now be more correct to say that young people have a different use for these new information and communication technologies. Eighty precent of young people between the ages of thirteen and twenty-four are on Facebook and 62 percent of those in the eighteen to twenty-four age group are members of four or more online social networks. On the other hand, they use an average of 2.9 websites. For this generation, social networks are becoming the entrance door to the web. They think if there is something important, they will know it from Facebook or Twitter or from another social network. Is it the same with religious news?

First of all, do young people use online social networks to communicate or to get information about their religion? In France and Austria, around one-third of young Catholics between fifteen and twenty-four are posting their religious affiliation on their Facebook profile. Facebook does indeed give the possibility of indicating it. Almost half of these young Catholics post messages of a religious nature on their boards or receive them. This allows the conclusion that young Catholics are religiously active on their social networks, and use them for religious purposes. Almost half of them say it is important for Christians to bear testimony to their faith on Facebook. This allows us to affirm that new media are playing a role in the way young Catholics are living their religious identity today. It also plays a role for young people entering monastic life nowadays. Novice masters have to take this into account, and reflect on it in order to propose a way to learn to use this new media from a religious point of view.

Does the Church Have to Use Social Networks to Be Heard by Young People?

Does the church have to do the same to reach young people? Some statistics seem to suggest this. For instance, Pelzer says that in Germany between 15 and 20 percent of people present at a church event found out about it on Facebook.[14] But maybe the question needs to be reversed: if the church would not be present on social networks and in general on the Internet, would it lose a part of its public only because it is now a habit to find out about news online? Also with regard to a person with a religious vocation entering monastic or religious life, Jean-Francois Mayer notes: "We are even arriving at the next step, where a monastery that does not have a website 'would be missing' potential vocations because all young people interested in religious questions will probably—more and more—go to the Internet as a first step in their quest."[15] It is now taken for granted that young people, before presenting themselves to become a postulant, as a first step, search communities on the Internet. Just as the church and religious communities adopted printing and television quite early, because they noticed that these could be useful for their mission, so the church of the twenty-first century has to find out how to use the new technologies to improve its communication with the public it wants to reach.

Has the church been, so far, successful in trying to reach young people through the new media? On the one hand, we found that readers of religious material online are often already active in the church; this also means that it seems difficult to reach people who are far from the church. For the online retreat of French Dominicans for Lent ("Retraite dans la Ville"),[16] we observed that the majority of people who participated in this retreat corresponded to the classical profile of the churchgoer (women above fifty) and not to the classical profile of the Internet user. But the question seems to be different if we consider the presence of the church on social networks. Sixty-seven percent of our sample says they are following the official profiles of the church on Facebook, and we could not find a difference according to the age. That means that young and less young people are following the profiles of the church a lot. Christian Klenk noted for Germany[17] that religious pages

---

14. Jürgen Pelzer, "Implizit religiös, Soziale Netzwerke und ihre Rolle für die kirchliche Kommunikation," *Communicatio Socialis* 45 (2012): 32.

15. Jean-François Mayer, *Internet et religion* (Geneva: Infolio, 2000), 73.

16. Isabelle Jonveaux, "Une retraite de carême sur Internet," *Archives de Sciences Sociales des Religions* 139 (2007): 157–76.

17. Christian Klenk, "Katholisches bei Facebook. Die Reichweiten kirchlich-religiöser Fanseiten beim größten sozialen Netzwerk," *Communicatio Socialis* 45, no. 1 (2012): 43.

on Facebook with the highest number of fans are those of the World Youth Days (7,703 fans in 2012), ecumenical meetings at Munich (6,429), Anselm Grün [a well-known Benedictine monk and author] (5,807), and the "Pope in Germany" (4,517). The first two are explicitly addressed to young people. Parallel to this, monks or priests have a personal Facebook profile to communicate with young people. Many of them told me in interviews that they began to use Facebook because young people of their parish told them they had to do it. Some of them also said to me that it gives young people who never came to a church or a monastery the opportunity to communicate with a priest or a monk. They can explain their problems and ask important questions about their lives, even if they are not always religious questions. In this sense, the communication of the church on social networks now seems to be central to reach young people who are already Catholics, and also those who would not come to a church but who nevertheless have an interest in religious questions.

Risks of Communication on the Internet Regarding Religion

Religions are therefore present on the Internet, and especially on social networks, and we can say that this presence is essential for their communication strategy. Online communication has its own codes, and it can entail some risks for the religious message. First of all, the church is present on the web, but it is not the only one. All religions are doing the same, and sociologists show that minority religions are proportionally more present than others because they try to get more visibility.[18] That means that the Catholic Church has to differentiate itself in its presentation on the web. On the one hand, young people are using the new media to present themselves as Catholics and to get information about their religion. But on the other hand, the use of social networks is naturally not only religious; it is only a small part of it, and religion becomes one thing among others. Just as they "like" the page of a brand or of a music group, they "like" the page of the church without making a real distinction.

Another risk of communicating on the web is for the actor of the church to adopt the production codes of the individual on a social network. How can the church, or an actor of the church, use the codification of the social network? We observe on the Internet that official pages of the church or of religious communities are often sober in their graphics, color, and sometimes have no advertising.[19] In this way the church can differentiate itself from other pages on the web and show the difference of the message it is trying to spread.

---

18. Christopher Helland, "Canadian Religious Diversity Online: A Network of Possibilities," in P. Beyer and L. Beaman, eds., *Religion and Diversity in Canada* (Boston: Brill, 2008), 127–48.

19. Jonveaux, *Dieu en ligne*.

It this sense, the sobriety of marketing would be the best marketing for the church. We can also find social network profiles of monks or priests who are using the production codes of ordinary individuals, and post a lot of pictures of themselves in all activities, religious and nonreligious, sometimes even in swimsuit.[20] On the one hand, it corresponds to the new marketing and also to the kind of communication young people are using on the web. But on the other hand, as it is not differentiated from the rest, this can be negative for the religious message. Because of the centrality of religious communication of the web nowadays, it has to use these means; but to protect the sense of the religious message, it must also find out how it might do it differently.

Conclusion

Mission and communication are a very important part of the identity of the Catholic Church, and communication necessitates knowing the characteristics of the public we want to speak to. Nevertheless, the Catholic Church has to find the right balance between the use of communication and the language of the young generation and faithfulness to its message. In reality, young people expect the church to use modern means of communication, but not necessarily to change its message. In this sense, young people also expect the church to give in its way of communication testimony of its difference.

Altogether it seems that the formation of young members of a diocese or congregation is a key point. First, the formation has to take into account the paradigm mutations of the general religious context that are now occurring, and especially of the new forms of Catholic identity and Catholic practice. Second, a formation for the use of new technology would have to combine the technical aspects of knowing how to use it and the pastoral aspect of learning how to communicate on such a medium. The Jesuit Andreas Schönfeld claims, "In order to have enough personnel for the missionary websites, it will be necessary for the future, that the church favors accompanied formation, which combines applied informatics, new media, and spiritual studies."[21] This can be also a part of the answer regarding the question of reforming of religious authorities, which we can also observe on the web. The position of religious institutions and the way they can assert the truth of their message have also to do with their capacity to use these media.

---

20. Isabelle Jonveaux, "Facebook as a Monastic Place? The New Use of the Internet by Catholic Monks," in T. Ahlbäck, ed., *Digital Religion,* Based on papers read at the conference arranged by the Donner Institute for Research in Religious and Cultural History, Åbo Akademi University, Åbo/Turku, Finland, on 13–15 June 2012 (Åbo: Donner Institute for Research in Religious and Cultural History, 2013), 99–110.

21. Andreas Schönfeld, "Christliche Spiritualität und Internet. Digitalisierung ZAM/GuL," *Geist und Leben* 84, no. 1 (2011): 6.

Index

Tutu, Desmond, 234
Twitter, 42, 47, 53, 258
two-spirited persons, 222,
223
Tyler, Edward, definition of
culture, xiv
Tyrrell, George, 163n5

Ubuntu, 141, 237
uncertainty
avoidance of, in interna-
tional communities,
143, 144
in postmodern culture,
167, 168
United Nations
Delegation of the Holy
See, interventions on
behalf of women, 220
on human rights of
LGBT persons, 224,
225
response to injustices
affecting women and
girls, 219, 220
unity, over conflict, 184
universe, in postmodern
culture, 165

vagabonds, postmodern
identity of, 166, 167
values, differences in, 100
Varghese, Elsy, on inter-
nationalization of
religious communities,
137, 138, 140
Vatican II
attitude toward the world,
173
and missionary nature
of the church, 71, 73,
149, 174, 177, 179
on other religions, 75
and struggle with moder-
nity, 163
Velle, Carlos del, passing
from being multi- to
intercultural, 54

verbal communication, and
intercultural studies,
246
Vethanayagamony, Peter,
on missionaries from
Global South, 68, 69
Vink, Niko, role of memo-
ries in international
communities, 140, 141
violence, against women,
218
VIVAT International, 154
Vlaïcu, Patriciu, on secularism, 43
vulnerability
attitude of, 88, 89
ethics of, 51, 52

wealth
as inherently dangerous,
32
as proof of self-indulgence
and greed, 32, 33
renunciation of, conse-
quences of, 34, 35
rights associated with,
and care for the poor,
30, 31
and social isolation, 29,
30
wealthy
church's relation to, 34
and issues of integrity and
credibility, 29
See also righteous rich,
theology of
whole, greater than parts,
184
Whorf, Benjamin Lee, on
cultural differences,
119, 120
Wiebe, Rudy, on thinking
differently, 5
Wijsen, Frans, on commu-
nity in African spiritu-
ality, 237
witchcraft, 238

women
subordination of, in
Roman Catholicism,
62
unjust living and working
conditions, 216, 217,
218, 219
See also clean energy;
corporations; domestic
responsibilities; drink-
ing water; government;
HIV/AIDS; human
trafficking; illiteracy;
missing women and
girls; poverty; violence;
workforce
women religious, abuse of,
by local bishops, 221,
222
Woolman, John, 150
workforce, women in, 217
World Bank, 33
World Council of Churches,
decision making and
intercultural differ-
ences, 141
World Union of Catholic
Women's Organiza-
tions (WUCWO), and
participation of women
in life and mission of
church, 221
Wright, Christopher, on the
righteous rich, 39, 40

Yin, Jing, and global intercultural communica-
tions, 248
Yina, Martin, on social communication and evan-
gelization, 49
youth, postmodern
as challenge for the
church, 255–57
characteristics, 253–55
religious practices of, 254,
255